FLINGS OVER FENCES

The Ups and Downs of Gay Kindersley

Gay Kindersley

FLINGS OVER FENCES

The Ups and Downs of
Gay Kindersley

ROBIN RHODERICK-JONES

Foreword by Lord Oaksey

To Flip —

*With many thanks
for all the help you have
given me with "Public Speaking"
Hope you enjoy the Book.*

*Gay
Marlborough
July 1995.*

Quiller Press
London

For Charlotte

First published 1994 by
Quiller Press Ltd
46 Lillie Road
London SW6 1TN

ISBN 1 870948 97 1

Production in association with
Book Production Consultants Plc
25–27 High Street
Chesterton, Cambridge

Typeset by Cambridge Photosetting Services
Printed by Biddles Limited, Guildford, Surrey

Front cover by Pierre Bellocq
The portrait of Gay Kindersley
on the back panel is by
Michael Corkrey and is
reproduced by kind permission
of Guy Hart.

Contents

Acknowledgements

I am grateful indeed for the patience and tolerance of those whose reminiscences, opinions and prodigious memories helped so considerably in the telling of this story. Among them were Michael Allsopp, Julian Lewis, Frank Mahon (who sadly died before publication), Dr Mark and Mrs Philippa Marshall and three racing journalists: Peter Scott, who has also tragically died and who for over twenty-six years was Hotspur of the *The Daily Telegraph*, Steve Taylor of *The Sporting Life* and Lord Oaksey whose contributions to the sport during his own riding days – in print and on television's Channel 4 *Racing* – are unrivalled and who has taken the time from his busy life to write a foreword.

I am grateful, too, to all those journalists (and their newspapers) whose accounts of particular incidents and descriptions of contemporary attitudes have illuminated my text and to Bruce Urquhart who helped Gay write up the original notes.

I particularly thank Oonagh, Lady Oranmore and Browne, for her welcome to me in Guernsey, her gentle patience during my interviews with her and for the use of her stunning photograph albums and scrapbooks. My special gratitude is also offered to Mrs Margaret Kindersley for recalling – and allowing me to share – memories which were sometimes less than comfortable for her.

I am indebted to my editor and publisher, Jeremy Greenwood, for his advice and to Philippa Kindersley for the unfailing hospitality she has shown to me and for the clear insights she contributed during our labours.

Most of all I thank Gay, not just for entering so wholeheartedly, into the spirit of the enterprise but for allowing me into his life so comprehensively. His generosity, his kindness and the laughs (sometimes tears too) we enjoyed together over the last eighteen months will always stay with me.

Robin Rhoderick-Jones
Middle St Andrew's Wood
July 1994

Foreword

by Lord Oaksey

Amo, amas, amat ... The word in Latin means 'love' – so to be an 'Amateur' of anything is to do that thing because you love it. When Gay Kindersley became Champion Amateur rider in the 1959–60 season, it was the high point of a long, hazardous, often painful love affair with riding.

But this is not just another book about another jockey – still less another account of a single love affair. For it tells the story of an all-round all-embracing 'amateur', a man who also loves wine, women, song, good fellowship and fun – and who, despite pursuing all those things with little or no thought for the morrow has still contrived to make, and keep, an army of devoted friends.

I have marched with that army for nearly fifty years – ever since Gay arrived at Eton heralded, for the first but not by any means the last time, by sensational headlines in the papers. The argument between his already divorced parents was just what England needed to take its mind off the war.

'Eton is sure to be bombed – much too close to London and Windsor Castle' was the view of Gay's adoring mother Oonagh Guinness. Her second husband, Dominic Oranmore and Brown had opted comfortably out of the war but her first, Gay's father Philip, survived Dunkirk only to be captured in North Africa. From a POW Camp in Italy his views on Gay's education came over loud and clear 'I do not want my son brought up a Sinn Feiner'.

That brand of Anglo-Irish conflict is central to this story and Gay was born with an explosive cocktail of blood in his veins. In my experience the only predictable characteristics of the Guinness family have been their great wealth and, to put it politely, their eccentricity. On the face of it the upper middle class English/Welsh Kindersleys were much more conventional. But Philip loved the thrills of raceriding, hunting and party-going almost as much as his son and one of Gay's uncles was killed riding on the roof of a Railway carriage. As with the Guinnesses there are more wives than husbands in the family and none called them dull.

If, like me, you have been lucky enough to watch, enjoy and even take part in some of the episodes it describes, this is a sad as well as an extremely funny book. In many ways, blessed with money, charm, courage and the loyal friendship of gilt-edged characters like Don Butchers, Cecil Bonner, Patrick

Cummins, Bill Tucker and a whole changing-room full of jockeys, Gay has been a lucky man. But again and again, often but not always his own fault, the Fates have demanded a high price for those blessings.

Even if some of Gay's injuries were partly self-inflicted, the fact is that they were far more frequent and painful than those which most of his contemporaries had to suffer.

And all that time, riding, singing, drinking or succumbing to what the author calls 'his incurable tendency to infidelity', my old friend has been a source of far more pleasure and amusement than sorrow and disappointment to his innumerable friends.

He never subscribed to the widespread view that I got tired before Carrickbeg. In fact he never blamed me for the whole long list of his disasters in which I had a share. Not when he got so drunk (and soaked in a friendly tart's perfume) at my Bachelor party that Magsie came to the wedding in mourning. Not when a tryst with one of the countless ladies with whom, under the spell of Luggala, he fell hopelessly in love was spoilt by midges – and not when our long happy drives-out to get-run-away-with round Bicester aerodrome shortened his career at Oxford.

What fun it has been to know him and how well this book describes an eventful and extraordinary life.

CHAPTER ONE

The Silver Spoon

There had been a cock-up. Some four hundred members of the British Sportsman's Club, drinks in hand, awaited with keen anticipation the arrival of the Australian cricket tourists. In a room a few yards away, a round-shouldered little man, with sparse sandy hair and eyes which managed at the same time to be both twinkly and dissipated, was engaged in amiable conversation with the literary editor of the *Sunday Express*. The door opened and in trooped the obviously misdirected Australians led by their captain, Allan Border, whose forbidding expression spoke of a marked distaste for formal receptions and particularly those perpetrated on him by Poms who would no doubt wish to rub in the fact (this was 1985) that they were in the process of winning the Ashes. The little man, quickly aware that the official welcoming party had somehow been bypassed, stepped into the breach and held out his hand.

'Hello,' he said, 'I'm Gay and this is my friend Graham.'

Border's moustache bristled almost audibly in the astounded silence. The cricketers behind him looked at one another. A stage whisper of a volume which would have reached every corner of Lords broke the tension; it was uttered by a hairy and hostile fast bowler not noted for social niceties.

'Strewth,' it said. 'Strewth; hang on to your strides, mate. The bastard's a poofter.'

It was his father's doing. On holiday in the South of France in the 1920s, Philip Kindersley had read of an American playboy who had fallen off a speedboat and been terminally minced by the propeller. The unfortunate man's name was Gaylord and Philip – despite the inauspicious circumstances – was much taken by it, determining then and there that this would be a fitting name for the son and heir that one day would surely be his.

Philip was the youngest son of Sir Robert Kindersley, a successful and altruistic financier who had been knighted after the First World War and who was, in 1941, to be elevated to the peerage as the 1st Baron Kindersley for his work as president of the National Savings Committee. Steeped in Victorian family values and a tradition of solid public service, he had high hopes for his six children, hopes that were shared by his equally duty-conscious wife Gladys. She was a tough and altogether uncompromising Welsh matriarch who interested herself closely in good works, becoming chairman (she would have had no truck with 'chairperson' or, worse still, 'chair') of two hospitals famous for their skill in repairing the faces of airmen who suffered terrible burns during the Second World War.

Of the Kindersleys' six children, Bow, the eldest, was killed in Flanders. His brother Dick proved to be both something of a trial and a disappointment to his essentially conventional parents. Persuaded to follow his father into the City, he quickly rebelled and took himself off to America where he felt he would have a freer rein for his artistic talents and a better chance of achieving the lifestyle he longed for. In Hollywood he attempted to act, wrote poetry for children, painted and seldom wore shoes. In Canada – rather less innocuously – he developed an unfortunate taste for riding on the roofs of railway carriages, a hobby which ended his life when, on a visit to England, he tried it from Victoria station and was swept off by the first bridge.

Hugh Kindersley – who eventually succeeded his father, having served with much distinction in both wars – became the paragon for whom his parents had fervently wished, rising in turn to the commanding heights of Lazards and Rolls-Royce. The girls, too, followed a happily predictable path, Betty marrying Jim Phillips, stud-owner and member of the Jockey Club, while Peggy bagged Algy Belmont, a successful stockbroker.

The family was brought up in Langley House at Abbots Langley in Hertfordshire and horses figured prominently in their lives, especially that of Philip, who developed an absorbing interest in both riding and racing. After his private school he was sent to Eton, where he found himself in the same house as Ian Fleming. It would seem that the company he kept and the influences on him there were not entirely to the family's liking, for when the time came for him to tread the well-worn path from Eton to Oxford, his father wrote cryptically, 'I'm not sending you there for academic reasons but more that you should rid yourself of those disgusting habits.'

At Oxford young Philip was able to indulge himself freely in horses, hunting with the Drag and venturing to ride in hunt races. He harboured ambitions to be a gentleman steeplechase rider of the first rank, but his height and weight precluded him from all but point-to-points and the occasional hunter chase. Nevertheless his patriotic colours (red cap, blue jersey with white spots) were often seen in the winner's enclosure and he once finished fourth in the Foxhunters Chase at Liverpool, a race for amateurs run over the stiff Grand National course. He had a number of horses in training, notably a successful hurdler called Blue Vinney with George Poole at Lewes, from which he derived enormous pleasure – but he was to remain immensely frustrated all his life that his size prevented him from being a more active participant.

At university he discovered women. Freed from the inhibiting confines of Eton, he was soon on the society circuit as a deb's delight, an activity he pursued with relish and energy both at Oxford and after coming down and following his father into Lazards. It was at a ball in London, when he was still only 21, that he met the 18-year-old Oonagh Guinness.

The Guinness family was extraordinary even by Irish standards. Oonagh's father, the Honourable Ernest, was the middle one of three brothers and the current power behind Arthur Guinness Son and Company. His elder brother, Lord Iveagh, owned extensive lands in Ireland and, leaving the brewing to Ernest, interested himself almost exclusively in matters agricultural. The youngest, who was later to become Lord Moyne, was a politician who rose to be secretary of state for the colonies and later minister of state resident in the Middle East, during which incumbency he was assassinated by Zionists on the steps of the British Embassy in Cairo.

Ernest and his wife Chlöe (known as Gar) owned two houses in England – Holmbury with three hundred acres in Surrey and No 11 Grosvenor Square (now the Irish Embassy) – and four substantial properties in Ireland. In order of grandeur, the latter were headed by Ashford Castle on the Mayo–Galway borders, followed by Glenmaroon at Phoenix Park near Dublin and two hunting lodges, Luggala and Loch Bray, in the Wicklow Mountains. All were lavishly staffed and Ashford Castle with its lake and woods was known as providing the best woodcock shoot in the world, good enough even to tempt a reigning monarch, George VI, to stay. In the event it was the shoot that was its downfall as the beaters, believing they knew a good thing when they saw one, went on strike in an effort to increase their day's pay from a shilling to one shilling and two pence. Ernest Guinness, who was as stubborn as he was rich, indignantly refused to countenance this extravagance and when the beaters failed to give way he sold his castle to a hotel chain almost overnight.

Glenmaroon, a vast town house so big that it spanned a main road by means of an enclosed bridge from which the family had once watched the fires of the Easter uprising, boasted one of the first indoor swimming pools in Ireland, an electric organ of Mighty Würlitzer proportions and a billiard-room the size of a basket-ball court. Luggala and Loch Bray, modest in comparison, were bought as places where Ernest's three daughters could be sent safely out of the way while the grown-ups were entertaining elsewhere. Finally there was the three-masted steam yacht *Fantôme* to escape to if a need for solitude became overpowering. Ernest occasionally apologised for its inadequacies – six state rooms and a crew of fourteen being embarrassingly unexceptional. Despite this apparently ostentatious display of wealth, the Guinness family, thanks perhaps to the diplomatic skills of all three brothers, remained the most Irish of the great Anglo-Irish dynasties. Even Brendan Behan, that most volatile and militant of nationalists, would have it that 'The Guinnesses are the only English aristocrats who have remained truly Irish.'

This was certainly true of Ernest's three daughters, Aileen, Maureen and Oonagh. Woven into their complex characters was all the laughter and the tragedy, the chaos and the circular logic, the generosity and obstinacy, the living for the day and the crack, the 'divil take the hindmost' and – above all – the deeply sentimental, uncritical love for Ireland that is the hallmark of its people. If, as James Joyce believed, Ireland is the old sow that eats her farrow, she would have found willing supplicants in these three heiressess to a Guinness fortune.

Oonagh was not only rich, she was small and slim and blonde and beautiful. Philip was tall, dark and strikingly handsome; he had impeccable breeding, sound prospects and enough money to lift him emphatically out the ranks of the gold-diggers who infested the London season; and he danced very well. Having almost nothing in common they fell in love and were married in 1929 at the fashionable St Margaret's, Westminster – the society wedding of the year. It was an occasion in fact to match the marriages of Aileen Guinness the year before to the Honourable Brinsley Plunket and of Maureen Guinness in 1930 to the Marquess of Dufferin and Ava. Oonagh's sisters were destined to live in two of the grandest houses in Ireland: Aileen at Luttrellstown Castle, County Dublin, and Maureen at Clandeboye in Ulster. All three seemed to have made marriages put together in an emerald green heaven but none was fated to be happy.

After a protracted honeymoon spent in a number of Europe's more fashionable resorts, Philip and Oonagh set up house in Rutland Gate, Hyde Park, from where Philip made a daily journey to his stockbroker's office in the City. Weekends were spent in the country, either at Plaw Hatch Hall, the Kindersley family home near East Grinstead, or in a succession of country houses rented for the summer. For Oonagh, Plaw Hatch was not much fun and she was seldom happy there. Golf, tennis and bridge were the older Kindersleys' preoccupations and Oonagh played none of them. She was made to learn golf with the resident professional and hated it; tennis was slightly more fun, although the velvet skirt in which she first appeared (not having anticipated the need for whites) aroused her mother-in-law's ire – as did Oonagh's infrequent attendances at breakfast, which were invariably greeted with a brisk 'You look seedy this morning.'

Philip, who was keen on all games and less than patient with his wife's lack of aptitude, also liked his hunting, going out so regularly with the Whaddon Chase that Oonagh thought she ought at least to try to share this passion. Fortified by unwise quantities of cherry brandy, riding side-saddle with her top-hat perched on the back of her head and braving what seemed to be interminable hail beating at her face, she trailed dismally after the field, terrified of jumping the obstacles that the others – particularly her husband – saw as a series of challenges to their nerve and ability. She never caught sight of Philip again after the various meets (he was always up at the front with the thrusters) and felt guiltily that he would be ashamed of her as she prayed passionately that she could soon go home. Amidst all these vexations, practically the only solace in what should have been a rural idyll was the occasional company of her gentle, artistic brother-in-law before the unforgiving architecture of the Southern Railway took him away for ever.

At Christmas the young Kindersleys would shoot at Ashford or join the Guinness gatherings at Glenmaroon. Just as Oonagh disliked Plaw Hatch, so Philip cared little for Ireland. He mistrusted the Irish and constantly complained that there was little or nothing to do. Taken to Luggala, which her father later gave to Oonagh, he called it a god-forsaken place – by which he actually meant that it had no golf course or tennis court to keep him actively amused.

This rather disheartening catalogue of incompatibility was alleviated by only two obviously shared interests: parties and their two children. Gay (his parents at the last minute had agreed that Gaylord was a little too much) was born by Caesarean operation on 2 June 1930 and Tessa arrived two years later. The usual succession of nannies came to Rutland Gate and went again – including the bossily barmy Nanny Skeet, who took to locking Oonagh out of the nursery as well as ordering her to have no more children. In the gaps between help, Oonagh took on a great deal of the bringing up herself and found that she enjoyed the company of Gay and Tessa rather more – she reflected sadly – than she did that of her husband.

The social round was unceasing, both in London and in the country where Philip rented Great Tangley Manor at Boxhill from Sir Frederick Ponsonby. David Niven, then a young officer in the Highland Light Infantry with an already highly developed taste for the good things of life, was a frequent visitor, as was Prince George, the Duke of Kent, who found the house useful as a private and congenial place to which he could bring his mistress, Edith d'Erlanger. Despite his unconventional love life, the prince was not entirely devoid of royal imperiousness. Finding one morning that neither Philip nor Oonagh had bothered to rise from their bed to see him off for an early engagement, he refused to come again – despite (at her husband's urging) a slightly half-hearted effort by Oonagh to seduce him to do so on the floor of a London nightclub.

Notwithstanding the children and the love that both Philip and Oonagh had for them, the Kindersleys were drifting apart. In public they remained an entity of sorts. At parties – four or five a week – they would drink too much and have their separate fun. For the sake of appearances and in an effort not to engage the interest of the gossip columnists too closely, they would always try to go home together, where invariably Philip would spend some time making himself sick so that he was fit – at least in his own estimation – to go into the office the next day. Oonagh found she could not master this arcane accomplishment and suffered increasingly debilitating hangovers. In this sea of alcohol, the remnants of romance slowly drowned.

Philip had in fact remained faithful to his wife for barely a year. Soon after the birth of his son, he began an affair with Valerie (known as Valsie), Lady Brougham and Vaux, who was a daughter of Field Marshal Lord French and, more poignantly, Oonagh's best friend and bridesmaid. Oonagh, slightly to her surprise, found that she didn't mind overmuch – until, that is, she happened to notice Valsie wearing her bridesmaid's dress at an assignation with Philip. This startling lack of sensitivity irritated her at the time, but more general lack of concern may be explained, at least in part, by the fact that she was in the process of forming an attachment of her own.

Dominick Geoffrey Edward Browne, 4th Baron Oranmore and Browne (Dom to his intimates), and his wife Mildred were often guests on the *Fantôme* as, of course, were the young Kindersleys and more occasionally (when engineered by Philip) the Broughams. This floating equivalent of Kenya's Happy Valley became a crucible out of which two new marriages were eventually forged. Ernest and Gar, secure in their own world, were at first slow to notice the irregularities but were moved eventually to remonstrate with their wayward daughter when she went home with Dom after Tramore Races, leaving Philip and Valsie to fly to London. Matters then became decidedly more public, and the press rumours which had started in 1934 turned into hard news when the papers in New York discovered Dom and Oonagh on a trip to Jamaica and Mexico a year later. Two divorces were embarked upon and the question then arose as to whom Dom was to sleep with in order to give his wife the necessary grounds. He flatly refused to employ any of the readily available professionals and decided instead that the statutory requirements could best be met by going with Oonagh to stay at a hotel in France owned by a Guinness cousin. The hotel manager, who had not been adequately briefed, baulked at giving evidence against such a distinguished kinswoman of his employer and the errant couple were obliged to move on to Austria and finally Nazi Germany in search of more compliant accomplices. Streams of German chambermaids and Hungarian waiters subsequently hurried to England to make the required depositions (and be handsomely rewarded) and the affair was speedily settled to everyone's satisfaction – everyone, that is, except Ernest and Gar. They hated the whole business, especially the publicity, and laid the blame squarely, and not entirely unjustly, at Philip's door.

These shenanigans appeared not to affect the children unduly; in fact they hardly seemed to notice. When his mother told Gay, then aged 6, of the register office wedding she had that morning undergone, he asked merely whether Dom had worn a nice tie. He and Tessa had already seen a great deal of the man who had become their step-father and they both liked and trusted him. Dom was very good with children (he had five of his own) and Castle MacGarrett, his home in County Mayo, was a paradise for the young, a magnificently turreted edifice set in 3,000 acres of best Irish grassland. None of the children was there permanently; the Brownes spent most of their time with their mother while Gay and Tessa made occasional visits to their father in England. But how they all loved it: there were ponies to ride and Daddy Dom built a show-ring on the lawns; there was the seemingly endless estate with little stone walls to be jumped and no barbed wire to impede progress; and, perhaps best of all for Gay, there was the river which wound its way lazily through the park and was a source of fine, fat brown trout left largely undisturbed by all save the local poachers. Dom's first – perhaps only lasting – love was shooting; he always wore plus-fours during the day and quite unashamedly described himself as the best shot in Ireland.

There was also the attentive staff led by Smythe the English butler: footmen in full livery, cooks, gardeners and grooms galore as well as Fahey the pig-man who looked like the Hunchback of Notre Dame and the Smiths (the labourer father, mother and twelve squabbling, tumbling, laughing, indescribably dirty children) who all lived in a two-room cottage and whose sleeping arrangements were an endless source of perplexed speculation for Gay and Tessa. But the family's favourite was Dom's valet, Patrick Cummins, who was soon to be promoted to butler and with whom Oonagh and her children struck up an immediate and lasting friendship.

During his search on the continent for admissible divorce evidence, Daddy Dom had become much impressed by the apparent orderliness and ability to get things done demonstrated by the German people under their new leader, whose name he could never remember. He had also been charmed by the beauty of the young Aryan women and persuaded Oonagh that a German nanny would be just the thing for Gay and Tessa. Quite clearly, he reasoned, German was going to be the important language of the future; why didn't the children start to learn it now? Accordingly an agency was consulted and Helga was engaged, complete with flaxen pigtail. She was not at her post for long. Completely failing to appreciate the haphazard charms of life at Castle MacGarrett and missing the flag-waving and discipline of the Hitler Youth, she became homesick within three months and pleaded for repatriation. Next came the dark and brooding Karen, a comprehensive Swabian sadist who – among other more violent preferences – would make her charges sick and then require them to clear the mess up with their own hands. She mercifully lasted only a matter of days until

Oonagh, noticing the lack of happy laughter, found her out. Elizabeth, on the other hand, was a resounding success – to such an extent that Oonagh began to suspect that some of Dom's male guests came principally to see the nanny, so much unexpected fuss did they affect to make of the children. Her instinct was accurate: one afternoon she came into the dining-room (usually deserted at that time of day) to discover the girl being energetically rogered on the polished table by a man with whom she herself had once enjoyed a brief flirtation. Elizabeth, tearful and imploring that it was all part of her wish to give entire satisfaction, was returned to the Fatherland to do her enthusiastic bit for the Führer's breeding programme and was replaced in due time by Maria.

Maria did not appear to have quite the same obvious attraction for men as her immediate predecessor and Oonagh felt that she could relax at last. This time her impulsive judgement let her down. One morning she was joined in her room by an excited and happily flushed small son. Oh, he explained, he'd had a lovely night. Maria had got into bed with him and blown into his mouth and then she'd asked him to tickle her ears and her front bits (aren't they big, Mummy?) and he'd found some soft hair in a warm place between her legs. And then she'd started to play with his flute and it all felt very nice. Then he'd gone to sleep and in the morning she'd done it all again. And what is this game called, Mummy, and will you play it with me? Oonagh felt that the German experiment had not been an unqualified success.

As his son's tenth birthday approached, Philip – who had married even sooner after the divorces than Oonagh and was now living at Rutland Gate with Valsie – decided that it was high time that Gay was sent away to school, and arranged for him to go to Cothill near Abingdon where he himself had been educated. His mother and grandmother Gar delivered the small Kindersley. At first he was homesick, so much so that he humiliated himself dreadfully by bursting into tears while sharing with his friends a birthday cake that Philip had personally delivered in a light aircraft. The sound of his father flying away overhead had been just too much. He loved his parents dearly and, despite his genuine affection for both Dom on the one hand and Valsie on the other, the realisation that his real mother and father were apart from each other for ever and that he was now away from both had sharpened his perception of loss almost unendurably.

Gay's first summer holiday from prep school was shared between England and Ireland. When they were at Castle MacGarrett he and Tessa were told that, as war had been declared, their father was to join the army and Gay was to be taken away from Cothill and sent to Castle Park near Dun Laoghaire, where he would be closer to his mother. The headmaster, Donald Pringle, although determined to run his school on 'English lines', was entirely unused to having quite such a notable sprig of the Anglo-Irish nobility in his care. He was much in awe of Oonagh and the trappings of wealth which accompanied her visits. He also found it difficult to cope with the quaint eccentricities which he came to recognise as an inevitable consequence of harbouring a Guinness. As time passed he found himself musing on the experience.

The Rolls-Royce, he thought, was fine; it added a bit of tone, in fact. Not so easy to regard with equanimity was the drunken driver who always seemed to be precariously at the wheel, or the same chauffeur's apparent keenness that young Kindersley should run away and do more important things such as going to the races. Then there was the time that the Garda came to interview him in the middle of prayers, anxious to know when he had last seen Lady Oranmore and Browne's car. It had later been found outside a Dublin bar, having apparently been there for three days and nights while the driver had enjoyed the mother and father of a bender. Mind you, he'd had to smile when her ladyship and the three young girls had arrived in the yellow brougham; pity it had to happen in the middle of the hockey match, which had never quite recovered its momentum once the girls had dismounted and descended on Gay – oblivious of the fact that Castle Park was winning its first game for two years.

The three young ladies whose behaviour had so agitated Mr Pringle were Tessa and her cousins (Aileen's daughters) Neelia and Doon. Aileen had parted company from her husband at about the same time as Oonagh left Philip and had taken to enjoying a series of lovers, including an Austrian – a Baron Pantz. The baron and his brother were much in demand on the social scene in Ireland, where they were known respectively as Hot and Wet. Aileen, suddenly becoming bored with Teutonic flesh, sailed to America and, after the outbreak of war, elected to stay there for the duration, leaving her daughters to be brought up by Oonagh. This was considered by all concerned to be a perfect arrangement (Oonagh was developing a taste for surrogate motherhood); it was blighted only briefly when Neelia and Doon had to be told that their father had sleep-walked out of a second-floor window with fatal results.

Like his sister-in-law, Dom elected to give the war a miss. This was surprising, given the fact that he had joined the Brigade of Guards for a short time in the 1920s, and the decision distanced him somewhat from the patriotic fervour generally rampant among the Anglo-Irish (who for the most part flocked to the colours) and even caused him a certain amount of unpopularity – to which he remained supremely oblivious. But it did mean that he was unable to travel freely to England and his neutral stance also surrendered to Philip a certain moral advantage when the latter joined the Coldstream. Philip came to Castle Park to watch his son play hockey and to say goodbye to both his children before sailing for France. Gay was very proud of him – he was one of the few fathers on the touch-line that day to be going off to fight.

Philip fortunately survived the horrors of the retreat to Dunkirk and eventually limped back to London, where the remains of his battalion were billeted at Buckingham Palace. Still covered in the grime of war and a layer of oil from the bilges of the fishing boat in which he had been evacuated, he was making his way across the royal forecourt late at night when the man with the loudest voice in the British army – Regimental Sergeant Major Tibby Brittain – mistook him for a guardsman who had been out on the tiles and was now desecrating what to the RSM was practically holy ground. The voice gave full vent to its owner's outrage.

'Come here, you horrible bloody scarecrow; what the bloody hell do you think you're doing? Come here. At the double.'

Philip turned and walked towards the near-apoplectic RSM, whose wrath slowly subsided as he recognised his target as, unbelievably, an officer of the Coldstream Guards. There was much apologising – the word 'sir' recurring frequently – and the two parted the best of friends. The encounter was to have a significant bearing on Gay's own military career some eight years later.

In early 1941, Philip came again to Ireland to say his goodbyes. He was now off to North Africa and, having had some experience of war, knew that this time he might not be so lucky. The feeling communicated itself to the children so that both Gay and Tessa clung to him as he got into the car to catch the mailboat to England. On Christmas morning 1942 he was captured twenty miles from Tunis, having spent a large part of that notably unfestive day snatching glances at his watch and wondering what the children were doing. Minutes after he had been taken he noticed a Coldstream soldier lying dead some fifty yards away and indicated to his captors that he would like to go and retrieve the man's identity discs so that the next-of-kin could be informed. A German, seeing that the British officer himself was slightly hurt, went instead on this humanitarian errand. As he got close to his objective a land-mine blew him to oblivion and Philip, gratefully taking that as an omen of personal good fortune, never doubted that one day he himself would somehow return safely.

He spent 1943 in Italian hands, escaping with two friends in September, on the day that Badaglio asked the Allies for an armistice – a circumstance which persuaded the always reluctant prison guards that they should pack up and go home, leaving their charges to their own devices and, more importantly, the gates wide open. Three months later he was recaptured by some somewhat less accommodating Italian fascists and handed over to the Germans, ending his war in a camp near Brunswick from which he was liberated by the Americans in April 1945. Years later he was to write a charming book (*For You the War is Over*) about his experiences; elegantly and painstakingly written, it remains remarkable for its complete absence of any account of his family's fortunes – a fact all the more extraordinary in the light of the dramas affecting his son, dramas in which, despite the circumstances, he was able to play a decisive role.

Gay's time at Castle Park was coming to a close. His last term was made particularly fraught by the fact that a boy in his dormitory had died of polio, then known as infantile paralysis. The boys were all sent home as a minor epidemic swept Ireland. When a case was diagnosed in Claremorris – a town close to Castle MacGarrett – Oonagh, again pregnant (she and Dom had already had a son, Garech, in 1939), moved to Ashford Castle with the children. From there she prepared to send Gay to a public school.

Philip had given much thought to this matter and had always planned that his son should go to Eton. Oonagh, at first happy with the arrangement, changed her mind at the outbreak of war. Eton was too close to London and even nearer to Windsor Castle, which she was firmly convinced would be a prime objective for German bombers. Not confident of the enemy's ability to hit a pinpoint target, she decided that Gay should continue his schooling in Ireland and entered him for St Columba's College in County Dublin, a Protestant foundation which was nevertheless fiercely nationalist, for example making the learning of the Irish language a high priority. Gay started there in September and word of this change of plan reached Philip in his prison camp in Italy. He was predictably furious and somehow (his book makes no mention of the incident) managed to wire his disapproval to both Oonagh and Lord Kindersley. The message was short and to the point: 'I do not wish my son to be brought up as a Sinn Feiner.'

He followed up this opening salvo with instructions to his father that he should go to the law if necessary to see that Gay went to Eton. A formal deposition was made to a firm of solicitors and Lord Kindersley applied successfully through the English courts for custody of his grandson. Oonagh, equally predictable in her reaction to this turn of events and feeling secure in her Irish fastness, ignored the order. The English judicial system, affronted at the flaunting of its authority over a British minor, applied to the Irish High Court, which granted a provisional writ of habeas corpus to Lord Kindersley (on behalf of Philip) calling upon Oonagh to deliver the boy to Plaw Hatch. In early November the story broke in the London evening papers and by the next day it had moved the war off the front pages in both England and Ireland.

Before confirming its judgment, the High Court in Dublin asked for written evidence from Philip Kindersley to the effect that he did indeed wish his son to be handed over to Lord Kindersley for the purpose of continuing his education at Eton College. This was forthcoming and despite (or perhaps because of) a twelve-hour speech by Cecil Lavery KC, Oonagh's counsel, the judge ruled that Gay should be handed over to his grandfather on 3 December. Oonagh was now very ill in hospital with pregnancy complications – a condition described coyly in court as 'a delicate state of health'. She roused herself to launch an appeal and her room at the Leinster Nursing Home soon resembled a barrister's chambers as counsel and solicitors consulted over the next moves. It was all to be in vain; the matter was referred to the Supreme Court and on 15 December it too ruled against her.

In its judgment the court made it clear that it believed that 'the mother's actions were motivated by nothing other than a genuine love for her son and regard for his safety and welfare'. It went on to stipulate that part of each school holiday was to be spent with Oonagh in Ireland and the remainder with the Kindersleys in England. None of this was any comfort to Gay's distraught mother. On 28 December she gave birth to a boy who died forty-eight hours later and, at her lowest ebb, her elder son came to say an emotional goodbye before leaving with Dom for the court, where he was to be formally handed over to his grandfather. Described in a contemporary account as 'this blue-eyed, red-cheeked lad of 13 years wearing a dark green muffler and brown overcoat', Gay wept when faced by the judge. So did Dom and the Kindersleys – even Cecil Lavery, with whom Gay solemnly shook hands, was seen to wipe away a tear. The large gathering of Irish women who had followed the case with mounting indignation did not weep. They preferred more positive action and their close interest, never less than 100 per cent partisan in Oonagh's favour, turned to outrage. Gay and his grandparents, trying to slip out of a side door, were trapped by a baying crowd who left the principals (and the press) in no doubt as to where their sympathies lay, hurling both abuse and handy projectiles at the 'English lord'.

After a disturbed night spent in the Gresham Hotel, the party sailed for Holyhead. The journey was rough, so rough that Gay – who had injudiciously tucked in to a plateful of bacon and eggs – was sick whilst being shown round the bridge by the captain, losing the wire plate round his teeth in the process. Reporters and photographers met the mailboat and there were more at Crewe. On the train to Euston, three forced themselves into the private carriage, demanding interviews and asking the now thoroughly alarmed small boy if he was happy. Lady Kindersley, who was as tough as she was determined, threw them out.

There followed a brief stay at Plaw Hatch where the Kindersley family had closed ranks and assembled in force. Apart from Valsie, her Brougham son Julian and Gay's half-sisters Nicky and Virginia were there, as were the Belmont cousins. (The Belmonts were themselves to have a particularly unfortunate time when their father, a wartime Ack Ack officer in charge of a sector of London's defences, fell out of his staff car while travelling at high speed from one gun emplacement to another and was killed). All were determined to make Gay as happy as possible and Valsie arranged that he should ride Sunny, the family pony. Equally concerned to show them that he could hold his end up, Gay rather overdid it, dismissing confidently cautions that the pony was far from easy to handle.

'I ride every day in Ireland and Tessa and I jump all the walls and Daddy Dom's show jumps,' he told them firmly.

Sunny, not having been exercised in weeks, was a little fresh and, not recognising this unexpected passenger as anyone very special, dumped him within seconds. Nothing was hurt save Gay's pride and the watchers were secretly pleased that he didn't appear to be quite as good on a horse as he had led them to believe.

Within three days, on 20 January 1944, he had joined his cousin Michael Belmont at Eton in the house of Mr A K Wickham (known to the boys, rather unkindly, as 'Prick'). Michael took Gay very much under his protective wing, shielding him from the many pitfalls laid out to trap the new boys, and he was lucky to have been assigned to the care of Wickham, who had once enjoyed the well-deserved reputation of being a Tartar but whose recent marriage to a stunningly beautiful Belgian princess had mellowed him considerably.

On his first day Michael took Gay to see their elder cousin Hugo Kindersley (later to become the third baron), who was a year ahead and in another house. As they stood talking outside the college, a photographer approached, waving his camera. Tail-coats flying, they ran to take refuge in a classroom. There, under siege, they were rescued by a master who suggested reasonably that they would do better to succumb in order to be rid of their pursuer quickly. From that moment on, Eton took precautions to protect its best-known pupil of the day from further press interest, but Gay was slowly realising that he quite liked being the centre of attention.

Throughout this whole sequence of events, with hundreds of column inches being devoted to it by the English and Irish national newspapers, the boys at Eton had followed matters every bit as closely as the good fish-wives of Dublin. The general sympathy had at first lain with Gay and Philip – the brave fighting man languishing in a beastly prison camp battling against all odds to see that his son was given an education befitting an English gentleman. Once the matter was resolved, however, attitudes changed perceptibly. All that publicity, it was assumed, was bound to have made the boy stuck-up; even parents could talk (boringly) about little else; no doubt he would need to be brought down a peg or two. The advent of Kindersley was awaited with the keenest anticipation. He was now a marked man, a creature which has always excited the greatest of suspicion in the public-schoolboy mind – he was different.

The fact is that he was indeed different, and not just because of the family row. Contemporaries remember him as a refreshing change from the usual product of the exclusive English prep schools which then fed Eton. His Irishness – extending to a soft Dublin accent and a fierce nationalism which led him to defend Ireland's neutrality and play rebel songs at top volume in the music rooms – caused him to be ragged without mercy, and his equally fanatical keenness for physical exercise made him anathema to the more aesthetic. On the whole, however, he charmed the waiting vultures off the twigs. His total lack of resentment at what had happened to him, the absence of any trace of conceit, his zest for life and his genuine ability to be interested in everyone and everything ensured that the teasing rapidly became good humoured. Another seven-day wonder had come and gone; soon he was able to merge into the background.

He made friends quickly and easily; his essentially trusting nature, his kindness and generosity – qualities that were to become characteristic of him in adulthood – were already evident. Apart from his cousins, he became especially close to Michael Allsopp, a life-long companion and confidant, and Bob McCreery, who was to become a great rival on the racecourse. He also made his first acquaintance with John Lawrence (later Lord Oaksey), with whom, like McCreery, he was to do battle over point-to-point and national hunt fences. Others, too, were to remain friends in need.

The courts having decreed that his holidays were to be divided between his mother in Ireland and (pending the hoped-for return of his father) his grandparents at Plaw Hatch, he soon became a veteran of the Irish Sea crossing – to such an extent that a steward, Tosh Ball, was permanently assigned to him. Tosh, a large and cheerful rogue in the best Irish tradition, would take him into the bar and fill him up with his Guinness grandfather's draught stout. Ball habitually travelled with a pound or two of Irish butter which invariably found its way into the ready hands of British Customs officials, no doubt in the hope that they would turn a blind eye to some of the other contraband the steward was running – notably silk stockings, for which most women in poor, blacked-out, blitz-torn Britain would give their all.

Gay entered into the spirit of this harmless smuggling with a will, often carrying in his suitcase many pairs of such stockings for his grandmother Gar. Suspecting that his Kindersley grandparents would not approve of this enterprise, he had not included them on his list of recipients. He was proved painfully correct in this supposition when one of his cousins discovered what appeared to be a silk mine in an open suitcase at Plaw Hatch and reported the matter. This resulted in a formal telegram from his grandfather to Dom: 'Kindly refrain from involving Gay in your contraband activities. They will cause much embarrassment on this side of the Channel. Signed Kindersley.'

While being questioned by Dom on the matter and relating the other events of his stay in England, Gay mentioned that he had unfortunately had a tickle in his bottom which had caused him to scratch quite a lot in what was probably rather an inelegant manner. His grandfather, suspecting piles or possibly worms, had caused him to be examined in a most intimate way by the family doctor – a proceeding which disconcerted the boy exceedingly. Dom, always sympathetic, saw his chance and composed a reply: 'Kindly refrain from poking about in Gay's arse as this causes him much embarrassment in his own channel. Signed Oranmore and Browne.'

Thus was the feud perpetuated.

Much as he liked – even loved – his grandparents, Gay's real joy was to go to Ireland and see again his mother and, especially, Tessa, to whom he had become very close. His sister had been born with an asthmatic condition which she did her best to ignore but which was serious enough to prevent her from going away to school. The great joys of this loving and exuberant little girl were her animals: her West Highland terriers, the guinea-pigs, the rabbits and, best of all, her pony Brown Jack. She was growing up into a first-rate horsewoman and keen was the rivalry between her and Doon. In the holidays Gay and the two girls would take part in the children's classes at all the shows, including the Royal Dublin at which Tessa won the 1945 championship. Gay and his own pony, Biscuit, were not nearly such an accomplished pair and he was sometimes reduced to tears of frustration as he failed to win a rosette. The cousins made up a highly competitive trio.

The holiday weeks were spread between Castle MacGarrett and Luggala, the hunting lodge in the Wicklow Mountains which was now Oonagh's. Tucked away in a deep valley in the shade of the hill known as The Fancy, Luggala was a place of enchantment. It cast its spell over all who arrived there down the long, winding, precarious drive from the road above and over the stream which fell gratefully into the deep waters of the black-as-night lough fringed with a circlet of white mica sand. In the eighteenth century The Fancy and the lough below had been the scene of many a skirmish between the redcoats and the rebel bands which roamed the mountains. For Gay and Tessa, it was their favourite place in the whole world.

At Castle MacGarrett Dom entertained in some state. Michael Allsopp was asked there and after protracted negotiations with his parents (who were not at all keen on his being mixed up with the wild Guinnesses), he was allowed to go. For a boy leaving England for the first time – and wartime England at that, with its deprivations and air-raids – it was an exciting and eye-opening experience. Met on the mailboat by Dom, he and Gay were tipped a crinkly white £5 note each and then nourished with an enormous steak. The sea trip passed quickly and then came the drive in the Rolls and the first heart-stopping view of the castle, with its turrets and the flag flying from the tower. At lunch a footman was stationed behind each chair, and afterwards the boys were given a glass of port. Mike, overawed by being treated like a grown-up and not wanting to spoil the dream-like quality of it all, had put aside the more mundane essentials of life until they caught up with him during his second glass and he began to wriggle on his seat. Dom, noticing his discomfort, suddenly broke off from a survey of the shooting prospects for the coming season.

He announced solemnly: 'I once had a friend who died out hunting because he didn't get off his horse to have a pee. He was so uncomfortable that eventually he fell off and burst his spleen. Off you go, my boy.'

The grateful Michael fled to the loo.

Dom had both a way with children and a magnetic charm for women, but his relationship with Oonagh was already under some strain; again the trouble was that the pair had very little in common. There was nothing private about their rows; indeed guests of whatever age were encouraged to take sides. Dom loved to surround himself with the sporting set whilst Oonagh – with whom the young Allsopp had fallen hopelessly in calf love – enjoyed the company of writers and artists, who would plead with her that they should not be subjected to the company of Dom and his shooting friends more than was absolutely necessary. She held court at Luggala, at which she spent an ever-increasing amount of time, and it was there that the disagreements were at their most spectacular. The servants found themselves in one camp or another, the Oonagh faction being led by Patrick Cummins who adored both his mistress and Luggala with equal intensity. He also loved Gay and Tessa, indulging them almost as outrageously as he did their mother.

In April 1945 the Americans reached POW Camp Oflag VIII F and Philip Kindersley was returned to London and to Valsie. He recorded the reunion as being 'As wonderful as I had always hoped it would be.' Gaunt and tired but deliriously happy, he took his wife, son and daughter to dinner at the Connaught Hotel with some of his closest friends from the camp, including Dicky Black, an amateur rider who was to win the first post-war Cheltenham Gold Cup on Fortina. Such was his exhilaration at being with his family again, Philip incautiously downed a brace of Dry Martini cocktails and had to sit for several minutes with his head in his hands. Gay and Tessa, worried about their father's state, were taken aside by Black, who explained to them gently the effects of alcohol on those who had been forced to abstain for some time. Still only 38, Philip soon recovered his health and vigour (as well as his capacity for drink and his addiction to bookmakers) and was quickly back in the City, working as a stockbroker for George Henderson and Company. He lived briefly at Plaw Hatch where he, Gay and Tessa spent many happy hours riding in Ashdown Forest, and soon found and bought The Grove at Turners Hill. From there he became master of the Mid-Surrey Farmers Draghounds, an all-consuming interest which was to give his son an early opportunity to ride over obstacles at a speed even faster than achieved when hunting in Ireland and confirmed in Gay an already half-formed addiction to racing.

At Castle MacGarrett Dom, too, had decided that racing was the thing. In partnership with Captain Cyril Harty, father of three jockeys, he bought a number of young potential jumpers. Bill Fogarty, the stud groom, and Gerry Madden (who went on to ride for Fulke Walwyn) backed and broke the horses in readiness for Frenchie Nicholson, one of the leading national hunt trainers in England, to look at and perhaps buy. Once the young horses were broken, Tessa and Gay would be allowed to exercise them – in itself an act of faith by Fogarty and a mark of the competence of the Kindersley children. The first actual racehorse that either of them sat on was Irish Lizard, who was to finish third in the 1953 Grand National, having survived an early incident during which he and Gay parted company and the then novice horse disappeared into the castle's park. He was found unhurt and the young jockey, fearing the worst, was mightily relieved when Fogarty allowed him to continue to exercise. What with the hunting with the South Mayo Harriers and now the chance to ride thoroughbreds, the racing seeds were well and truly sown. They flourished in the climate of competition with Tessa who, although two years younger, was so accomplished that in March 1946, at barely 14, she was allowed to ride in the cob's race at the South Mayo point-to-point, finishing an excited and much acclaimed third.

In January 1947 there was an outbreak of diphtheria in the west of Ireland. Dom was in London, ostensibly on horse business but in fact seeing a woman whom who he had taken as a mistress after the war, and Oonagh decided that she ought to call in the ancient family doctor to decide how best to protect the children. He advised an inoculation of anti-toxin and that evening he administered the injections. At about 1 o'clock in the morning Tessa staggered into her mother's room, complaining that she felt awful and was finding it difficult to breathe. Oonagh put her back into bed, alerted the household and recalled the doctor. By the time he arrived, Tessa's breathing had deteriorated and the old man seemed helpless. He diagnosed a massive asthma attack, probably brought about by a reaction to the inoculation, but had no resources with which to do anything about it. Patrick Cummins tried the only remedy he knew, getting the now desperately weakening child to sip some brandy, but in a few more agonising minutes she was dead. Only those who have seen a child of their own die can know Oonagh's immediate and overwhelming grief. She woke Gay, who stood forlornly in his dressing-gown while the memory of the pale face on the pillow, framed by its flowing blonde hair, became indelibly etched on his memory – his first death, his sister.

Philip, summoned by telephone, arrived the next day and was greeted by Gay on the steps of Castle MacGarrett; father and son collapsed weeping into each other's arms. Gay led him to the room in which Tessa lay and Philip kissed her gently on the lips before turning to comfort Oonagh who, knowing how Tessa had hated the dark, had not left her daughter's side. She was to sit with her for each of the three nights that preceded the funeral.

Dom was eventually contacted and arrived, both grief-stricken and burdened with guilt. He felt then – and for the rest of his life – that had he been there he might have had the presence of mind to have quizzed the doctor on the possible effects of an injection and perhaps have prevented the tragedy.

The household went into the deepest of mourning. Patrick Cummins and Bill Fogarty in particular were inconsolable; even the horses seemed to hang their heads. Philip met the man who, it appeared, had been responsible for the death of his daughter. There were no recriminations as the two of them, father and doctor, each wrapped in his private cloak of misery, shook hands.

The manservants carried Tessa the one-and-a-half miles to Crossboyne Church, the family following on foot as is the custom of Ireland. Halfway down the long Castle MacGarrett drive, Gay heard the sound of galloping hooves. It was little Brown Jack, who had broken out of his box and now took station on the park rails alongside the coffin. He kept pace with it until it reached the gates, then stood and watched patiently as the melancholy procession wound slowly out of sight.

She was buried in newly consecrated ground at Luggala – the enchanted house – where Oliver Messel later designed a light-filled dome resting on four classical columns: a white marble shrine set against the black, cold waters of the lough in the green fold of the Wicklow Mountains.

The coroner's verdict was death by misadventure.

CHAPTER TWO

The Making of a Corinthian

At Eton, Gay worked and played hard – characteristics inherited from his father who was nothing if not wholehearted in all his undertakings. Not blessed with an academic brain, the young Kindersley channelled his considerable energy into the sports field. He practised assiduously and began to make his mark. At athletics his aim was to win the Eton Mile – the blue riband race – and in his final year he failed only by inches, being awarded his colours for a brave attempt and for being placed in a number of other events. He captained the gentlemen's cricket team (a euphemism for the 4th XI), represented Eton at rugby and his house at the field game, being particularly pleased when Philip raised a team of contemporaries to take on his house XI. He also rather fancied the stage and took part in a production of a melodrama called *Ten Minute Alibi*, produced by Tim Brinton – later to become a television newsreader. This venture did not go entirely to plan as Gay, whose key role as the villain required him to commit a murder and then turn the clock back to establish an alibi, turned it forwards instead, thus irredeemably confusing both the cast and the audience as well as causing severe anguish to the producer. Despite this lapse, in his last year he was elected to Pop, the Eton society – the pinnacle of social acceptability.

At about that time it became clear that he was now Ernest Guinness's favourite grandchild. The old man became determined that the boy should join him in the family business. With that in mind, he had mapped out a career plan which he now unveiled to Gay. First was National Service in the Foot Guards, then Oxford to read for a chemistry degree and next spells in various departments of the company to prepare him for the grave responsibilities that would be his in due course. He would, Ernest explained to him during dinner at Holmbury, inherit a great deal of money when he was 25; meanwhile he was to receive a small farm in Ireland which would provide a modest income. If that proved not to be enough bearing in mind the regrettable fact that he seemed determined to own and ride expensive horses, some Guinness trust or other could probably be tapped to keep him going. Gay, who had never thought about money – there always seemed to be a ready supply – rather diffidently felt obliged to point out what seemed to him to be a couple of flaws in this otherwise excellent scheme. First, he didn't know a thing about chemistry (at Eton he was concentrating rather haphazardly on modern languages) and, secondly, his father had proposed that he should do his army service in a cavalry regiment – preferably one that still recognised that horses were every bit as important as tanks. Ernest, who was not in the least used to having his judgement questioned, brushed aside these tentative objections and switched on the 9 o'clock news, which he listened to every evening at the table, commanding both his family and the hovering servants to keep quiet. The meal over, he wiped the Jersey cream from his moustache and, as always, retired to watch Laurel and Hardy films on his cinematograph. The matter was closed.

At the age of 17, Gay seemed set fair for a future for which most young men would sell their souls: an assured career within the protective confines of one of the world's most prosperous companies; enough money (with a great deal more in prospect) to live comfortably and embark if he wished on a notoriously expensive hobby; and an indulgent and provident family to fall back on if necessary. What more could any young man require?

Gay's preoccupation, however, was not with the future but with a far more pressing problem. What he wanted most, and wanted urgently, was a proper experience with a woman – one which he could parade in front of his friends at Eton. Irritatingly, an increasing number of them would return from holidays boasting about girls they had kissed, fumbled with (they phrased it differently) and even made love to. It was obvious even to the artless Gay that a lot of this sort of talk was prompted by a natural desire to be one up, but having had no such adventure himself since the blessed Maria ten years before, he found himself ill-equipped even to make up a plausible story. He had, of course, been to one or two dances and on occasion had even been alone with a debutante as nervous as himself, but had found that he had little to say once they had explored the weather and the vagaries of parents. He didn't know where to turn for advice. Should he ask his father? Should he, perhaps, try to find a brothel – he understood from his more sophisticated friends that there were discreet establishments in London that would take care of his needs. As he dithered in indecision, a shapely windfall fell into his lap; her name was Simone and, miraculously, she was French.

Daddy Dom had found her on one of his trips to London and invited her to stay at Castle MacGarrett where she was, as it happened, the only guest. Around 30, she had long, shining red hair, a tiny waist and the neatest of ankles, and she was gratifyingly fascinated by the Irish countryside. In particular she was enthralled by the hundreds of 'leetle rabbits' hopping about the lawns ('I shoot the buggers,' said Dom dismissively) and by the 'ver beeg 'orses' on which Gay, who had fallen in love at first sight, showed off madly to impress. After Dom and Oonagh went to bed Gay took to playing her his records which, being in the main rebel songs delivered at a brisk pace, were not of a tempo entirely conducive to romance. There were, however, some of Oonagh's which appeared to be suitable for dancing and one evening Simone suggested that they should do just that. Clutching her firmly, closer and closer, Gay felt the excitement welling up inside him and then, hazarding a guess at what should come next, he lunged forward to kiss her on the lips. Simone responded enthusiastically at first and then disengaged gently, murmuring, 'Oh Gay, you are ver' sweet but you are still only a leetle boy.' The leetle boy, however, feeling far from leetle in any department, was thrilled at this taste of the real thing; how many of his boastful friends could talk authoritatively of an experience with a grown-up? He wanted more. He would show them.

The following day Gay was to travel to England for the second half of his holidays and by happy coincidence Simone had to return to France. They travelled together on the evening mailboat, the sea calm, the moon bright and Tosh luckily absent. After dinner they walked the deck hand-in-hand, pausing now and then to kiss in a darkened corner. For Gay it was blissful; in racing terms his love-making had come on more than a few pounds in the last twenty-four hours.

Arriving at Holyhead at midnight, they transferred to the Euston train and were allotted adjoining sleepers. In a fever of excitement Gay undressed, only to remember with sudden dismay that he had no overnight bag. He was forced to slip between the sheets wearing his Eton pattern underwear – an unattractive combination of dirty yellow woolly vest and long pants. He lay in his bunk, heart racing with a thrilling anticipation of he didn't quite know what. The connecting door opened and there was Simone, hair flowing over a long white nightdress.

'I tink, my dulling,' she whispered, 'we will keep the door open.'

She turned off her light and shimmied over to her bunk where she lay in the dim light, looking expectantly over at Gay only a yard or two away. If ever there was a clear indication that he should join her, this was it, and even Gay recognised that his moment had come. Instead he froze. He couldn't do it. If Simone saw him in those awful clothes she would laugh at him. His romance would be shattered. He shut his eyes tightly and tried to think what a man of the world would do. When he opened them again, Simone had turned over and in the morning the door was closed.

Hours later she stood on the platform in the thin light of London's dawn, waiting for him to finish dressing. He tumbled fearfully out on to the platform and she kissed him on the cheek. She shook her head slowly, looking deep into his eyes so that Gay should see in their clear green depths a hint of what might have been. He never saw her again and later his father found him strangely subdued. Back at Eton his friends readily believed his story; they could recognise the truth when they heard it. They laughed.

It would be difficult for even the most insensitive of young men not to appreciate the contrasts between life as a member of Pop at England's leading public school and that of a National Service trooper in the 4th Royal Tank Regiment at Catterick Camp in Yorkshire. At Darlington railway station there had been no Guinness Rolls or deferential chauffeur. In their place stood a grim military three-ton lorry and a harassed sergeant whose sole aim was to tick off the names of the apprehensive conscripts as quickly as possible as he packed them into the back of the vehicle. The barrack-room – one arm of a wooden single-storey structure called a spider – held thirty metal-framed beds on which sheets and four folded blankets awaited their new owners. The tall steel lockers were painted battleship grey and the shining lino floor was cold and uninviting. Gay's next-door neighbour – lately out of Wandsworth after a misunderstanding with the Metropolitan Police over a case of GBH – occupied a bed-space only three feet away. He eyed the Old Etonian with marked disfavour, reminding Gay strongly of an alarming illustration he had once seen in a mythology book. Affecting not to notice the unwinking stare, he turned his back and continued with the disagreeable process of changing into his newly issued blue-and-white-striped army pyjamas.

'Oy,' said the basilisk. 'Oy. Get your arse 'ole covered up. Whaddyer think I am, a bleedin' shirt-lifter?'

The 4th Royal Tank Regiment was charged with turning out crewmen for the Royal Armoured Corps. From Catterick newly trained recruits would join cavalry and tank regiments stationed all over the world, from the United Kingdom to Hong Kong. It was also responsible for initiating the special training required by those who, by virtue of their supposedly superior education, had been designated potential officers (or fucking POs as they were more usually known by Skinner of the next bed) in order to prepare them for the rigours of a War Office selection board. WOSB, Gay had been led to believe, was the final hurdle to be successfully negotiated before he could be commissioned into the 7th Queen's Own Hussars, a regiment chosen for him by Philip as having sound horsy traditions. There was, he knew, also the matter of four months at an officer cadet school, but everyone at Eton had said that this was little more than a formality.

First, though, there were the three months of basic military training to be undergone by everyone, irrespective of their military destinies: a seemingly endless round of drill, small-arms training, PT and fieldcraft exercises conducted on the parade square, in the gym and on the Yorkshire moors. For the POs there was also the unofficial intelligence test devised by 4RTR, who had learned from bitter experience that some of those considered to be officer material by the War Office were about as suitable as a well-bred Labrador – a test, in fact, to try to weed out the educated idiots.

Gay, in common with a dozen or so of his intake of 120, took this examination and, despite completing it with an easy confidence, found that his name did not appear among those listed as having passed. It seemed that he had fallen at the first fence and was doomed to spend the next eighteen months in the less than appreciative company of Skinner and his mates. In some despair, he steeled himself to ask his troop sergeant for an interview with a demi-god known as the Squadron Leader.

'Waste of fucking time,' the sergeant assured him cheerfully, 'but I'll see what I can do.'

The Squadron Leader, a rotund major equipped with a luxuriant moustache to match his beret and blackthorn walking stick, seemed oddly pleased to see him.

'Kindersley, is it?' he asked. 'Not Philip Kindersley's boy by any chance?'

Gay confirmed that this was indeed the case.

'Good God,' the man said, 'he was in the bag with me. Splendid chap. Now what's the trouble?'

Gay explained that he would like, please, to take the test again.

'No need for that. You probably passed the first time what with being Philip's son and all that. Some sort of administrative balls-up, I expect. Don't worry about it, I'll add your name to the list. Give my regards to your father. Kindersley, eh, well, well, well!'

The War Office Selection Board was held in a country house not far from Catterick. The army, on taking it over, had tried successfully to remove any vestige of gracious living, putting up signs in such profusion that they served only to confuse. Gay and thirty-nine other hopefuls were issued with number-plated vests ('We never use names here') and sat down in the gothic hall to listen to the opening address.

'Some of you will fail,' said the colonel. 'But don't worry; it's not the end of the world. Some are born to be officers, some can be made into officers and some will never make it. It doesn't mean that you will not succeed later in life.' He paused, searching for an example. 'As a doctor or an artist or something. It's no disgrace.'

He clearly did not believe a word of it and neither did his audience. He outlined the programme for the next three days. Gay and his fellow candidates were to be subjected to a round of tests designed to sniff out unofficer-like flaws in their characters. There were essays to write and more intelligence tests to be taken. Outdoors there would be command tasks, conducted in syndicates of ten; each would take his turn at leading the others through complicated manoeuvres involving crossing crocodile-infested rivers with poles that were too frail and scaling supposedly electrified fences with ropes that were too short.

When affairs finally got briskly under way, officers scribbled maniacally on millboards as candidates fell in, tumbled off, shouted unworkable orders at each other or merely stood in mulish incomprehension. On the assault course, at which Gay excelled, a potential Guards officer broke his arm, giving rise to much speculation as to whether this meant an automatic pass for keenness or a fail for ineptitude.

Indoors again, the aspirants were warned of a five-minute 'lecturette' during which they would be required to deliver an informative talk on a matter dear to them for the educational benefit of the rest of the syndicate. Stamp collecting, bullfighting etiquette and the future of the Empire were among subjects chosen confidently by members of Gay's group; he himself was agonisingly undecided. Eventually he settled on the politics and history of Ireland and began to condense that complicated subject into the required three hundred seconds. Not surprisingly, he found this difficult and compromised with a stout defence of Irish nationalism with particular emphasis on the heroism of Eamon de Valera's stance on neutrality during the Second World War, all transmitted to his audience in a nervously wobbly voice pitched several octaves above his usual one. This was not a subject that endeared itself to his listeners, his performance being roughly akin to delivering a talk on the Roman sense of fair play to a room full of gladiators. Fellow candidates and examiners alike looked at each other with increasing disbelief, one of the latter allowing his clip-board to drop to the floor from nerveless fingers as he recalled his own father's service with the Black and Tans.

The final interview with the colonel seemed to go a little better. The contingent from Catterick had been carefully briefed on the questions that were likely to arise. 'Why do you want to be an officer?' was favourite, followed, it was confidently forecast, by a cursory canter round the aspirant's school career and a probe into his hobbies ('If you haven't got one, start one now'). The colonel was wily; he knew perfectly well what was expected of him and avoided all such predictable topics, varying his questions to suit what little he knew of each man. To Gay he seemed to be pleasingly interested in matters Irish, then he asked about fox-hunting before finally enquiring keenly into the form of the runners at Sandown Park that weekend. He had a facility for creating an easy self-confidence in his victims and each came out of the interview with the opinion that it had all gone rather well. Gay thought that he might even have done well enough to pass.

He had not in fact passed but neither, it appeared, had he failed. He was left sitting in solitary limbo as the others, having been given their results, departed either cheerfully brash or blankly disappointed. At last, the red tabs reappeared.

'Come inside, Kindersley.' He indicated his office and Gay, now fearing the worst but still clinging desperately to the fact that he hadn't been given the slip of paper which had so recently determined the moods of his companions, entered and stood trembling in front of the desk.

'Sit down. Now what I've decided to do is make you a borderline case, which means that all being well you will have passed, but ...'. He paused and looked appraisingly across his desk. '... there are one or two things I must check up on. Your mother's Irish and, I understand, lives in Ireland. The War Office is concerned about the IRA and you did make some pretty odd remarks in your lecturette. In fact the whole tone of your talk was not one I expected from someone who apparently wishes to be an officer in the 7th Hussars. We'll let you know.'

Gay, wondering just how they were going to investigate Oonagh – and remembering that she numbered among her friends Brendan Behan and one or two of his more silent associates who always seemed to wear dark glasses and military-looking berets – made his way despondently back to Catterick. Four weeks later he was informed by the stout major that he had, after all, passed and would be leaving for the Mons Officer Cadet School in Aldershot, home of the British army.

Hoping that he had put the worse of the square-bashing and barrack-room polishing behind him, he was pleased to see that among those in his platoon's wing of the now familiarly shaped spider was Michael Belmont, who had been there for some time but had been relegated because of illness and made to start again. Belmont quickly reassumed the role of mentor to his cousin that he had adopted so willingly at Eton and began by disabusing Gay of any notion that he might be harbouring as to the comparative ease of his new life.

Catterick, Mike explained, was a holiday camp when compared with the regime at Mons; punishment in the form of extra drill and shining parades was commonplace; relegation – or back-squadding as it was known – was frequent; and their lives were regulated twenty-four hours a day by a man bent on the pursuit of perfection, Regimental Sergeant Major Brittain of the Coldstream Guards, a man of such fanatical military exactness (the fastidious Belmont shuddered) that even the vegetables in his garden were dressed by the right. The Brittain philosophy was simple; the cadet was to be broken down into his component parts and then reassembled to produce an officer worthy, if not of a commission in the Coldstream, at least of playing the part of an officer in some lesser regiment. This ethos, Michael continued, was enthusiastically approved by the non-commissioned officers at Mons and no one endorsed its more uncomfortable manifestations more diligently than the man who was about to march into his young cousin's life at 120 paces to the minute – the man he was to know as Staff. Staff (short for Staff Sergeant) was the NCO responsible for the turn-out and drill of Gay's platoon and he didn't like cavalry cadets – it was widely supposed that he had been run over by a tank in the advance from Normandy.

Michael was earnestly advising his cousin to watch his step when the door flew open and, with a stamping of feet, the subject under discussion swept into the room. Nobody moved except Belmont, who sprang to attention. Staff surveyed the chaos of kitbags and suitcases from under the peak of his hat; the creases in his battledress trousers gave the appearance of having been sewn into place (they had); he held a pace-stick diagonally across his bulging chest and the brightness of his belt brasses menacingly matched the glittering of his eyes.

'Stand up. Room shun. From now on you're officer cadets, God help you. In the next hour you will draw your bedding; get your hair cut; have yourselves measured for uniforms by the tailor; get your boots, beret and white discs and be back here sorting yourselves out. Outside in three ranks; now move.'

Gay collected extra drills as others collected cigarette cards; endless evenings were spent repolishing boots which Staff had not considered up to standard and which had been further dulled by their frequent journeys through a window on their way to the nearest flower-bed, propelled thither by the tip of an ever-active pace-stick. He was relegated to the very back of the platoon where the awkward squad was invariably placed, the more effectively to hide their blemishes from the watchful eyes of the RSM. His drill deteriorated rapidly from indifferent to a stumbling shambles as he strove to shake off the constant reminders from his tormentor that he marched like a ploughboy. Staff was a bastard and Officer Cadet Kindersley bore the brunt.

Salvation arrived in a most unlikely form. There was a full school parade conducted in a cacophony of shouted commands as the various staffs yelled at their platoons while the company sergeant majors outdid each other in their own exhortations for perfection. From his position on a dais overlooking this kaleidoscope as platoons marched and counter-marched, the hitherto silent figure of the regimental sergeant major suddenly brought proceedings to a halt with a command which soared effortlessly above those of lesser mortals. He called for Officer Cadet Belmont. Mike marched stiffly towards the huge figure, watched by four hundred pairs of eyes whose owners fervently thanked their Maker that they had not been singled out. The parade held its collective breath but the expected explosion failed to occur as, remarkably, cadet and RSM were seen to be engaged in almost animated, if one-sided, conversation. Belmont returned to his platoon and Mr Brittain swelled into action.

'STAFF,' he roared. Twelve staffs stiffened and eleven imperceptibly relaxed as it became apparent that it was Gay's Staff who was under attack.

'STAFF. BRING MR KINDERSLEY TO ME.' Staff had mixed feelings as he doubled his least favourite cadet to the waiting RSM. On the one hand, this cavalry wart was clearly going to get his comeuppance; on the other, he himself was responsible for bloody Kindersley and might not therefore escape unscathed. He halted, breathed deeply and reported: 'Officer Cadet Kindersley, sir.'

Brittain looked down at the dishevelled figure in front of him. 'Mr Belmont told me who you were. Your father was a great friend of mine. The Hon. Philip Kindersley, wasn't it?'

Gay gulped and affirmed that that was so.

'Great man, your father. He's in good health, I trust? I'm glad to have you here.' His eyes sought those of his disbelieving subordinate. 'Staff, see that you move Mr Kindersley to the front rank of your platoon. Can't have him in the back with the ploughboys now, can we?'

Gay doubled proudly back to his place, his heart singing and a new-found confidence already clearly visible in the bounce in his step. For the second time in a few weeks, he was grateful to be his father's son.

As the first part of the Mons course drew to its dreary conclusion, Ernest Guinness died – another victim of medical incompetence. A pain in his leg was diagnosed as a blood clot and the doctor advised him to have an immediate hot bath. He did so and suffered a fatal heart attack.

For such an astute businessman, Guinness had been peculiarly short sighted in his plans for the provision of his family after his death. His two brothers had taken precautions to unload a great deal of their considerable personal wealth on their heirs in good time to avoid inheritance taxes. Ernest, in a mistaken belief that he had plenty of time, failed to emulate them and the Irish government was pleasantly surprised to receive around two-thirds of his fortune. At the time his grandchildren, inured against any trace of poverty by their indulgent mothers, hardly noticed the difference.

Gay now moved into G Squadron, where he and his fellow cadets destined for the mechanised cavalry regiments of the Royal Armoured Corps carried out the specialised training designed to fit them to lead a troop of tanks or armoured cars. Life became a little easier, much of it being spent in the dark as they peered sleepily at films of the internal combustion engine and the mysterious ways of firing mechanisms. Drill, though, still played a significant part in their routine as they strove to reach the state of perfection demanded by RSM Brittain for their final pass-off parade. Under-officers were appointed from among them and further layers of polish were applied to their boots. Gay managed without serious mishap and really rather enjoyed the theory of tactics of armoured warfare that was also a feature of the course. His major problem was navigation across country which, conscientious to a fault, he attempted to master by glueing his eyes to a map; as a result he was frequently lost while others did better by following sign-posts.

The tactics training – indeed the whole course – climaxed with Exercise Trek on Salisbury Plain, when each cadet was invited in turn to command a troop of armoured cars. Gay, who had recognised that his uncertain performance under Staff together with his map-reading difficulties made him a borderline case, determined that when he was appointed to one of these key positions he would put in an exemplary performance. His chance came when, as a troop leader, he was ordered to withdraw in contact with an advancing enemy. As the opposing force came over the hill to his front, Gay realised that their tactics were far from perfect. Even to his unpractised eye they looked to be something of an uncoordinated rabble and, far from withdrawing and keeping them under observation, as his directive required, he ordered his troop to attack. The consequences were predictably disastrous. The directing staff were furious; they had written the exercise not to give bloody Kindersley the chance to win a Victoria Cross but to assess the performance of all the commanders within a carefully prepared scenario. It had not gone according to the script; Kindersley, despite his stuttered protestations that he was using his initiative, had ballsed it up.

The immediate future looked bleak. The realistic choice seemed to be the sack and a return to the ranks or, at the very least, a relegation to begin that part of the course again. Mons decided on the less draconian alternative and Gay watched his companions pass-off up the famous steps to the strains of 'Auld Lang Syne' and away to join their regiments. He returned to the empty billets of G Squadron to await the new intake.

As he had discovered from Mike Belmont, there were advantages in a repeat performance. Practice made, if not perfect, a useful approximation of it and he began to enjoy himself as his new colleagues, struggling with unfamiliar technology, sought his advice. Navigation became easier as he recognised familiar landmarks; it was all rather a doddle. He begun to organise the end-of-course party in a local hotel and persuaded Philip to part with a case of vintage port to help matters along. He had asked the RSM to join them and Mr Brittain had been graciously pleased to accept.

Exercise Trek came round once more and because Gay was well liked and no one wanted a complete failure on their hands, he was again given command of a withdrawal in contact. This time the directing staff had even taken the precaution of filling the other seat in the turret of Gay's armoured car with the most accomplished student on the course; they were taking no chances.

The enemy came over the hill just as before but, if anything, in an even greater state of disarray. The budding military genius alongside Gay became very excited.

'Look, Gay,' he yelled. 'Look at them; they're a complete heap. You can't just withdraw. If we attack now, we'll annihilate them. Go on, do it. I promise you it will be all right.'

It was not all right. Flags waved; whistles blew; urgent messages were transmitted on a dozen radios. The Squadron Leader, purple in the face, led a frantic charge of umpires' scout-cars up to Gay's vehicle.

'I cannot believe it. I just cannot believe it. You've done exactly the same thing again. I give up. I bloody well give up.'

The military genius curled himself up in the bottom of the turret in an effort to make himself invisible. Gay's world caved in.

Certain now that he had finally failed, he started to hand over responsibility for the leaving party to another cadet. In advance of the interview he knew would soon follow, he began to pack and wondered what might be in store for him at Catterick or wherever it was they would send him. Inexplicably however, he had in fact passed. The Squadron Leader, in listing his weaknesses, left him in no doubt that he would have to work hard if he was to gain the respect of the soldiers in his regiment. Nevertheless he was a trier and that was something. He wished Gay good luck and then abruptly switched to other matters.

'Tonight, Kindersley, at the party. Grahams '26 isn't it? Ah yes, good.' He flicked his whip in dismissal.

The guest of honour was in good form as he sat at Gay's right. He reminisced fondly about Philip's and his own days in the Coldstream. He sympathised deeply that Gay was not going to join the Brigade but indicated that, while not quite the same thing, of course, he understood that some cavalry regiments were really quite good. He drank a great deal of port and mentioned that he and Mrs Brittain were intending to go to Ireland for their holidays next August.

'Ah,' said Gay. 'I shall be asking for leave then; it's Dublin Horse Show week. Why don't you come and stay?'

And, because he too had drunk a lot of port, he then forgot all about it.

For Gay, and indeed for Michael Allsopp who followed him shortly afterwards, joining the 7th Hussars was rather like going to a new school. There was a sense of excited anticipation and a feeling of growing up. The regiment was stationed at Barnard Castle but there was also a move to look forward to as in late 1949 it was to be posted to Luneberg on the North German Plain to become part of the occupying allied forces.

As an officer Gay was hopelessly inefficient. He had little clue about the art of command and only a tenuous grasp of tactics. He was frequently lost on manoeuvres and required close and constant supervision by his squadron leader.

But as is so often the way, he was popular with both the soldiers in his troop and his fellow subalterns; with the former because he did his best to look after them, was always cheerful and unfailingly generous; and with the latter for his good comradeship, his enthusiasm and – human nature being what it is – for the fact that he could be unfailingly relied upon to attract to himself whatever official censure was on offer.

His good-natured ineptitude obtained for him the job of regimental messing officer, a punishment appointment which involved the supervision of the routine ordering of the daily rations in barracks and the holding of fortnightly meetings with a representative body of soldiers to discuss their complaints about the quality of the food. Of these there were many and there would have been more but for the brooding presence of a Scottish cook sergeant, who would fix the habitual moaners with such a threatening eye that they subsided, saving their comments for anonymous and profane unofficial additions to the posted minutes on the squadron notice-boards. For a time, when Gay was away for a week in Ireland, he handed over his duties to a regular officer and was panic stricken on his return to find that his stand-in had failed to put in the next batch of orders; the regiment was faced with having no food for three days. He foresaw mutiny. In a state of some agitation he telephoned a friend in the Catering Corps and asked for help. The man was as obliging as it was possible to be under the circumstances and sent over a thousand large pork pies and half a ton of potatoes. The cook sergeant looked at them gloomily. 'I'll no' be able to make ma porridge with that lot,' he said. 'There'll be riots the morn.'

For seventy-two hours the 7th Hussars lived off pie and chips. There were no riots and few complaints; the soldiers hated porridge and Gay was greeted with approving cheers on his frequent visits to the cookhouse.

During his week away he had arranged to have his first ride on Balheary Boy, a horse he had bought in Ireland to be trained by Cyril Harty. Gay revelled in the atmosphere at Mullingar racecourse as he changed for the first time into proper breeches, racing boots and his brand new colours (green, mauve sash). The race was a bumper, but despite that there was plenty of distinguished company in the jockeys' room. Gay, heart pounding, walked out to the paddock to join Oonagh and the captain. Harty had done his work well; the grey stood gleaming with health as his owner was given a leg up into the saddle. He finished third behind two well-known amateurs and was to dream the race over and over again.

Back at Barnard Castle he laid his final plans for the Dublin Horse Show. He asked some brother officers to stay, first at Luggala and then at Glenmaroon for the show itself. He included one whose sister he fancied greatly – on condition that she came too – and arranged with the captain to run Balheary Boy at Phoenix Park at the end of the week so that she could admire his dash and his courage. Invitations to hunt balls and other equally splendid and alcoholic events showered in. It was all very satisfactory, and as August drew nearer his excitement mounted. And then the letter arrived. Post-marked Aldershot and written in the formal and courteous manner of a senior Buckingham Palace official, it was from RSM Brittain and said how much he and his lady wife were looking forward to staying with Gay for the horse show.

Fighting off his immediate panic, he telephoned his mother to ask her whether the pair might stay at Luggala where Oonagh was now in residence – Dom having pushed off permanently with the actress Sally Gray, whom he was later to marry. Oonagh, evincing little surprise, was as vague and accommodating as ever. 'How nice, darling,' she said. 'Yes, of course; I don't think I've ever met a sergeant major before.'

Patrick Cummins rose to the occasion magnificently; his reputation as the best butler in Ireland had not been lightly earned. He fussed round the Brittains as if they were royal personages, deftly rearranging little tables and precious ornaments as the vast couple trundled majestically round the small drawing-room. Mrs Brittain all but matched her husband in bulk and the only bed large enough to take them was in the room above Oonagh's own; she wondered in passing whether the Luggala floorings were up to the combined weight.

Gay's friends were terrified of the RSM – most had also recently suffered the regime at Mons – and sat quivering as he quizzed them boomingly about their subsequent military careers. At dinner that evening, with the Brittains each overflowing their allotted delicate Chippendale chair, conversation was sticky. Mrs Brittain was clearly fascinated by the mechanics of running the Luggala household (some twelve in number), enquiring interestedly of Oonagh where she bought her lamb and what make her vacuum cleaner was. Oonagh, becoming rather faint at this domestic inquisition and having no idea what a vacuum cleaner was, let alone its provenance, waved frantically at Patrick to bring another large glass of sherry for her guest. Kath and Cotty Mordaunt-Smith (Kath was Dom's sister, who had washed her hands of her wicked brother) had been drafted in to help matters along, but were mesmerised by the proceedings and hardly spoke. Mrs Brittain, alert to the fact that she was now moving in elevated social circles but also not unaware that she had the edge when it came to claiming acquaintanceship with members of the royal family, sought to change the subject.

'Tell me, Mrs Mordaunt-Smith,' she essayed, 'we know the royal princesses quite well; which do you like the best?'

Kath, taken unawares, and ever more furious with Gay for having inflicted this intolerable situation on Oonagh, snapped that she thought they were both quite poisonous and then, immediately regretting her discourtesy, fell to chattering incoherently about the war. Sam White, the Paris correspondent of the *Evening Standard* and an old friend of Oonagh, tried to break the tension by standing on the table after dinner and giving his lavatorial rendition of 'The Red Flag' – a party piece which had been previously well received in some of the great houses of France and Ireland. Here it died a predictable death. The RSM twirled his moustache and Mrs B gazed at her napkin; neither joined in the half-hearted applause. Sam took another glass of port.

The next morning Gay and the 7th Hussar contingent left for Glenmaroon, leaving Oonagh, the Mordaunt-Smiths and the unrepentant White to cope. That night the Brittains' bed collapsed, covering their hostess in a layer of plaster flakes as she cowered in the room below.

'Never mind, me lady,' said Patrick. 'It might have been themselves that landed on you.'

Gay's week in Dublin did not go well. Guilt-ridden at leaving the Brittains at Luggala, he was also frustrated by the fact that the girl whose presence he had so cunningly engineered clearly did not return the passion he nursed for her. Grinding his teeth, he watched her dance at ball after ball with the queue of young bloods who had quickly homed in on this ravishing new adornment to the Dublin scene. In desperation he confessed his love, only to be told forthrightly that he was being silly. He felt he had a lot to learn. To cap it all, Balheary Boy – his last card in the campaign to engage her undivided attention – did not run at all well, finishing second last. He was mortified when an acquaintance enquired, in the most patronising of tones and in the girl's presence, what Gay thought he was doing riding a hunter in a flat race.

Having dispatched his party back to England, he prepared to return to Luggala, fearing that he had some explaining to do. He was met at Glenmaroon by Oonagh and the Mordaunt–Smiths, who had fled, leaving the Brittains in the care of Patrick Cummins. Kath set about him. He had been selfish and unthinking; how dare he leave his mother to field his guests; how dare he ask them in the first place knowing that he would be otherwise occupied? She gave him an uncompromising rocket which would have left the RSM himself open-mouthed with admiration. Gay burst into tears.

The Brittains were due to stay for another week and in a little Ford motor car he drove them to see every sight in Ireland from Glendalough to Killarney. They kissed the Blarney Stone and stood on the edge of Galway Bay. They drank champagne and ate lobster; he hoped earnestly that they enjoyed it all. Under his ministrations and those of the unflagging Cummins the Brittains blossomed, so greatly that they proved too much for the little Ford. On the last day of the visit it sighed gently and collapsed on its springs, worn out by the effort of it all.

Gay's last few months in the army were spent with his regiment at Luneburg, where the 7th Hussars were required to train harder and more professionally than had been possible in the north of England. Gay, however, had other matters on his mind. It had now begun to worry him obsessively that he still remained a virgin whilst his fellow subalterns seemed able to boast continually – and sometimes even convincingly – of their exploits. He turned his attention to breaking his sexual duck; Germany seemed just the place and Hamburg was only a few miles away. Sometimes with a friend but often when alone, he engaged one after another the services of a number of enthusiastic fräuleins, who at that time still dispensed their favours for little more than a square meal and a night in a warm hotel bedroom. From them he learned at least some of the tricks of the trade. Becoming more confident, he extended his activities to include the bored wives of RAF pilots whose husbands always seemed to be away on some mission or other; they were flattered by the attention paid to them by this expensively dressed and handsome young cavalry officer who clearly had much money to spend and certainly knew how to show a girl a good time. His repertoire was expanding rapidly.

As his leaving date approached, his fellow subalterns – who enjoyed his easy-going company and mindful, no doubt, of the general benefits that could accrue from having an inheritor of the Guinness millions in their midst – were keen that he should extend his service with the regiment. His superiors, recognising that he was not suited to a military career, were equally determined that he should not. Gay himself, perfectly well aware of his lack of martial talent and remembering his promise to his grandfather that he would give the brewery a go, had no doubts. Besides, he wanted to have a proper chance at race-riding and Germany was no place for that, despite the ready availability of horses liberated from the Germans and the excellent tuition ('forvard with yor hands, forvard I say') he obtained from the regiment's Prussian riding-master. He had enjoyed his service and the comradeship of the soldiers and his friends in the mess, but it was time to move on.

During his final days, he helped to organise a point-to-point for British officers over natural country on Luneburg Heath. Selecting his own ride with some care, he navigated the course safely; it was his first race over obstacles and he loved it. This, he firmly decided, was the life for him.

CHAPTER THREE

Early Days

The sport which was to play such a dominant part in the life of Gay Kindersley makes its first appearance in print in 1752. Mr O'Callaghan of County Cork, out hunting with his close friend and neighbour Mr Edmund Blake in the shadow of the Ballyhoura Mountains, paused on his way home to admire the view. From the little village of Buttevant they could clearly see the steeple of St Leger Church rising into the sky some four-and-a-half miles away across the emerald green fields. O'Callaghan was brimming with contentment; they had enjoyed a grand day. He sighed and then observed somewhat complacently – and half to himself – that there never was a horse in Munster could touch his own when crossing such a country. Mr Blake demurred sharply; his friend, he suggested, had clearly failed to appreciate that he, Edmund Blake, possessed an animal which, if not the best in the whole of Ireland, would certainly leave that poor old thing of O'Callaghan's trailing in his wake. The wager was struck, the course set: start at Buttevant, finish at St Leger. The steeplechase had made its debut in recorded history.

That there had been similar contests across natural country before that time can hardly be doubted, but it was to be another forty years before a steeplechase (or steeplehunt as it was sometimes known) for more than two runners was documented as taking place in England. It had become fashionable to arrange races during boastful flights of after-dinner fancy, and such contests soon caught the imagination of Mad Jack Mytton, squire of Halston near Shrewsbury. Of all the sporting eccentrics of the early nineteenth century, Mad Jack was the most flamboyant. Born rich, he made light work of disbursing his fortune, being so careless with money that while returning from Doncaster Races in an open carriage he fell asleep counting the proceeds, allowing several thousand pounds to blow away along the roadside. He loved racing, chiefly for the gambling opportunities it afforded him, and is credited with inventing the midnight steeplechase by challenging his dinner guests to race him by moonlight from Halston to the Raven Hotel in Shrewsbury for a sweepstake of £100 a head. Jack, who knew the country far better than any of his friends, held a comfortable lead until he inadvertently jumped into a duck-pond. By the time he had extricated himself and completed his now soggy journey, the winner had roused the hotel staff and the party was once again in full swing.

For four years Mad Jack served as a cornet in the 7th Hussars, having decided that he would not go to university as his guardian had planned – at least, not for any length of time. The only evidence that he went to Cambridge at all is an order for three pipes of port to be addressed to him at his college – which, being equivalent to some 2,500 bottles, gives some credence to the theory that he had intended to appear for at least one term. Mytton's fine disregard for money, his addiction to gambling, his love of racing, his unbridled enthusiasm for a party, even his choice of regiment and brief flirtation with university, all have echoes in the life of the young Gay Kindersley some century-and-a-half later. There, it is hoped, the coincidences end, for Mytton died in a debtors' prison shortly after setting fire to his night-shirt in an attempt to cure himself of hiccups.

The first steeplechase to be run over a purpose-built course was held at Bedford in 1810. During the thirty years that followed, the events gained rapidly in popularity. The Grand Leicester Steeplechase became an annual fixture and when Tommy Coleman of St Albans gave a semblance of organisation to the series of annual races he promoted with the support of influential – even royal – patrons, owners began to realise that to be successful their horses needed speed as well as stamina. By 1837 Coleman had his imitators all over the country, one of the earliest and most unlikely being a Liverpool publican with a reputation as the best fish cook in England. As fond of the racecourse as he was of his kitchen, William Lynn organised two 'Great Liverpool Chases' at Maghull in 1837 and 1838. His meetings attracted nationwide interest, including that of the Jockey Club, and this may have unnerved Lynn for he retired before the scheduled 1839 race to devote himself to coursing and the Waterloo Cup. In his place a syndicate was formed from some of the greatest names of the turf, including Lord George Bentinck, Lord Robert Grosvenor and the Earls of Sefton and Derby. Their lordships moved the venue to Aintree, already an established flat course. Under this new and patrician management Lord Sefton waved away seventeen runners in 1839 to negotiate twenty-nine untested obstacles, which included three brooks – one of which did for the redoubtable veteran, Captain Becher.

The race was won by Lottery, ridden by Jem Mason, a dandy so concerned about his appearance that he had the legs of his boots made by Bartley of Oxford Street and the toes by Wren of Knightsbridge. Lottery was a character too – the first to be publicly acclaimed in a tradition since illuminated by household by-words such as Golden Miller, Arkle and Desert Orchid. By their very presence on a course, Mason and Lottery could draw thousands to watch them perform in a wildly successful partnership made all the more unlikely by the fact that the horse so hated his rider that complicated subterfuges had always to be employed to allow Mason to climb into the saddle.

In 1843 the Aintree race was renamed the Liverpool and National Steeplechase, and at the same time it became a true handicap. Shortly afterwards the first adverse comments appeared in print, criticising the fact that each year horses were killed; the chorus reached a crescendo six years later when three died. Unlike the press campaigns which were to follow intermittently over the next century, the cause for complaint at first was that some of the fences were so small that horses treated them with a careless contempt which could – and often did – lead to disaster.

The Grand National, studded as it is with controversy and attended by its rich history of glamour, romance, courage and not a little tragedy, has a worldwide appeal that far transcends interest in racing or even in horses. For Philip and Gay Kindersley it held a fascination which translated itself into a yearning to be a part of that history. Philip had long given up any ambition he might once have entertained of riding in the race himself, but he saw in his son the means by which he could perhaps still be closely concerned. Gay, from the moment that he decided finally that he would try to become an amateur rider of the first rank, simply wanted to win it. In the years immediately before and after the Second World War, father and son found a focus for their interest as they followed the career of a sportsman who foreshadowed all their own racing dreams and was to come heart-breakingly close to success in his attempts to take the greatest prize of all.

Anthony Mildmay was born in 1909, the only son of a Devon family that, three generations earlier, had married into Baring Brothers, the great City bank. After Eton and Cambridge, he naturally joined the family firm, where his uncle was senior partner. Not enjoying business life and positively hating London, he cast around for something that would engage his interest, and his search finally led him to Peter Cazalet, whom he knew slightly from Eton. Peter had some jumpers in training at his home, Fairlawne near Tonbridge, and Anthony was soon riding out there in the early mornings before leaving for his office in the City. The two rapidly became close friends and Anthony, supported by his father, bought a number of horses to be trained at the Cazalet establishment. In 1933 his quest for the National began.

At this time, Mildmay stood 6 foot 2 inches tall but – unlike Philip, whom he knew well and who was only a fraction taller – he weighed under 10 stone. In his early days, he was an indifferent horseman but he possessed two priceless assets: he had a single-minded determination to do well and he was completely fearless. In his first full competitive season, having ridden only one winner, he entered himself for the National on the 8-year-old Youtell. They fell at the first fence and Anthony broke his nose, the race being won by the incomparable Golden Miller barely two weeks after he had triumphed in the third of his five successive victories in the Cheltenham Gold Cup. This remarkable double remains unique, but for Mildmay the race was only the beginning of a long and unforgiving battle with the Aintree fences.

Two years later, having narrowly escaped death in the 1935 race, he bought Davy Jones, a 7-year-old entire who had won three times over a mile on the flat before succumbing to the respiratory problems which led to his being sold and later tubed by his new owner, for whom he then won a few hurdle races. By the time Mildmay entered him for the 1936 National, he had been given only two more runs, winning once over two miles – not the most suitable of preparations.

The field of 35 for the great race included two former winners, Golden Miller and Reynoldstown, but the former – who had always hated Aintree – fell at the first and by the second circuit only eighteen were left standing. At Becher's, Davy Jones and Reynoldstown with Fulke Walwyn in the saddle were well clear. Three fences from home and with nothing to choose between them, Reynoldstown made his only mistake. He hit the top of the fence, had the stuffing knocked out of him and only a horseman of Walwyn's skill could have retained his seat; even so he lost a stirrup iron. To the crowd – and to Anthony Mildmay – it was clear that Davy Jones had only to jump to last two to win.

Reynoldstown, with magnificent courage, fought back and began to make up ground on the leader but Davy Jones, although hardly bred to stay, was still on the bit. At the second-last he pecked a little on landing and Anthony let the reins slip through his fingers to give his horse every chance to recover. Recover he did, but in a nightmare moment Mildmay saw that the buckle had come adrift from its prong and the reins were flapping irretrievably loose. Frantically he tried to guide the big chestnut towards the last fence with his whip but all to no avail; they ran out, leaving the tired and gallant Reynoldstown to win his second National in successive years. Like the true sportsman he was, Anthony did not allow his bitter disappointment to show – after all, before the race he had thought that they would do well to complete two circuits – and in the evening he was at the traditional winning owner's party at the Adelphi Hotel.

After the war the Cazalet–Mildmay combination again took up the running and to such good effect that Anthony was leading amateur rider for four seasons. In 1949–50 he rode thirty-eight winners, a record that was to stand for over twenty years. He had become something of a cult figure with journalists and the racing public, and after his father died in 1947 the cry 'Come on, my lord' was taken up with a will every time he rode. A year later he had a fall that injured his neck muscles so severely that occasionally during a race, cramp would grip him in such a vice that he would be unable to lift up his head. This affliction probably cost him the 1948 National, striking at a vital moment and causing him to ride the last mile virtually blind.

Lord Mildmay did not confine his love of racing to taking part. He was a member of the National Hunt Committee and a steward of that organisation for four years; in 1947 he was elected to the Jockey Club, an honour that he felt reflected on his sport rather than on himself. To both Kindersleys he was a hero who had played a significant part in raising steeplechasing to a popularity it had never before enjoyed, and in May 1950 Philip Kindersley arranged a City luncheon in his honour. Two weeks before the day, Mildmay, a shy man who was not at all happy in the presence of pomp and circumstance, telephoned Philip to ask him to cancel the event. Thinking the request rather odd and certainly very disappointing, Philip complied. A few days later Anthony Mildmay went down to the sea at his home in Devon for his customary swim before breakfast and was never seen again. As he grieved for his friend, Philip speculated, not for the first time, whether his son could ever emulate the racing successes of this great Corinthian. There were to be circumstances in Gay's life which would evoke memories of Mildmay as they did of Mad Jack Mytton. Inevitably they would not always be what Philip had hoped for.

In that same May, Second Lieutenant Kindersley was officially demobilised. He crossed to Ireland to ride Balheary Boy in a race at Punchestown which, although described as a steeplechase, included a stone wall and several banks. He got round safely but without distinction and returned to London to see what Guinness had in store for him.

Since his grandfather's death, the directors has taken over the management of his future with the company. Bearing in mind the need to instil into him some basic knowledge of chemistry, they sent him to a crammer in Aldgate, at the same time issuing instructions that he was to lodge for the time being in one of the Guinness houses next to the Park Royal Brewery. Dauntingly, he found that he was to share this residence with the brewery's managing director, who made it quite clear that he expected young Kindersley to spend all his waking hours memorising his text books and none of them scanning the racing pages of the *Daily Express*. Furthermore, he said, he strongly disapproved both of horses and those who were silly enough to ride them. In his experience, he added, people on horses looked ridiculous and gave themselves airs.

In this uncongenial presence, the reluctant chemist dutifully wrestled with bunsen burners and molecular structures, becoming even more disheartened by the less-than-pleasing news that physics was also to be on the curriculum. His tutors found him unreceptive and were not surprised, when he came to take examinations designed to check on his progress, that he achieved only 17 per cent in chemistry and 18 per cent in physics. Gay did not need the managing director to tell him (although he did – and at some length) that the Guinness board had concluded that his future lay elsewhere.

Farming appeared to be an attractive alternative and he went to stay with his grandmother Gar at Holmbury, where he was allotted to Mr Knott the farm manager for milking duties with the Jersey herd, an activity which began each morning at 4 o'clock. This took some of the steam out of his normally unremitting pursuit of an energetic social programme and even his equestrian activities were confined to days with the Mid-Surrey Drag and an occasional point-to-point on Potheen, a horse which taught him a lot about staying in the saddle while hitting the tops of fences. After three months he went to Ireland to work on his own farm at Clonsilla and there put a horse called Cardinal Puff into training with Dennis Baggallay with a view to riding in bumpers in the summer. Baggallay – who had been a successful amateur rider – had been chosen by Oonagh, who insisted that the family connexion with Cyril Harty should be severed on the grounds of the captain's suspected connivance with Dom while the latter was conducting his clandestine affair with Sally Gray.

By this time Gay had, for the first time, a regular girl-friend. Dilly Radford had been introduced to him by Michael Allsopp and was everything that he could have wished for. Her blonde, soft curly hair and huge blue eyes had captivated him so completely that Allsopp was convinced that his old friend was in love. She came to Ireland frequently, often to stay at Luggala where Oonagh's own social programme was now in full swing. Without the restraints imposed by Dom, the house had become a glittering epicentre for the literati: Claude Cockburn, Lucian Freud (married in 1953 to Oonagh's niece Caroline), Nell Dunn and John and Rikki Huston were frequent visitors together with Xan Fielding and Patrick Leigh Fermor (endlessly reliving and recounting their 'black-turbanned, booted, sashed, silver-and-ivory daggered' guerrilla warfare days behind German lines in Crete), as well as Robert Kee, the author and broadcaster who became Oonagh's lover, and the ever-present Brendan Behan. It was indeed a heady mixture. The parties were wild even by Irish standards; Oonagh never saw anyone before noon but thereafter lunch, the centrepiece of her day, would go on well into the night, people coming and going as they pleased. To Behan, Luggala was a place where 'anyone could say what they liked [where had he not?] as long as it didn't take too long and was said with wit'. To others it was a sanctuary where every gentle human aberration was tolerated without question – if indeed any was ever noticed. One regular guest liked to take all her clothes off and dance on the table amongst the gold plate and the crystal glasses. Sex there was in plenty, especially of an extra-marital nature, and Gay – often asked by temporarily loverless ladies of his mother's generation to help them through an otherwise lonely night – entered into the prevailing spirit with a will.

The ban on contraceptives in Ireland meant that he had to indulge in minor smuggling operations which sometimes involved his friends. One evening, swimming at the Lansdowne Club in London before leaving to catch an evening plane to Dublin, Gay shouted across the pool a request that Michael Allsopp should get him some Volpar gels, a spermicide in tablet-like form then popular with those who didn't much like the principal product of the London Rubber Company. Allsopp, who was to join his friend in Ireland the next morning, had never heard of the stuff and tried to ask for some clarification. In mixed company and over the width of the pool this wasn't at all easy but he eventually gathered from the coded and rather garbled messages yelled at him that he was being asked to obtain a tube of lozenges from a chemist. He arrived at Luggala bearing three packets of winegums.

Presiding over this hedonistic scene was the magnificently imperturbable Patrick Cummins, now leading a team of hand-picked servants who treated everyone (even the wildly unpopular) with benevolent impartiality – except, of course, for Oonagh and Gay for whom he reserved the right to pamper without restraint. Marco Marshall, a doctor who was married to Gay's cousin Philippa, arrived with Gay at Luggala for the first time at 3 o'clock one morning to find Patrick and the maids lined up on the steps. Even at that hour there was a shining pleasure in their faces as they helped their favourite to his bed, making sure that the fire in his room was piled high and that he and Marco had the requisite number of hot-water bottles and pots of strong sweet tea.

Gay's twenty-first birthday party in June 1951 was an affair of epic magnitude. Marquees were erected on the lawn; extra staff were procured and Tommy Kinsman, the most popular dance-band leader in London, was engaged to provide the music. The guest list was impressive: the embassies in Dublin were represented by the ministers of Spain, Argentina and Belgium and the American chargé d'affaires. Irish society turned out in force as did the glitterati (known by Marco as the arty, crafty and downright dafty). Gay's friends from England and Ireland, drawn mainly from the cavalry and racing worlds, were accompanied by a coterie of beautiful girls led by Dilly. As usual proceedings began with champagne; the evening sun shone strongly; the lough sparkled within its fringe of white sand and Luggala, seeming to know that it had been created for such splendid occasions, basked contentedly in the glory of it all. Patrick moved here and there seemingly without hurry; but there was never an empty glass or an unsightly plate.

As dusk began to fall, proceedings warmed up when Roderick More O'Ferrall made a badly judged pass at the well-proportioned and sexually enthusiastic wife of an Irish poet. Her husband had consumed a bottle of Moët & Chandon in a brave attempt to determine whether he really enjoyed the stuff; concluding that he did, he went in search of fresh supplies, coming across the errant couple behind a marquee in the first throes of passion. Pausing briefly to lay O'Ferrall out with a remarkably accurate right hook, the poet sat down on the grass to consider the matter further. Deciding that his act of spontaneous retribution did not begin to meet the case, he went to find his car. Revving hard, he drove it through that part of the wall of the tent which he imagined was adjacent to the spot where he had last seen his wife mopping her aspiring lover's bloody brow. His aim was uncertain and the car was brought to an eventual halt by a table at which Oonagh's middle-aged and rather prim secretary was sitting, pitching her to the ground and inducing a sharp pain in her lower back. An Italian doctor who had just discovered that Jameson's whiskey was much to his liking insisted that the proper – indeed the only – cure for an injury so serious, so prejudicial to the signora's continued good health was a suppository. The unfortunate woman was scooped up and, before she had time to make even the feeblest of protests, found herself laid out on a bed in a downstairs room of the house. There the doctor performed his self-imposed task to the cheers of a fascinated crowd that had flocked to the windows. The secretary took only a few days to recover from her physical hurt but the memories of her public treatment were slower to fade; she could never think of Italy again without a shudder.

That party and countless others like it persuaded Gay that, much as he loved the country and its people, he should no longer seriously contemplate living and working in Ireland; it was all too much of a good thing. Luggala, with its womblike embrace and its unremitting opportunities for self-indulgence, would lead nowhere except, perhaps, to early liver failure. It was marvellous to know that he could always return and be cossetted by his mother and the wonderful staff, but life – real life – must be tackled in England. The Mildmay in his character was, temporarily at least, getting the upper hand over the Mytton.

He sold the farm at Clonsilla and went up to Christ Church, his father's old college at Oxford, to read agriculture. Too late he discovered that a sound knowledge of chemistry was a pre-requisite for academic success in the theory of farming; hydrocarbon chains again began to haunt his dreams. He shared rooms with Peter Alexander, a friend from Eton who, when he was sober, was joint master of the University Drag Hounds. Peter and his fellow joint master, Tim Beaumont (later a priest and Liberal spokesman on the arts in the House of Lords), were determined that Gay should join them – but for very different reasons. Alexander, a good horseman and keen on his racing as well as the Drag, was fonder still of evenings in London, while Beaumont's pleasure in his appointment stemmed largely from the social prominence it gave him. Neither was prepared to undertake the considerable work involved in recruiting new subscribers, organising the hunting country and arranging the meets; Gay, they felt, would have profited from the experience gained with his father at the Mid-Surrey and would be ideal for the job.

He threw himself into the Drag enthusiastically and in his first season also began to point-to-point. He kept two horses, Cardinal Puff and Flicko, at Cecil Bonner's livery yard at Bicester where he and John Lawrence (who was up at New College) would ride out every morning, travelling the nine straight miles up the A43 in Gay's 1937 Wolseley Hornet. Lawrence, who had been a year ahead at Eton, had completed his National Service in the 9th Lancers and in the long term shared Gay's ambition to be a first-class amateur. He had not been riding seriously for very long and, at this stage, was neither as experienced nor as accomplished as Gay. For both, the immediate preoccupation was to avoid being carted round Bicester aerodrome where Bonner had his training gallops. Under the tutelage of the trainer – and much encouraged by his father – Gay had an excellent first season, riding several winners both for himself and for others, of which the best was Ruby Holland Martin's Questrin. He was developing into a competent jockey, perhaps lacking a little style but, like Mildmay, absolutely fearless.

The highlight of the university hunting scene was the Drag point-to-point known as the Oxford Grinds. Philip was anxious to take part in the Past and Present race and Gay, who was partly responsible for the organisation, was determined that not only would he find his father a ride, but that he should win the event. Accordingly, when Major Bill Pilkington telephoned to ask Gay to ride his horse Martial Law in the race, he explained that he was already booked for Questrin but asked if his father could have the ride. There can have been few such requests, and a lengthy silence followed as Pilkington tried to remember how old Kindersley senior was and whether he was both fit and good enough for Martial Law, who was no mean performer. Eventually he agreed and a delighted Philip began to prepare himself.

On the day there were five starters: Alexander (who had conscientiously remained sober for some of the preceding twenty-four hours), Philip, Gay, John Lawrence and Robert Higgin, an intellectual undergraduate better known for his academic ability than for his horsemanship. Higgin had poor eyesight and sported expensive pebble-lensed spectacles which he was not prepared to risk either out hunting – where he was known as Blind Bobby – or on the racecourse. All the riders, except Philip who had not been let into the secret, were in no doubt that the main aim was to give the old man (he was 45!) every chance. In the weighing-room the subject of the conspiracy was greeted fondly by the clerk of the scales, a bookshop proprietor called Mr Hedges who had performed these duties at the Grinds for more years than most could remember. Hedges was so pleased to see Philip that the cigarette which was stuck habitually to his lower lip fell to the ground in the excitement. He invited the formidably large figure to sit on the scales and the needle revolved rapidly past the 13-stone mark. Mr Hedges coughed: the correct weight for the race was 12 stone 7 pounds but he was not about to allow his old friend to be disqualified. 'Just about spot on,' he muttered, ushering Philip quickly away and waving to a considerably lighter Lawrence to take his place.

The day was fine – so fine that the sun shone out of a cloudless sky, casting uncompromising black shadows in front of the first six fences. It was the shadows, combined with Blind Bobby's affliction, that did for the race plan. From the start Higgin set off, quite inadvertently, as if the devil himself were on his tail. What in fact was on his tail was Martial Law, a front runner by inclination who took such an exception to being upstaged so early on in proceedings that Philip found him impossible to hold. Higgin never saw the first fence and his mount, deceived by the dark void into thinking that this was an obstacle of such fearsome proportions that it would be prudent not to attempt it, ducked out to his right and stopped dead, decanting his surprised jockey into the birch. Martial Law, trying to avoid the stationary horse and confused by the blackness as well as alarmed by the frantically scrabbling Higgin, skidded into the bottom, depositing Philip on the far side. Bobby remounted quickly, not in any spirit of wishing to rejoin the contest – he'd already had more than enough – but in order to escape the vengeful figure pouring blood from a broken nose which now advanced upon him. To the astonishment of the spectators, all four remaining competitors, forgetting the race in the quest to allow Philip to continue, set off in pursuit of the loose horse. Martial Law, however, was not to be caught and, as the stewards began to despair, the race resumed a recognisable form. The carnage however continued: the shadows claimed another victim in Lawrence and Alexander (whose hangover had now both caught and overtaken him) also fell, bringing down Questrin. All five starters had, by this time, come to some form of grief but Gay remounted to win, followed some minutes later by Blind Bobby, who had some difficulty in finding the post. Philip was never to ride in another race.

Heartened by his success in point-to-points, Gay felt that he was now ready to begin riding under national hunt rules. His father encouraged him to go for advice to John de Moraville, who had a training yard at Childrey. De Moraville (who had also been a prisoner with Philip) and his stable jockey Dicky Black were anxious to help and Gay immediately felt at home, riding out on the downs with the first lot and then eating the traditional trainer's breakfast over which plans were discussed for the horses in the yard. De Moraville found him a selling chaser for £450 and set about getting both the horse and the rider fit. Tight Knight was a bouncy chestnut, keen to get on and take a friendly hold, but clever enough to measure his fences – in short a near perfect schoolmaster. In December 1951 he and Gay were ready for their first outing at Lingfield.

Gay drove down from Oxford with John Lawrence and met Philip on the course. The race, although a selling chase, had attracted a number of top jockeys and Gay was the sole amateur. Among his rivals were the formidable Bryan Marshall and the even more awe-inspiring Fred Winter. Philip went into the weighing-room to speak to Marshall.

'Look here, Bryan,' he said, 'my boy's having his first ride today. He's done a fair bit of point-to-pointing but do you think you could just keep an eye on him for me? Shout at him if you think he needs some advice.'

'Don't you worry, sorr,' came the reply in the soft brogue of the Irish professional who was to win two Grand Nationals in successive years. 'I'll look after him right enough.'

Gay's instructions from his trainer were uncomplicated: 'Let the old horse see his fences and go out and enjoy yourself.'

His father was even more succinct: 'Do what Bryan Marshall tells you!'

At the top of the hill with three fences to go, Gay was lying third and coasting. As they went round the left-hand bend into the straight, he heard Marshall from behind him. 'Gay, me boy, pull over to your right, will you.'

It was more an instruction than a question and Gay hauled in on his right rein. Marshall came through on the inside, getting a clear run at Winter as the latter made for the post and beating him by a short head. Tight Knight finished third.

In the unsaddling enclosure, both Philip and de Moraville were complimentary. Philip went to thank Marshall as the jockey headed for the weighing-room.

'That's alright, sorr,' he said with a wink. 'I looked after him all right.'

Fred Winter's view was a little less sanguine.

Gay and Tight Knight had three more engagements that season but failed to fulfil the promise shown at Lingfield. The final outing of the year was at Chepstow and was to lead to his first brush with racing's authorities. The plan was that Gay and George (an American friend from Oxford) would stay the night before the race with a girl who had a flat in a country house near London. They would get up early the next day and pay a quick visit to the Turkish baths in Jermyn Street, where Gay would shed a few pounds before driving down to Chepstow. With the optimism of youth, timings were going to be cut a little fine and events did not precisely follow the script.

The girl was attractive and, despite his still undying love for Dilly, Gay thought that a little dalliance would be good for him. He knew that his attentions were not unwelcome and had every reason to believe that, all being well, he would not have to sleep alone. George would be consigned to the spare room. Matters began to go wrong during dinner; George fell heavily for his hostess and slipped into an easy line of transatlantic chat, the like of which Gay had only heard at the movies. The more George laid on the charm, the more the girl glowed with evident pleasure. Gay, now very much on the side-lines, began to glower as he saw his prize slipping away. The second blow fell when it emerged that there was only one bed. Gay resigned himself to (at best) sharing the sitting-room floor with the American. The girl, however, had a better suggestion; they were all friends and the boys had a long way to go tomorrow. Why not all share her bed?

Undressing briskly, she slipped between the sheets and watched interestedly as Gay and George, embarrassed in each other's presence, struggled awkwardly out of their clothes and climbed in on either side. She reached up and put out the light. The silence enveloped them. Nobody moved. The men hardly dared breathe; sleep appeared to be out of the question. At last she sighed.

'Oh well,' she said. 'Come on then, Gay; it had better be you. After all, you are my cousin!'

By the morning matters had fallen more than a little behind schedule. In the Wolseley, George showed none of the conversational sparkle he had deployed at dinner. Eventually he spoke.

'I guess,' he said, 'God just isn't an American after all.'

As he left the Jermyn Street baths, it finally dawned on Gay that he was not going to make Chepstow on time. Frantically he searched for a telephone-box and rang the course to leave a message for his trainer. De Moraville was not amused, being forced to put up a professional who thought he knew more about Tight Knight's little preferences than either the trainer or the horse itself. Tight Knight, used by now to amateurs who left him alone to get on with things, did not find his new jockey's close supervision to his liking and fell. Gay, when he at last arrived and had been given short shrift by a tight-lipped De Moraville, was invited into the stewards' room to explain his absence. He had prepared, he thought, a convincing case, launching into a complicated recital involving severe traffic problems aggravated by a flock of sheep and the taking to hospital of a stranded and heavily pregnant farmer's wife. The stewards listened carefully but were not impressed. One even went so far as to remind his colleagues that they had heard similar stories from amateurs at the last three meetings. Was there perhaps a shop that dealt in such fairy-tales? They fined him heavily.

At Oxford Gay's work had not been given the undivided attention to which the university felt it was entitled. Soon after his arrival, he and his censor, Hugh Trevor-Roper, had come to the conclusion that his lack of enthusiasm for chemistry would require a change of direction. Accordingly they had agreed on a course of politics, philosophy and economics – PPE, Gay being given until the end of his second term to show that he had mastered the basics. But the Drag, the racing and his and Peter Alexander's proclivity for extended parties (they would draw the curtains at noon and turn the hands of the clock to 8 to produce an appropriate atmosphere) had relegated his studies to a priority so far down the line as to be hardly discernible. Trevor-Roper stuck to his guns and demanded that Gay should complete a written progress examination.

Unbelievably this was to be conducted at the student's lodgings and Gay saw a solution. He engaged a second-year PPE undergraduate to do the test for him and left his would-be saviour hard at work while he went off to discuss next year's hunting plans with a friendly farmer. When he returned he found that his essays had been written with an erudition which was breathtaking; they would be sure to please. True, he found that he was unable to understand more than a fraction of the theory and there were an alarming number of words in the elegant paragraphs which he didn't quite recognise. Never mind, doubtless it was all good stuff and well worth the money. Assiduously he copied out the neat pages, adding the occasional original thought. This may have been a mistake, for he was awarded the now familiar 17 per cent.

Trevor-Roper was very civilised about it all. He pointed out that there had not been much headway up to date and that any sign that matters might improve was sadly absent. He advised Gay to cut his losses (and those of his trustees) and find something else to do which more closely suited his undoubted talents. It was simply that he, Professor Trevor-Roper, couldn't quite put his finger on what that might be.

Gay went to see Philip to discuss his problems. As he saw it, there were two matters which needed to be resolved. First, he was more convinced than ever that he was in love and wanted to marry Dilly; second was the business of what he was to do next with his working life. Philip was appalled at the thought that this eager boy, still not quite 22, should be contemplating marriage. Something must be done. He went into urgent conference with the trustees and emerged with a scheme which seemed to cover all the angles – at least for the immediate future. Gay could go to Canada to view the Guinness operation there. This would remove him neatly from Dilly and, as the trip was to last for only three months, he would be back for the national hunt season. Philip was as determined as Gay himself that his son should pursue a racing career – but first he could rough it a little.

CHAPTER FOUR

A Bachelor Gay

Still only 21 and with an educational track record that hardly endeared him to the directors, Gay enjoyed surprising status within the family firm – as is clearly illustrated by the fact that he travelled first class to New York on the *Queen Mary* in the august company of Peter Candler, the head of the Guinness operation in Canada. The trip was uneventful, Gay largely devoting his time to fruitless attempts to separate a succession of heavily chaperoned American girls from their vigilant parents. After a few days in New York and a short stay at Candler's Montreal home, he was put on a train for Calgary – a journey which amply vindicated his late Uncle Dick's much quoted description of Canada as 'all rocks and bloody Christmas trees'.

He was booked to work for six weeks at Duke Petroleum, the Alberta-based company which represented the Guinness group's main interest in the west of the country. Within hours of getting off the train he was on his way to a wild-cat oil rig some hundred miles to the south to take his place at the bottom of the installation's hierarchical pile, his duties being those of a general labourer or roughneck – the dogsbody of a five-man crew. He worked an eight-hour shift which varied between the relatively civilised daytime hours and the aptly named graveyard stint which began at midnight. He lived (or more accurately slept) in a grim concrete blockhouse – which the owners, with misplaced optimism, had called the Grand Hotel – in Coleman, a town built primarily to house the Polish miners who worked its many pits. They were not a sociable bunch and Gay, anxious though he was to be friendly, did not fit easily into the hard frontiersman atmosphere relieved only by bouts of self-destruct drinking on a Saturday night. Life was far from easy on the rig site either; there were those of his workmates who harboured a resentful suspicion of his limey accent and the fact that he was a boss's man. The most vociferously objectionable of the critics – a lanky Canadian of about Gay's age – had taken an immediate dislike to the newcomer and lost no opportunity to goad him. Insult followed insult until at last, patience exhausted, Gay went for his oppressor. He had to be dragged off by the foreman as he was resolutely engaged in rearranging his tormentor's features to an unattractive pulp. The fight brought him some rather grudging respect – not least from his opponent – but he was glad that his stay was not to be prolonged.

The six weeks passed slowly until at last he was back in Calgary in time for the annual stampede – an event in which he was determined to take part. Fearful for his safety, the Duke management was reluctant to pull the strings necessary to wangle him a rider's licence but his persistent cajoling eventually wore them down and they capitulated; he would be able to take his place in the Bucking Horse Championship alongside such local notables as Casey Tibs, Lawrence Dodging Horse and Leo Red Crow. The city newspaper, under the headline 'Around the Corrals', reported his first appearance:

An English boy, recently arrived from the old Country, proved himself a game sport in the novice riding championship but he had no luck.

At that, Gay Kindersley, now of Calgary, didn't do any worse than many a native son as a horse named Lazy Boy dumped him into the dirt six jumps out of the chute.

Gay looked like a real Westerner – mostly when he ruefully picked himself off the ground and brushed the dirt from his blue jeans.

Unlike the roughnecks, the veterans of the exclusive rodeo circuit, far from resenting this strange, slightly built Britisher with an apparent death-wish, seemed keen to help. But they were also practical men who harboured no illusions. 'You see that crowd?' one said to Gay, pointing at the thousands sitting in the main stand. 'I've seen as many guys come into this game and leave it limping – or worse.'

Two days after his disagreement with Lazy Boy, Gay was introduced to Coyote, a raw-boned, wall-eyed grey who greeted his new acquaintance with bared teeth. The veterans were free with their advice. 'He's real mean,' they said. 'Jest about did fer ole Kit.'

Gay put the spur (used to rake the shoulder of the bronco when it first leaves the gate) on his left boot and climbed up on to the chute. The two cowboys employed to make everything ready had done their work: Coyote stood motionless. Gay lowered himself into the saddle and gripped the leather handle with his left hand. He nodded – giving the signal that he was ready – and the gate shot up. Coyote came out fighting – and, for good measure, twisting and bucking, ducking and diving. The same reporter was again on hand:

Gay Kindersley, the young English boy who gamely attempted a bronc ride a few days ago, was back again despite the rough ride he was given before being bucked off.

This time he got it even rougher. He started well, aboard a horse named Coyote, but Coyote really warmed up to his work.

Gay was thrown high in the saddle, came down hard on the horn and was a dead pigeon when he was tossed into the dirt.

He was revived in the arena hospital after being carried off on a stretcher.

He had lasted some eight seconds in the saddle and was out for four hours; not an encouraging ratio.

To recuperate – and finish off his stay in Canada – he was dispatched to a dude ranch – a sort of Western-style holiday camp with a bunkhouse to live in, pork and beans to eat, horses to ride, lakes in which to swim and a promise that the women would outnumber the men by 8 to 1. Horses for the moment held little appeal and the lakes were cold, but the odds on landing a lady companion for the week seemed attractive. Sadly, the damage done by Coyote's unforgiving saddle horn proved to be a little longer lasting than forecast and Gay found it impossible to raise anything other than his hopes.

As he prepared to leave Canada he was offered a job with Duke Petroleum. Candler had been impressed by his young protégé's performance; he had acquitted himself well at the rig, had been something of a success in the offices at Calgary and had shown undoubted courage at the stampede. Gay was tempted; indeed, had it not been for his financial independence, his long-term racing ambitions and the fact that Tight Knight was waiting to begin a new season, he would have gratefully accepted. As it was, he returned home, horizons broadened, tougher in body and in possession of greater self-confidence. He felt a new degree of freedom too; he was able to cope better, he thought, with whatever life had in store. Canada had been good for him.

While he was away, Philip had moved to Coldharbour, a property not far from Plaw Hatch which conveniently included a three-bedroomed cottage in the garden. In this he installed his son, for whom he had found a place in the City working for George Henderson and Company. He had been busy with the training arrangements too, moving Tight Knight from Childrey to Don Butchers's yard at Lewes, only twenty minutes away, and he now awaited the start of the national hunt season, particularly Gay's part in it, with considerable anticipation. He was pleased to see the changes that the few months away had wrought in his son; most of all he was happy that the thought of marriage to Dilly – or anyone else – had apparently been forgotten. The boy could now concentrate on his racing.

Don Butchers had been a moderately successful jump jockey in the years either side of the Second World War and now trained some twenty-five horses. He and Gay hit it off immediately, admiring in each other a cheerful disposition for hard work. On Gay's part there was also a willingness to learn. By September 1952 he and Tight Knight were ready for their first outing of the season – a two-mile selling chase at Newton Abbot. They won by fifteen lengths; so impressively had the horse run that Gay (acting on the strict instructions of Butchers as to how far he should go) was outbid in the subsequent auction and lost him to a bookmaker. He was disappointed but in the event Tight Knight won only two more races before going wrong in the back, vindicating Don's strong advice that Gay would do better to look for a younger horse to bring on.

In pursuit of that aim, owner and trainer flew to Ireland, returning from the Ballsbridge Sales with Sandymount, winner of a useful bumper and a classic chasing type who was probably fast enough to win over hurdles. And win he certainly should have done at Sandown in December had Gay – taken unawares in the excitement – not been left at the start, eventually finishing third and fairly flying as he passed the post. Butchers's punishment for his sleepy owner (the trainer had backed Sandymount to win £1,650) was to put up a professional in the horse's next attempt over hurdles but, like Tight Knight, Sandymount was used to amateurs and objected to the more bossy style favoured by the pros. He ran worse than he had under Gay and the latter was reinstated for the rest of the season, being placed twice. A golden opportunity, though, had been lost.

Despite that early setback, he was now gaining a reputation as an amateur who could hold his own in almost any company and he began to accumulate rides. A friend of his father owned Tommy Traddles, a veteran who had already run in a Grand National, and promised Gay that, should he get on with the animal in a handicap at Windsor, he could have the Liverpool ride that year. Gay, who had spent the previous night dancing furiously to Humphrey Lyttelton's band and then bonking a drinking-club barmaid (all in the interest of losing three pounds in weight), negotiated the obstacles impressively and was duly booked for Aintree. Sadly, that enticing prospect evaporated when the old horse went wrong and had to be withdrawn.

The barmaid grew curious about racing (she may also have been a little flattered by the attention she was being paid) and persuaded Gay to take her to Lingfield on the following Saturday. In the dim light of the club – and indeed in her bed – she had seemed almost young and certainly desirable. In the members' enclosure at Lingfield she was electrifying: her leopard-skin coat, stiletto heels and tight black skirt served only to emphasise her forty-plus years. Gay, slightly taken aback by her appearance, nevertheless determined that he would go through with it – the ticking-off he had received from Kath Mordaunt-Smith as she had stridently reminded him of his obligation to the Brittains kept leaping to his mind – and escorted her loyally, pretending not to notice the sniggers and the whispered comments of his friends as they queued to be introduced. They thought the situation hilarious but hilarity was not one of the emotions chasing each other through Philip Kindersley's mind as he eventually steeled himself to greet the ill-assorted pair.

'Pleased to meet you, Mr K,' the lady chirruped as they came face to face in the bar. Philip's natural good manners prevented him from tackling Gay on the spot, but so public a lack of judgement on his son's part could not be allowed to pass unchallenged. Michael Allsopp, barely able to restrain his amusement, was sternly ordered to pass on to Gay that there should be no repeat performance.

The racing career was proceeding rather more smoothly than the love life and, in particular, Gay's ride on Mr S E Homewood's handsome grey Silver Shadow II in an amateur race at Newbury in January gave rise to favourable press comment. The *Sporting Life* correspondent wrote, 'Mr Kindersley could not have ridden a better race ...'

These words of encouragement and many like them led to offers from other owners, the most important being John Bailey, whose useful 13-year-old Merry was trained at Dorking by Alec Kerr. Gay, again suffering from a severe hangover, rode Merry in a hunter chase at Lingfield and impressed the connexions to such an extent that they booked him for the Foxhunters at the Cheltenham Festival. He didn't let them down, dead-heating at 100 to 8 with the hot favourite. Merry was now booked for the Past and Present Steeplechase at the Grand Military Meeting at Sandown (then held after Cheltenham) and Gay was delighted when Peter Cazalet rang to ask him to ride a horse at the same meeting, summoning him to school alongside the Fairlawne stable jockey. This invitation from a man he had so long admired thrilled Gay – a euphoria which lasted only until he was left at the start of a line of fences and received a bollocking from the trainer which, in its ferocity, outdid anything he had suffered in the army. Cazalet's mild appearance masked an unremitting professionalism.

At Sandown Merry started favourite and set off on his three-mile quest with a determination which Gay found hard to curb. The horse was foot perfect, attacking his fences with an assurance that signalled that he was on top of his form. But when they came to the final open ditch he galloped into it as if it didn't exist, turning a violent somersault and lying motionless on the far side. It was later established that he had suffered a haemorrhage and was almost certainly dead before he actually reached the obstacle. Gay woke up in the racecourse ambulance room with severe concussion, unable to ride the Cazalet horse the next day; instead he went wearily home to Coldharbour Cottage to recover, surfacing briefly to be Mike Allsopp's best man.

Mr Pickwick was very pleased that his young gentleman was not badly hurt and looked forward greatly to keeping an assiduous eye on him. As butler, valet, cook, gardener and general factotum to the cottage, he had, on many recent occasions, administered to Mr Gay after wild parties such as those held by the hunt. There was the time, for example, when Dr Marshall was staying and he and Mr Gay had gone off to do the cabaret at the Earthstoppers' Dance; they had sung all those terrible Irish songs and the young gentleman had apparently put so much effort into his performance of 'Slattery's Mounted Fut' that he passed out. Somehow the doctor had got him home and woken Mr Pickwick to give him a hand with his burden up the winding, narrow stairs. It had been quite a struggle and, within one step of their goal, the three of them had tumbled all the way down again in a tangle of arms and legs. It was a mercy no one had been killed, although he had felt a passing pang of regret that the doctor had escaped unscathed when he had quite unnecessarily complained that Pickwick had obviously not wished his feet for a month.

Pickwick's real name was Joe Roe, but his appearance and name had been Dickensian for so long that very few people remembered the one he first enjoyed. It was true that he had smelly feet – indeed there was not much of him that did not hum a little on a warm day – but he looked after Gay with such a touching solicitude that it was simpler for the latter to freshen the air by opening a few windows than to run the risk of giving offence. Pickwick's only hero (no man, after all, can be a hero to his valet) was P G Wodehouse's inimitable Jeeves – but there were, in truth, very few characteristics he shared with that doyen of gentlemen's gentlemen other than the facility with which he mixed a hangover cure. The ingredients were never divulged to the patient but no one was ever long in doubt as to the sureness of Pickwick's touch on any given day, for one of the most unforgettable features of his particular recipe was that the slightest inaccuracy in the amount of one of its key constituents turned it into a laxative of such ferocious power that it took only seconds to act.

Pickwick soon learned that the death of Merry and the subsequent loss of the Cazalet ride were not the principal causes of his young master's unusually prolonged gloom. The fact was that, like Anthony Mildmay, Gay hated the City and the monotonous daily routine that working there imposed upon him. Pickwick advised him to have it out with his father. With some misgiving, Gay did so, pleading that he could not be really happy unless some way was found of allowing him to work with horses full-time. Philip, who had been anticipating some such approach, had already given the matter a little thought and suggested that Gerry Langford might be willing to take him on as an unpaid assistant.

Langford was an eccentric vet in his mid-60s who had bought the 300-acre Ardenrun Stud, which was near to Lingfield racecourse and close enough to Don Butchers to enable Gay to ride out when required. Philip telephoned Langford and put the proposition to him. The vet-turned-breeder said 'Yes,' he was delighted – 'send the boy straightaway.' Gay was soon to see why he was quite so enthusiastic.

Langford's capriciousness did not extend to his own rigidly imposed routines. He kept both his property and the horses that occupied it in accordance with the very highest of standards. The paddocks were fenced with imaculately manicured natural hedges; not for him the artificiality of post and rail. In addition to the horses, he kept a few cattle and a flock of sheep to balance the grazing and some of the outer fields were arable. The whole formed the cream of the country hunted by the Mid-Surrey Drag Hunt and the Old Surrey and Burstow Foxhounds. However, like so many sticklers for detail, he failed entirely to get on with people, making no allowance for personal foible or human frailty, so that staff came and went with terrifying rapidity – often arriving on a Friday and leaving on the following Monday. He also had a frightening temper which he exercised impartially on his wife and daughter as well as on the transient workforce. The only permanencies when Gay arrived were the two Alfs, a father and son combination from Yorkshire who ran the farm and coped with the Langford tantrums by the simple expedient of completely ignoring them. Gay was to be the sole long-term addition to the staff, supplemented from time to time by unwary itinerants who had not done their homework before seeking employment and who rarely stuck for long the fearsome regime imposed upon them.

Although Gay's primary duties during the twelve-hour working day were seeing to Domaha and Flag of Truce (the two stallions) and their visiting mares, he was often invited to muck out ten or more boxes as well as ride the teaser round the paddocks to see which mares showed more than a passing interest. The act of covering took place in an enclosed yard into which the mares were led to have their hind legs shackled securely before receiving the stallion. Occasionally Langford would become impatient with the time the operation was taking and would dispense with the restraints. Gay, leading in Domaha to do his stuff during one such frantic burst of activity, was able only to stand by helplessly while the mare lashed out and caught her intended mate squarely in that part of his anatomy which was most exposed as he mounted her. He squealed with pain and his testicles quickly swelled to the size of footballs. For days Gay sat in his box playing a hosepipe on them to hasten their recovery. As Domaha struggled to regain his virility, Flag of Truce became the busiest stallion in the south of England, coping admirably with his increased load. Gay wondered enviously how he managed it quite so often.

During his time with Gerry Langford, Gay had two horses with Don Butchers – Sandymount and a selling hurdler called Pascaval who gave him a winning ride at Fontwell in September. Sandymount, however, continued to be unlucky, being beaten narrowly twice before Christmas. In January 1954 he was booked for a novice chase at Newbury, but barely seventy-two hours before the race a schooling accident at Ardenrun caused Gay to suffer the first of a cumulative series of injuries which eventually were to be instrumental in ending his riding career. It was Langford's fancy to show off one or two of his best jumpers to potential clients by putting them at an enormous tree trunk lying in one of his fields. In doing so on a slippery surface, the horse Gay was demonstrating fell and he dislocated his right shoulder. If he was to race that week the injury required urgent treatment and this imperative brought him into contact for the first time with Bill Tucker, a London doctor with a practice in Park Street known to the racing world as the Jockeys' Garage. In fact Tucker did not confine himself to jockeys but dealt with all manner of sporting injuries, concentrating on athletes whose primary concern was to be back in action as soon as possible. His surgery was a fully equipped diagnosis and treatment centre where he and his physiotherapist, Jean Cooper, wrought miracles, patching up their customers at a speed which often horrified the more orthodox of the medical profession. Tucker would turn out, often in his dinner jacket, at any time of day or night and travel miles to render assistance to anyone who felt it necessary to be back in the saddle or out on the cricket field the next day.

The doctor strapped Gay's shoulder securely back in place, and so comfortable did it feel that he was able to assure Don that he could do the ride at Newbury. Taking Marco Marshall with him for last-minute adjustments, he changed with some difficulty before being helped up into the saddle. Sandymount responded magnificently to the one-armed urgings of his young rider. The now fairly experienced campaigner shot round the two-and-a-half miles, flying the sixteen fences without a suspicion of a mistake. Taking up the running two fences from home, he finished four lengths clear. Gay came in for some fulsome praise. Michael Belmont and his wife sent a telegram: 'Congratulations. Let us know when you ride without the use of your legs as well and we'll back you!'

The racing correspondents, too, were impressed: Richard Baerlein of the *Evening Standard* and Captain Heath of the *News Chronicle* were among those who praised both his skill and his courage, but they were less sure of his judgement when it became clear that he intended to ride Pascaval for the horse's first trip over fences at Lingfield the next day. How right they were; Pascaval was brought down and out went the right shoulder once more. Out too went Kindersley, who fainted from the pain.

Despite Tucker's best efforts, he was not able to ride again for several weeks and went to Cheltenham for the National Hunt Chase still not fully fit. This race – for amateurs only – was then over four miles and until the 1930s had been the most important race on the card, attracting more prize money than the Gold Cup; it was still a prestige event with a high-class field. Sandymount had been prepared with a three-mile chase in mid-February and both Gay and some of the more knowledgeable tipsters felt that he had a favourite's chance. The bookmakers and public didn't agree and he started well down the betting at 100 to 7. Again the horse jumped well, but at the fifth one of the runners baulked and ran up the fence, bringing down half-a-dozen others – including Gay. The result was multiple bruising in his left knee and thigh and an ear hanging on by the merest thread of skin. Cheltenham Hospital dealt with the ear – but in such a way that the fastidious Duque de Albuquerque, the great Spanish amateur rider who was staying with Gay at the house of a mutual friend, turned green as he saw the results, pushing his porridge away and hurriedly leaving the breakfast table. Tucker was enlisted the same day to free the knee so that Gay could take a ride at Sandown the following week, but this time the treatment was not a success, the pain being so intense that he fell off almost unconscious, having been bumped hard as he jumped the second last.

He was now accumulating injuries at such a rate that together they posed a serious problem. In addition to the right shoulder on which repairs had been effected, he was having regular treatment for the left, which was prone to dislocate at the most inconvenient moments – invariably coming adrift, for instance, during the dramatic climax of 'Slattery's Mounted Fut', a performance requiring histrionic use of the arms and a final stripping off of the shirt. Tucker had at first believed that Jean Cooper's expert therapy would be able to deal with it and Gay had undergone many sessions with her at Park Street. He was leaving one day as Denis Compton, the England batsman, came in for treatment on his knee.

'Who's that chap just going out?' the cricketer asked. 'I'm sure I've seen his face somewhere.'

'Oh, that's Gay Kindersley,' said Jean. 'He's an amateur gentleman!'

The injury, however, was beyond physiotherapy and by the spring of 1954 the shoulder was slipping out of its socket so easily that even a sneeze disturbed it. He found that he could not carry out the simplest of manual labour at the stud with any certainty that it would not go again and so he went back to the Garage for more advice. Bill's unrivalled reputation as a diagnostician and short term patcher-up did not extend to his surgical abilities; when he told Gay that he should have an operation which would involve the shortening of the muscles in the upper arm so as to keep the shoulder in its socket and that this would mean the loss of some external rotation, his friends all warned against Tucker carrying it out. But Gay, loyal as ever to those who had helped him in any way and as usual allowing that loyalty to influence his judgement, insisted. He was admitted to Sister Agnes (The King Edward VII's Hospital for Officers in Beaumont Street) and Bill went to work with his knife. Oonagh, who had come from Luggala to see her son, was a little surprised when the surgeon, his hand still encased in blood-soaked gloves, wandered into the waiting-room.

'All is well, Lady Oranmore,' he said. 'But it was a little more difficult than I thought and I've had to use a stronger gut than I would wish.'

Gay's three weeks in Sister Agnes were devoted (without success) to attempting to persuade the day and night sisters into his bed in turn. They were Irish and had responded encouragingly to both his indelicate suggestions and the renditions of the more sentimental love songs in his repertoire; neither, however, was prepared to risk the wrath of matron by going beyond the occasional snatched kiss. So taken was he by Maureen, the night sister, that after his release he arranged to take her out for the evening and, with some difficulty, managed also to persuade her that she should stay the night in the small flat he had taken off Belgrave Square rather than trekking home to north London. Maureen – despite the theatre, the dinner, the dancing and the soft lights – suddenly remembered at the critical moment that not only was she Irish, but she was also a good Catholic and, clamping her legs firmly together, she reduced him to a frenzy of frustration which was never to be eased by either of his nurses.

While recuperating at Luggala he was rescued from this period of enforced celibacy by being able to renew his much valued and intimate association with Rikki Huston, who was staying while her husband and Gregory Peck (who for a long time was convinced that Oonagh, Lady Oranmore and Browne, were three separate people) were shooting some scenes for Huston's movie *Moby Dick*. Even more demanding, when he got back to London, were the attentions of the Volga Boatwoman, an exotically dressed White Russian whom he met at a drinks party and who saw him as a valuable and perhaps even long-term meal ticket. She was gratifyingly practised and worked enthusiastically at making herself sexually indispensable, applying techniques which were not only outside Gay's experience but often beyond his wildest flights of imagination. The combination of the Volga Boatwoman's excesses and the less-then-delicate surgery on his shoulder made healing a long and painful process which was only completed when he fled to France to stay with his mother and was admitted to hospital at Menton. It was to be six months before the hole finally closed up and he was fit to return to England.

In January 1955 he was able to start work again, this time as a pupil to Don Butchers, having found that he could not face the thought of resubmitting himself to Gerry Langford's outbursts. There was the added complication that Her Majesty had temporarily taken custody of his driving licence, making daily travel restricted. He and Mr Pickwick took up temporary residence within bicycling distance of the Lewes yard while he set about getting himself fit and finding a more permanent home.

During the previous autumn he had replaced Pascaval with a rogue of a hurdler called Ben Tinto who provided him with the first win of the season in a seller at Kempton. The afternoon wasn't an unqualified success, however, because Ben Tinto – who never won another race – beat a hot favourite from the north of England whose connexions had invested heavily with the bookmakers. They were keen on buying the animal who had been responsible for their misfortune and bid Gay up to at least twice the horse's worth before giving him best. He would, as Don Butchers pointed out irritatingly often when Ben Tinto regularly let them down, have done better to have let the beast go.

Apart from that race and a win on Sandymount in the fittingly named Corinthian Chase at Kempton, he was finding success hard to come by. As the season drew to its close, all that seemed left to tackle were point-to-points. Then, unexpectedly, he was asked to take the ride on Manx Cottage in a hunter chase in the May meeting at Stratford. He knew nothing about the horse and, in his eagerness to accept, he neglected to do his homework; had he done even a little he would have discovered that Manx Cottage had failed to get round safely in six attempts. True to form, at the open ditch in front of the stands the horse failed to rise an inch; most of the field of 25 galloped over Gay's prostrate form and he woke up in Stratford Hospital with a broken back and spinal concussion. The doctor in casualty was disgracefully unsympathetic, crudely encasing the shattered body in plaster in the manner of a builder rendering a particularly rough wall. In his carelessness he put the plaster on too tight and during the night holes had to be drilled in it to allow Gay to breathe properly. In the morning, as is often the way in the aftermath of accidents of that nature, he found that he couldn't pee and a catheter had to be inserted by the same incompetent practitioner, with as little finesse as he had employed the night before. The patient's morale was decidedly low.

By breakfast-time Michael Belmont had discovered his cousin's whereabouts. He quickly arranged a transfer to Sister Agnes and alerted Bill Tucker. The latter removed the plaster and substituted a metal corset, warning Gay that he would have to remain flat on his back for at least a fortnight. Immobile and fractious, the patient found it difficult to renew his approaches to the nursing staff and was rescued from boredom only by the fact that he was sharing a room with one of the Brigade of Guards' more unconventional products – an officer known as the Streetfighter. He had acquired this name, he told an interested Gay, because of his expertise in the specialist skills necessary for successful hand-to-hand combat in the bazaars of the Middle East. He had been in the Scots Guards during the war (and had been decorated more than once for bravery) and was now, he said, engaged on secret duties for his friend the King of Jordan. He had come to Sister Agnes to have a gangrenous finger removed after leaving some of it behind in a crashed jeep in the desert. The Streetfighter's accounts of his own and others' military exploits were related with an engaging verve which held his captive audience of one unfailingly enthralled. The soldier became a close friend, resented by some who saw him only as a sponger but very much liked by Gay, who appreciated his companionship, his humour and his uncomplicated views. At a time when good fellowship and fun were at a premium, the Streetfighter provided liberal quantities of both.

One of the more frequent visitors to his bedside was an attractively buxom actress whom Gay had met briefly in London and who had, it seemed, not only welcomed his attentions but given out ample promise of more favours to come. Never one to pass up such an opportunity, he resolved that on his release from hospital he would put her to the test, notwithstanding the inconvenience that would undoubtedly be caused not just by his corset but by a more serious complication which he earnestly hoped would cure itself speedily. He had developed a distressing medical condition which the Streetfighter delighted in describing graphically as a weeping willy.

'Must have been with a tart, old boy; can't be too careful. Never touch 'em myself,' he assured Gay cheerfully as he helped himself to a further glass of his room-mate's champagne and the remainder of the grapes.

Not having been near a prostitute, Gay put his affliction down to an infection caused by the catheter with which he had been fitted at Stratford. He had to resign himself to wearing a nappy, which hardly enhanced his sexual allure and even constrained him to be uncharacteristically diffident in his pursuit of the actress. In the event she didn't seem to mind either the condition or the impedimenta. As she was appearing in a play at Folkestone, he went to stay with Philippa and Marco at their house in Bletchingly, dragging them with him night after night to watch her excruciating performances on stage. It was at dinner after one of these expeditions that Marco first noticed an unpleasant and pervasive smell. To begin with he put it down to Gay's condition, making a mental note that he should see that the nappy was changed before he went to bed; presumably the actress too would appreciate this attention to personal hygiene. It was only when Gay left the table temporarily that it became apparent that it was the girl herself who was at fault – an impression confirmed at subsequent meetings, after which she became memorably known as Iced Ink.

Bill Tucker, monitoring his patient's progress through what was intended to be a relaxing recuperation, concluded that prolonged exposure to hot sun coupled with a rest from the unrelenting attentions of Iced Ink would be more beneficial to Gay's general health than spending each evening in the front stalls followed by an all-night work-out for his still delicate spine. He prescribed a holiday at Portofino on the Amalfi coast, preferably alone but at least without the actress. The Streetfighter – whose return to the desert could, it seemed, be postponed for a time – volunteered enthusiastically to join this arduous expedition, in order, as he put it, that 'you should not have to drink alone, old boy'.

Within minutes of their arrival in Italy and barely having consumed his first Campari, Gay had fallen in love. The recipient of this instant attention was Isobel Baird, the Irish widow of a racing driver, but he had only one evening to make his mark (and that with the Streetfighter at his elbow) before she was due to fly home. Succeeding in his quest, after extracting a promise that she would return (at his expense) as soon as possible, he devoted himself daily to composing lyrical protestations of undying love.

The Streetfighter, soon bored with the heavy sighs of his friend, mentioned suddenly that he had now received the expected instruction to report for his next mission; the situation in Jordan needed urgent attention. He must leave immediately; Gay would have to moon alone. Deprived of his companion and looking round for alternative sources of amusement, Gay met John and Deirdre Clark, who persuaded him to travel to Cannes with them, where they proposed to put up at the Carlton. Pausing only to fire off a wire to Isobel advising her of his new location, he travelled to the Riviera, arriving at the hotel in time to witness an increasingly acrimonious argument between the manager and his intended hosts. All the rooms were, it seemed, occupied; as neither Mr and Mrs Clark (nor Mr Kindersley) had booked and this was August, there was nothing that could be done. In vain did the Clarks protest that they had in fact booked some weeks before; there was an impasse. A helpful Englishman, overhearing the problem and obviously possessing some influence, interceded and a large double room (with a dressing-room bed for Gay) was instantly conjured up. John Clark, a captain of industry who was later to become chairman of Britain's largest manufacturing company, found himself wrestling with decidedly mixed feelings when he discovered that the good Samaritan was a Labour Member of Parliament taking a well-earned rest from leading a successful waiters' strike in London hotels.

Cannes was fun and the remainder of the holiday was all that Gay would have wished. As the Clarks went home, Isobel arrived and he was able to take over the larger room. Smart boats cruised in and out of the fashionable harbour, bearing acquaintances of either himself or his parents. All were generous with their hospitality, and what with the sun, the uniformly excellent food and Isobel's gentle restraint of his alcoholic intake, Gay was soon restored to the top of his physical form and eager to sample each and every one of the hedonistic pleasures on offer. When his romantic companion had once again to return to Ireland, he too felt that it was time to go home. Although he was no great enthusiast for the gaming table, he went to the Casino for a final sentimental throw. There he met the heiress Sarah Chester Beatty and her friends, who were cruising the Mediterranean on her father's yacht. Among those in the party was a stunningly attractive English girl called Margaret Wakefield.

CHAPTER FIVE

Leading Amateur

On his twenty-fifth birthday in June 1955, Gay inherited three-quarters of a million pounds from the estate of Ernest Guinness. He immediately bought Hullers, an eighty-acre farm at Beare Green near Dorking, and then the Priam Lodge training establishment at Epsom to which he persuaded Don Butchers to move – charging him no rent but opting instead to keep two horses in training there free of any fees. He now had four animals with Don: Sandymount, the four-year-olds Friarspark and Brian Oge, and finally Prince Eyot, bought by his father from Bob Turnell. The immediate plan was to run Sandymount in the 1956 Grand National.

Hullers, although modest in size, was a comfortable house, decorated and furnished – with Valsie's help – in expensive good taste. The farm possessed two cottages, one occupied by Gay's housekeeper, Mrs Norris, and her husband (Gay had parted with Mr Pickwick) and the other by George Woodman who did most of the farming. Only a few easily motorable miles away, the functional 35-box Priam Lodge had four flats which housed Butchers, his two head lads and the stable jockey, Alan Oughton. The close proximity of the properties allowed Gay to ride out regularly in the early mornings and still put in a day on the farm when his other engagements allowed. Since returning from France his social life had been both complicated and hectic. Although he persevered with Isobel for a time, she had seemed not to be quite so irresistible in the grey light of an English autumn, and Philip – whose list of qualities desirable in a serious girl-friend for his son did not include flat vowels and a previous husband – glowered so effectively from the side-lines that the affair ended within a few weeks. She was replaced by the Flying Fornicator, a lady master of foxhounds with a pilot's licence, lustrous black hair and legs that were the stuff of a bootmaker's dream. But despite this agreeably arcane distraction, he found his mind constantly reverting to thoughts of the lovely Margaret Wakefield. He made arrangements to see her in London and she was everything he remembered. Soon he was spending every possible minute in her company. She came to Hullers and met his friends. They raced together four days a week; quickly they became inseparable.

Magsie was different from anyone who had gone before. Apart from Dilly – the exquisite and romantic will-o'-the-wisp who had flitted in and out of his life making few if any demands – he had never experienced anything approaching a stable relationship. The succession of one-night stands, bored wives and widows on the make had not prepared him for this rather aloof and apparently virginal vision who had once harboured ambitions to be an actress but had realised that she had neither the talent nor the driving ambition to succeed. Unlike most women of his acquaintance, she had a mind of her own and the more he saw of her the more certain he was that she was the one who should be his wife. He felt instinctively that his mother would approve ('Just as long as she makes you happy, darling') but he knew from the view that his father had taken of Dilly that any long-term plans were unlikely to be welcomed quite so uncritically by Philip, for whom no woman would ever be good, rich or well bred enough to marry his son. A little apprehensive but nevertheless determined, he proposed to Magsie in January 1956 – after the third race at Kempton Park – and was duly accepted.

Magsie, despite Philip's prejudices, came close to passing his rigorous vetting procedure. He had two reservations: first, she was far from rich and therefore, he reasoned, must be a gold-digger. Secondly, her father was a run-of-the-mill character actor who was unlikely to climb the thespian heights whereby – in Philip's judgement – social acceptability could be attained (just); in summary, she was not out of a distinguished enough drawer.

It has to be admitted that Hugh Wakefield did little to endear himself to the Kindersleys. In an interview published by the *Sunday Express*, he appeared irritatingly patronising: 'She has a lot of famous friends,' he was quoted as saying about his daughter. 'I always knew she'd find me a first-class son-in-law. Very popular, my daughter; stayed last week with the Duke of Rutland; before that at Warwick Castle and she's a friend of the Duke of Kent.'

The words, although grating, were perfectly true. Magsie was indeed a close friend of Edward, Duke of Kent – such a close friend that he had talked to her of marriage. She had also been engaged to an aristocratic flat-mate of Michael Allsopp and had come to know the Earl of Warwick through Sarah Chester Beatty – who was later to marry his heir, Lord Brooke. But to Philip and Valsie such boasting amounted only to bad taste. There was also the matter of the luncheon party.

Gay had arranged a weekend at Hullers at which both sets of parents could meet. The Wakefields were to stay, while the Kindersleys would motor over to Sunday lunch. An old RAF friend of Hugh lived close by and on the Sunday morning the house party went out to have drinks, leaving Mrs Norris in charge of the roast beef. The retired wing commander was garrulous and lavishly generous with his gin. He had a lot of catching up to do and was loth to let his guests go; the day was beginning to run a little late. By the time they extracted themselves and rolled back to Hullers in high good humour, the senior Kindersleys had been waiting for over an hour and had been left far behind in the refreshment count. It was a sticky start and rapidly became a quagmire.

Hugh Wakefield was a peppery little man at the best of times; when fired up by drink and a sense of occasion he was inclined to brook no argument. Philip, socially sensitive, defensive on behalf of his son and worst of all severely sober, was not prepared to be benign. At the table Gay switched the conversation desperately from one subject to another in an attempt to engineer harmony; he was wasting his time. Hugh pontificated about hunting; Philip doubted loudly that the actor had ever hunted in his life. Philip mentioned that in the Western Desert he had noted that the RAF apparently went home at weekends; Hugh wondered whether Philip had ever heard of the Battle of Britain. Finally, Wakefield demanded that, if the marriage was to go ahead, he would need some concrete assurances that his daughter would be properly looked after. Philip said that he had heard that she had already been well looked after by a succession of people. The meeting was a disaster and when Valsie announced over the pudding that in her opinion Magsie would make an entirely unsuitable wife for her step-son, the women – and Gay – burst into tears. The engagement was off.

Magsie returned to London with her parents. Gay followed the next day, having spent an unsatisfactory evening with his father (whose jubilant relief at the turn of events was hard to bear), followed by a sleepless night and, to cap it all, an incoherent breakfast with Don Butchers who was interested only in Sandymount's preparation for Aintree. He and Magsie had lunch at the Savoy, and after a second bottle of claret they decided to ditch the wedding arrangements and elope, telling no one but Oonagh and Magsie's mother Vi. The venue chosen for this clandestine tying of the knot was the magical Luggala. That evening they flew to Dublin.

Their timing was less than perfect. At round 4 o'clock the next morning, an electrical fire broke out in the 16-year-old Garech's room and the flames spread quickly. Garech alerted the household, and Patrick Cummins with the rest of the servants began to heave the most valuable of the pictures, furniture and silver out on to the lawns while Robert Kee tried to telephone the fire brigade about twenty miles away in Bray. It took some time for the sleepy voice at the other end to come to grips with the problem.

'And which brigade exactly would you be wanting?' it enquired interestedly. Kee looked at the instrument helplessly. Cummins seized it.

'The nearest one, you eedgit. Would you want her ladyship's house to burn to the ground completely?'

In the event, three engines were dispatched but none appeared as promptly as might have been hoped. Each in turn had steered off the edge of the steep

Luggala drive and into a snow-filled ditch, having to be dug out by hand and shovel. When the firemen eventually arrived, already mightily dishevelled by their exertions and shaking their heads sympathetically at the destruction, they made their preparations. Slowly – desperately slowly, it seemed to the impotent watchers – they joined the hoses together and lowered the pump into the stream. At last they were ready.

'Switch it on,' the chief officer ordered. 'We will,' his henchman at the water's side responded with a welcome note of urgency. The engine coughed protestingly into life. No water appeared.

'Now will you look at that?' said Cummins disgustedly. 'Can they not see that the engine is disconnected to the pipes?'

Somehow the flames were put out and at dawn the firemen, loaded with liquid souvenirs pillaged from a rescued sideboard, departed in a clatter of self-congratulation. The tired little party sat silent and dejected on the gilt, smoke-blackened chairs that now furnished the courtyard, sipping tea magically conjured up by the butler. Oonagh, mink coat over her nightdress, tried to console Kit the shepherd, who had appeared over the hill to help but had been seduced by the contents of the sideboard and was now hopelessly, sentimentally, drunk. Kee had re-entered the house in search of his wallet but there was a weary lethargy over the rest of them as they gazed up at the ruins of what had been the best-known – and the best-loved – house in Ireland. In time it was to be restored to its former glory by Oliver Messel. This night it was merely forlorn.

The disconsolate household made its way to Dublin, where the next day Gay was disappointed to learn that, despite assurances in London to the contrary, Irish licensing laws precluded a swift conclusion to his marital odyssey. He, Magsie and Oonagh went on to Paris, where his mother was confident she could arrange matters quickly with the help of the British ambassador. That, too, turned out to be false optimism and the drawn-out little farce entered its final act as they trailed into London to stay at a small hotel in Little Venice sometimes used by Oonagh when she wished to keep her visits to the capital from the press. From there Gay organised a special licence at Caxton Hall and he and Magsie were married in the presence of the two mothers, Garech and Tara (Garech's 10-year-old brother), and two of Oonagh's friends. Despite the secrecy, the *Daily Sketch* had been tipped off and a number of photographers lay in wait. Gay and Magsie ran in different directions in their panic to escape, meeting later at the brief reception before flying to Paris for a short honeymoon. The whole business of getting married – far from the society wedding that both had expected and, indeed, wanted – had turned into a travesty.

No one had been left out of proceedings more comprehensively than Philip. For this he was at least partly to blame; it was, after all, his opposition that had triggered the whole unfortunate series of events. Oonagh, relishing a conspiracy, revelled in the secrecy, taking particular delight in her ex-husband's exclusion. Gay had in fact written to his father the evening before the wedding in an attempt to explain and had paid the hotel's hall porter handsomely to deliver the letter. Philip never received it and only knew that his son was married when asked by a newspaper for his reaction. 'It was a crashing surprise to me,' he said. 'I thought Gay was in Ireland with his mother.'

Crashing it may have been; crushing it certainly was. On their return from Paris, Magsie and Gay found a letter from Valsie telling them how deeply wounded Philip had been at having to read of the marriage in the popular press. He had always expected a great deal from Gay, hoping not only that his son would live out his own unfulfilled racing dreams but that, somehow, he would also be able to fill the awful void created by Tessa's death. Gay, painfully aware of his father's longings but recognising from an early stage that he was neither blessed with extraordinary riding skills nor temperamentally suited to the conventional lifestyle that he knew his father wished for him, had from boyhood lived in a state of anxiety to please which made his present guilt all the more troublesome. But Philip, whatever his faults, could not for long bear a grudge against Gay; mollified by his son's contrition and content to delude himself with the fiction that the whole episode had been engineered by Oonagh, he and Valsie were soon regular visitors to Hullers, pleased that Magsie tactfully approved of its furnishings and that she showed no sign of attempting to curb Gay's racing plans.

Magsie played her cards beautifully – not perhaps without a modicum of calculation, but principally because she was deeply in love with Gay and wanted to please him and his family. Oonagh she found easy; in some ways the women were very alike: both were feminine to a fault, aware of their good looks and the effect they had on men; both basked happily in the interest that the press (which in those days knew where the lines were drawn) showed in Gay and in themselves. But where Oonagh was vague and curiously unworldly, Magsie was shrewd and organised enough to inject a little much-needed discipline into her husband's life. As for Gay, although he believed himself to be happy in his new state, he found that he was oddly unsettled. He craved to be like other men who, when they married, had to move up into another gear of responsibility; had to sharpen the focus of their career ambitions, needing to acquire a mortgage and to work hard to support it. These were the ingredients of other people's lives that seemed to be both normal and worthwhile – but they were absent in his own. He already had a house; he certainly didn't require a mortgage or even a job, come to that; marriage would make little difference to any of his plans. He seemed to have done things back to front. He wished he wasn't quite so different. But – not given to prolonged introspection on this scale – he quickly put his misgivings aside and prepared to resume his life.

For Magsie, though, much had changed and she loved the excitement of it all.

Being part of a high-profile family was fun and the publicity the Kindersleys and the Guinnesses seemed to generate appealed to the actress in her. She found Gay's easy familiarity with people from all walks of life lovable and stimulating. She had never experienced such gregariousness before: they had only to step on to an aeroplane to acquire a dozen new friends. She was dazzled by the sparkling cocktail of poet and peasant, literary lion and political polymath she found at Luggala – even (once she had suppressed her initial alarm) to the extent of good-humouredly tolerating a drunken Brenden Behan chasing her round the courtyard apparently intent on rape. She relished, too, the more formal atmosphere at Luttrelstown and Clandyboye – where to her delight the Queen Mother was an occasional visitor – and felt happy and secure in a milieu where her husband was so obviously liked by everyone they knew and admired by so many more for his dash and courage on the racecourse.

Gay began to ride again soon after Christmas, winning twice on Prince Eyot at Fontwell and Plumpton. At the latter he was in fact clearly beaten by at least a neck, but at holiday meetings judges were hard to come by and the temporary incumbent had obviously lunched exceedingly well. A fortnight later the *Racing Calendar* reported that the official had relinquished his licence.

Sandymount's preparation for the National was giving his trainer some anxiety. The horse had never quite been on top of his form since being brought down in a fall the season before and, although he won a handicap chase at Newbury in January, Don felt that something was not as it should be. The *Daily Mirror*'s racing correspondent, Newsboy – who was Don's nephew Bob Butchers – did not share his uncle's misgivings. Under the headline 'March 24 is the Big Day for Gay', he wrote:

> Courage and enthusiasm win the Grand National. Sandymount and his owner-rider Mr Gay Kindersley are not short of either quality. A good thing too for you will find Sandymount among the big race entries out later today.
>
> Falls and disappointments have not blunted the enthusiasm of Gay, a true amateur rider. He was full of it after winning on Sandymount at Newbury last Saturday. He instructed trainer Don Butchers to enter the horse for the Aintree event on March 24.
>
> Gay is no kid-glove amateur; he gets full enjoyment out of the back-room jobs of racing. Early each morning he goes to Epsom to exercise his horses and then grooms them. Hunting is another part of his life and he has also ridden bucking broncos in Canada. Now the thrills of tackling Aintree fences lie ahead.
>
> Sandymount is sure to be weighted lower than Gay can manage

comfortably but you can bet, though, that a spell of road running will trim the Kindersley bulk on the big day. The best of luck to Gay and Sandymount.

Don's premonitions proved to be more accurate than those of his nephew. Soon after his Newbury triumph, Sandymount went off his food and a prolonged investigation at the Newmarket Research Station – a leading equine hospital – confirmed that he had a long-standing injury to a gland at the back of his tongue which prevented him from swallowing properly. It was inoperable.

Friarspark, on the other hand, won several times as a four-year-old – usually with Alan Oughton on board; Gay and the professional jockey Dave Dick landed a substantial gamble on him at Worcester. Feeling duty bound to celebrate, they arranged to meet Magsie in London and embarked on a binge, the staple ingredients of which were oysters and Brandy Sour. The mixture did not sit happily in the Kindersley tummy and he disgraced himself in a cinema by being comprehensively sick over the row in front. His only consolation in the resulting embarrassment was that he had been so ill that it was no longer necessary for him to lose weight by finishing the evening at the Turkish baths in Jermyn Street. For Dick, however, the trip was essential if he was to be in good enough shape the next day. As he relaxed in a cubicle he was astonished to hear voices he recognised as two well-known – but far from well-liked – professional punters criticising loudly his riding of a failed favourite at Fontwell the day before. Not feeling disposed to argue the case, he prepared to leave when he realised that not only were the men alone in the hot-steam-room, but that someone had left a small coil of rope outside their door. He tied it securely shut, turned the heat control up to maximum and left, taking the men's trousers with him.

The next day at Lingfield – where Gay rode Brian Oge to his first win over hurdles – the precious pair turned up glowing as pinkly as boiled lobsters and had to endure not just the aftermath of their scalding but unrestrained hilarity from those in the know. News travels fast in racing and Dave Dick was one of the best-liked figures on the circuit.

Before the season ended, Prince Eyot and Friarspark won again and Gay rode his point-to-pointer Fezzan to victory in the Past and Present Steeplechase at the Grand Military meeting at Sandown. Altogether he had ridden five winners since his marriage and, apart from the sadness of Sandymount, all seemed to augur well for the autumn. That year his old friend Bob McCreery had been leading amateur with thirteen winning rides and Gay was giving serious thought to how he might challenge him in the not-too-distant future.

During the summer the Kindersleys settled down happily into the age-old squirearchal roles demanded of them by the conventions of English village life.

Magsie was able to add to the general contentment by being pregnant with Robin – the first of their children, who was eventually born in October. Domestically things could hardly be going better but the next national hunt season, in contrast, was an anti-climax. None of the horses ran up to expectation and Brian Oge, having won a high-class Manor Chase at Windsor and appearing to mature into a serious contender for the Cheltenham Gold Cup, lost his form entirely. In all Gay was able to muster only three winners and again McCreery took the title, sweeping the board with twenty-three.

During the summer of 1957 Gay bought Magsie a four-year-old hurdler called Gama II from Alec Head in France, with the long-term aim of turning him into a steeplechaser but meanwhile riding him to a win in an amateur's flat race at Worcester. Also that summer the Kindersleys went on holiday to the South of France (so popular than with the national hunt world that Cap d'Antibes was known as Lambourn-by-the-Sea) with a gang of those who were to become regular companions on many subsequent jaunts, among them the Fulke Walwyns, the Winters, the Marshalls, Dave Dick and Bob McCreery.

The 1957–58 season began well. Fezzan won convincingly at Wye and Fontwell while Brian Oge, back on song, won five out of six races before suffering severe tendon trouble from which he never entirely recovered. To replace him Gay bought a successful point-to-pointer, Tartary, and after a couple of encouraging warm-up races, entered him in the Foxhunters Chase at Liverpool – a race run over one circuit of the Grand National course. Don Butchers was not pleased; he hated Aintree, considering the then unreconstructed fences not to be a fair test of any horse other than a specialist. He feared for both Gay and Tartary and, in the event, Tartary seemed to share his feelings, rapidly losing enthusiasm and falling further and further behind despite Gay's frantic urging. Eventually the horse shed his tiresome burden, the race being won by Merryman II, who went on to win the National itself in 1960.

Soon after her husband's abortive attempt to conquer the Liverpool fences, Magsie gave birth to Catheryn. Shortly afterwards she was to be able to go with Gay to Spain for a race meeting advertised as a part of the amateur world championships and organised by the International Federation of Gentlemen Riders – the Fegentri. Although Great Britain was not an official member of the federation at that time, there was a strong turn-out of owners, trainers, riders and racing correspondents, all of whom shared a keen nose for an outstanding party. John Lawrence (writing as Marlborough in *The Daily Telegraph*) described the invasion as the most powerful force to enter Spain since Wellington broke out of the lines of Torres Vedras. And not only did the pleasure-seekers come from England; entries and their connexions arrived in large numbers from Germany, France, Switzerland and Italy to give some credence to the claims being made for the meeting as a truly international occasion.

The two principal events on the card were a valuable flat race over a mile-and-three-quarters and a steeplechase run over big but soft birch fences; together these were to make up the Spanish leg of the world championship series. Gay had flown out Gama II for the flat and was to ride Flashaway for trainer Ivor Herbert over the fences. Ten other English horses had also travelled by air at the host country's expense, including mounts for Lawrence and Bob McCreery. The Duque de Albuquerque – who had kept horses with Peter Cazalet and had himself ridden in the Grand National – was amongst those representing Spain.

A non-stop supply of gin fizzes at their hotel and a succession of unstintingly hospitable receptions did much to ensure that any advantage the British riders may have enjoyed by virtue of ability and experience had all but evaporated by the morning of the meeting. Six haggard amateurs with red-rimmed eyes – and twice that number of equally ill-used owners and trainers – assembled at the beautiful Madrid course. The setting was magnificent. The flat and jumping tracks were separated not by rails but by manicured privet hedges; the paddock resembled an English lawn complete with rose garden, and the arched and cloistered washed-pink stand soared skywards in the style of a Moorish palace. The women were as elegant as any seen at Royal Ascot and the men, freed from the tyranny of stiff collars and top-hats, sported the air of genuine graciousness that is the mark of the grandee.

The English thoroughbreds – the horses, that is – stood out among their rivals. The journey and the subsequent indignity of being packed closely in the cattle trucks which took them to their stables seemed to have done them little harm. Their coats gleamed with health and, as they paraded for the first of the featured races, none looked better than Gama II. In a field of 19 he was probably the best known, having raced in both France and England. The Tote quickly sold out of tickets on him – he was the hottest of hot favourites.

His rider was far from feeling in rude health as he wearily climbed aboard in the paddock. The added responsibility of carrying the bulk of the racegoers' money – a development he had not foreseen – weighed heavily upon him as he cantered down to the start. The comments of the other British riders – glad to be relieved of such pressure – were kindly meant but restored only a little confidence. Lawrence remarked that their foreign rivals hardly looked up to much and Gama II must surely have the beating of those out from England. McCreery wished him well and said he would try to stick close but he was by no means sure that his own mount would get the trip. Perhaps, Gay thought, as they began to line up, all would be well – despite his throbbing head.

The start was a shambles and the widely varying standards (and temperaments) of the competing nationalities ensured that the tight bends were negotiated successfully only by using the roughest of riding-off techniques, more usually seen on the polo ground. Lawrence made the early running on the Doug-Marks-trained Duet Leader and, hearing the schemozzle behind him as they rounded the first turn, concluded that he ought to stay there. Duet Leader, untouched by the bumping and boring and terrified that the unseemly noise would catch him up, agreed and bolted for home, winning by a distance with Spaniards second and third. Gama II finished fifth and the punters looked thoughtfully at the Englishmen as they tore up their tickets.

In the two miles over the lush fences that came next, a German entry that had won the year before started an even hotter favourite than Gay. Flashaway was top weight and took the lead but was unable to sustain the pace. McCreery on his own Gold Wire won with John Lawrence on Siamois second (both trained by Ryan Price) and the German a disappointing third. The betting public had had a bad day.

That evening the phenomenally generous Albuquerque gave a party for five hundred at his estate outside the capital. There, amidst the bands and the flashing flamenco dancers, sustained by vintage champagne and the best of the ducal table, they danced under the velvety Madrid sky until the first streaks of dawn called them reluctantly to their beds. Later that day Gay and Magsie flew to France to join Oonagh on a boat in the Mediterranean. The pace of the last few days had reminded him strongly of Luggala and as they crossed the Pyrenees he wondered with a sudden apprehensive lurch in his stomach exactly what his mother had got herself into.

His unease was well founded. Oonagh had married again in 1957 and there were already signs that this was to be disaster transcending any unhappiness she had undergone during her time with either Philip or Dom. Staying with her niece Caroline (Maureen's daughter) in the United States she had met a Cuban couturier who worked for the American designer Charles James. Miguel Ferreras, a great bull of a man ('Should be kept chained to the bed-post,' said Philip when they met some years later) was professionally ambitious and seventeen years younger than the woman who now fell in love with him. They married in Drake's Hotel in New York and she brought him back to Luggala for Garech's eighteenth birthday party, where he met her family and friends for the first time. They were uniformly appalled, the more so as Oonagh let it be known – in an almost casual way – that even at the wedding itself she had wished that she was marrying someone, anyone else. Yet, fascinated and trapped, she was unable to free herself of the thrall in which she was now apparently held. In a matter of months she opted for a compromise: she would remain married but not live with the husband she now suspected of being sexually equivocal. The first physical estrangements began in 1958 but she was unable to break away entirely and, as much as three months later, the Cuban retained enough influence to persuade her to fund a fashion house in Paris – the Maison Ferreras in the rue de Faubourg – through the medium of a Canadian company in which Oonagh had a five-million-dollar holding.

Maison Ferreras might have succeeded in New York – or even in London; in Paris it was an intolerable irritant to the great French houses. Talented as he undoubtedly was, Ferreras could not begin to cope with the squeeze that they exercised on him and the operation began to lose money at an ever-gathering speed. In 1964 Oonagh decided that she could do no more either for the salon or for the husband whom she hardly ever saw. Ferreras, in an announcement to the press, stated briefly: 'My wife wants a divorce; I have been told to close down the business.' The worst seven years of Oonagh's marital life were lightened only by the reassuring comforts of Luggala where she still inspired undying devotion from her family and the admiration of her friends – causing Claude Cockburn, for example, to write:

> she has an extraordinary skill in assembling a seemingly random collection
> of guests, some of whom may have been feuding for years until the magic
> of Luggala gets to work. Where else could the Duc de Brissac [sic] and
> Brendan Behan have a row with a director of the Bank of England about
> the Grand National and be soothed by a man singing a poem in Gaelic?

In pursuit of some strand of personal happiness and to satisfy her constant longing for small children to be about her, in 1963 she began proceedings in Mexico (where her friend John Huston was filming *Night of the Iguana*) which were eventually to enable her to adopt baby twins.

As Gay nursed his hangover in a Spanish airliner most of this sad story was still to unfold but, in a momentary flash of unusual prescience, he felt certain at that moment that the misery caused by his mother's marriage would not be confined to her alone. Somehow it would affect his own family and its future well-being. At that stage he couldn't quite see how but it worried him considerably. Seeking comfort, he took Magsie's hand and went to sleep.

Back at Beare Green, village cricket was in full swing and Gay, taking his duties as president of the club seriously, had organised a celebrity team to come and play the home side. He was determined that this should become an annual fixture and after a post-match drink in the King's Head he had invited everyone to Hullers to continue the evening. After supper and before the dancing had properly got underway, there was a demand that the host should give of his party piece. Gay, never averse to performing in the service of 'Slattery's Mounted Fut' (and pleased that the climactic tearing of the shirt would present him with an opportunity to show off his Mediterranean tan), gave it his all. Off came the shirt with even more than the customary vigour and, simultaneously, out with an audible snap went his remaining shoulder. John Lawrence drove him to London and Tucker arranged to operate immediately, sewing this – the right – shoulder joint together in the same way (but rather more tidily) as he had the left some five years before. Although less messy, the healing process still took five months and Gay was out of racing action until after Christmas.

This period in hospital had been enlivened agreeably by an attractive nurse who responded to his advances with a commendably greater wholeheartedness than had the Irish sisters. So mindful of the need to look after her favourite patient was she that, returning from holiday some time later, she noticed with pleasure and anticipation from an examination of the admissions book that Gay was once again in residence.

Thinking to surprise him as she came on night duty, she crept into his room, undressed and slipped into bed. It was not she, however, who provided the ultimate surprise. In her enthusiasm she had misread the name in the book and was now between the sheets with 80-year-old Guy Kindersley, Gay's great-uncle. The old boy was gratified. Relating the experience to his bemused wife the next day, he admitted that: 'I like it in here; awfully friendly lot the nurses.'

Alan Oughton took the rides on the four fit principals of the Kindersley string: Tartary, Fezzan, Handsome Prince (a selling hurdler) and the nine-year-old hunter chaser J'Arrive bought from Arthur Stephenson. By the Cheltenham meeting a rejuvenated owner was back in form, having ridden a double on Tartary and Handsome Prince at Windsor in February. He had three rides at the festival: Tartary and J'Arrive in the Foxhunters and United Hunts Cup respectively and, most exciting of all, Irish Coffee in the prestigious Kim Muir, then restricted to serving and ex-serving amateur riders – a wide field in the days of National Service. Irish Coffee had come over from Ireland for the race and Gay had picked up the ride by chance, never having sat on the horse until that day. He started second favourite to the 1956 Grand National winner ESB and won at 100 to 30 – a surprisingly short price for a horse that had not been placed first in any of his previous seventeen outings. The noisily enthusiastic acclaim from the huge Irish contingent – who looked upon Gay as their own – as he and Irish Coffee entered the winner's enclosure did much to explain the odds.

In the Foxhunters, Tartary fell but J'Arrive finished second in his race, pleasing everyone except Philip Kindersley who had backed him in a multiple bet involving four runners, only J'Arrive failing to oblige. The horse, however, more than made amends by winning three times in the spring to help Gay to a total of seven for this unfortunately short season.

During the summer it became evident that Magsie was again pregnant (Kim was to be born in January 1960); what was not so evident was that her marriage was already beginning to founder. At the root of the incipient problems was Gay's hopeless inability to be faithful and Magsie's determination to keep him in line. He had – as was the case with his father – an incurably roving eye. He also had money and charm as well as the glamour associated with putting his life constantly at risk: for many women an irresistible combination, especially when deployed with a complete lack of self-consciousness. Most of all he was over-sexed almost to the point of priapism and actively sought out complaisant partners. At this stage of his life he envisaged no commitment outside his marriage; there was no thought then of any permanent arrangement involving a mistress or mistresses tucked away in quiet mews houses. What he felt he needed – and with an ache that amounted to compulsion – was not much more than a constant succession of one-night stands, a reversion to his pre-Magsie days. With whom it hardly mattered; almost anyone would do. This, he persuaded himself naïvely, had no connexion with his wife; it stood on his own. His desire for other women did not, as he saw it, affect his marriage.

It is hardly surprisingly that Magsie failed to grasp this logic. She first had evidence of her husband's activities on the morning of John Lawrence's wedding. Gay had been to the stag party organised the night before by Bob McCreery at the Stork Room – a club known both for its saucy floorshows and the sexiness of its hostesses. The Old Etonian racing fraternity was out in force: Kindersley, Lawrence, McCreery, Piers Bengough (later Her Majesty's representative at Ascot and a fine amateur rider) and Gay's cousin Hugo forming the hard core. After dinner and several gallons of champagne, the Stork's fleet of girls began to infiltrate the party. Champagne gave way to multi-coloured cocktails. There was dancing; there were earnest protestations of undying friendship made in incoherent little speeches attempting gallantly to express the party's collective wish that good fortune and happiness should attend the marriage of the future Lord Oaksey; there was, in short, the usual bonhomie attendant on such rituals. But not all was innocent and altruistic, for these were rich young men well able to indulge their rising lusts as they felt the warm well-rounded flesh of the girls on their knees. Gay, never for a minute able to contemplate resisting such temptation, gathered up his companion, bundled her into a cab and soon found himself in a bedroom in Soho. His lady was friendly and compliant; she was anxious to please – a girl didn't always get so lucky, this one was a gentleman, rich and good looking. But she also wanted to get on with the matter in hand. Time was money. Her gentleman had, however, drunk not wisely but far too liberally for his now struggling libido. The more she coaxed him, the more difficult he found it to respond. What he really wanted was to go to sleep. Perhaps a little later ... He failed on all counts to come up to scratch. The girl's pleasure at her catch now changed to irritation. She needed quickly to free herself of this encumbrance and get back to the club; with a bit of luck there would still be a few punters left. She told Gay he must go; if he didn't leave immediately, she would call her brother who was a bouncer. Gay guiltily gave her £15 for her trouble and staggered home to his in-laws where, thankfully, Magsie was safely asleep. He undressed as best he could and fell into bed.

In the morning his headache was stupendous. Magsie was not surprised; she expected as much when the boys went out together. She sniffed – and sniffed again. That smell, though; that wasn't alcohol; that surely was cheap scent? Gay appeared to be drenched in the stuff. She shook him out of semi-consciousness and taxed him with it. He groaned. She telephoned Hugo and asked him what had happened at the party. Had there been any girls? Hugo – off his guard – said yes, of course, loads of girls. Had Gay gone off with one. Yes, of course, nothing unusual in that; that's what they were for. Magsie couldn't believe her ears. She consulted her mother. Vi said that boys would be boys. Her daughter found no comfort in such pragmatism and returned to the attack. Gay, not sure what his cousin had or not said, denied everything. He felt quite righteous in so doing; after all he hadn't actually slept with the bloody girl. But the seeds of discord and mistrust were sown; soon they were to have fertile ground in which to flourish.

It was a relief to be able to turn aside from marital friction and make careful plans with Don Butchers for the 1959–60 season. To the string they had now added a chaser, Donino's Serenade, and three hurdlers, O'Connell, Gallant Barney and Speedwell; he now had fourteen horses of differing ages, experience and ability at Priam Lodge, the most expensive being Gallant Barney, the seven-year-old winner of an impressive number of bumpers in Ireland. He had been bought in the summer for £2,500 – a huge sum at a time when training fees were £10 a week and the entire prize money at a meeting such as Wincanton would total well under £1,000. Dick Francis, in the *Sunday Express*, forecast a determined attempt to do well:

> The unofficial role of premier owner-rider vacated by the late Lord Mildmay eight years ago is at last being filled – by quiet, fair, 29-year-old Gay Kindersley.
>
> Owner-trainers abound but owner-riders on the Kindersley scale are almost extinct. Single-minded devotion to racing, ability, courage and cash seem so seldom now to coincide in one person. Gay ... should start this season well at Newton Abbot next Friday and Saturday.

The season did indeed start well but the first day's racing at Newton Abbot was not without its attendant social drama.

Gay and Magsie had asked themselves to stay at the Devon home of Johnnie and Jose Bastard, friends Gay had met in the South of France. Johnnie was cast flamboyantly in the Kindersley mould of womanising, and consequently there was frequent tension between him and his unforgiving wife. The Kindersleys had hardly arrived when it became apparent that there was a serious note of discord in the air; Jose was in a glowering temper and the Bastards were not communicating with each other. A strangely unsteady Johnnie (it was barely tea-time) took Gay aside to explain the problem while Magsie found herself the recipient of a similar confidence by the aggrieved lady of the house. The ingredients of the story were familiar – at least to Gay.

Johnnie, spending a couple of days in London earlier that week, had become carried away on a high tide of champagne consumed in the company of a night-club hostess and, on discovering that she lived not far away in the West Country, had asked her to join the house party for dinner. When sober again he had optimistically taken the view that she would either forget or just not turn up; he had not informed his wife. Shortly before the Kindersleys had arrived he had gone out on to his lawn and was not able to take a telephone call from the lady confirming that she would indeed be among those present that evening and asking if she could stay the night. Jose, not knowing who she was and not wishing to appear impolite, said yes, of course, and set off down the garden to make enquiries. When she dragged the embarrassing truth out of her reluctant husband, she hit the roof. Her verbal assault was vitriolic; by the time Gay and Magsie arrived, Johnnie had sought refuge deep in a bottle.

To complicate matters, Jose's 80-year-old father – a retired Indian Army major with sternly old-fashioned standards of morality – was also staying and had not been, even partially, apprised of the situation. When the lady arrived and was relieved of her fur coat, she displayed a sequinned little black number with a cleavage so precipitous that Gay, leaning forward eagerly to introduce himself, was able to snatch a view of both pink-tipped nipples. She smiled at him, accepted a cocktail and began to make herself agreeable to the rest of the party. Jose and Magsie froze as Johnnie – his nightmare a reality – half-heartedly attempted to respond with the strictly limited small-talk of which he was by now capable. The major, however, was much taken. Noting Gay's close attention to the new arrival and not wishing to be in any way stand-offish in the way his family seemed to be, he joined in an animated discussion of London's better-known watering-holes. 'What a splendid girl,' he thought. She seemed to know all the clubs he'd read about in the gossip columns. Assuming she was a friend of the Kindersleys, he wandered over to Magsie.

'Lively gel, that,' he enthused. 'Known her long, have you? Reminds me of someone I once knew. I forget where. Not your sister by any chance?'

At dinner the spectacular spectre at the feast was placed between Gay and the old soldier. The former, seeing that his host was now so drunk as to be incapable of playing a useful part in proceedings, did his best to jolly things along. Magsie and Jose were huffily unreceptive and only the octogenarian appeared wholly at ease, treating his dinner companion to an earnest monologue relating the pleasures of life on the North-West Frontier and, in particular, a detailed account of the all-India pig-sticking tournament at Peshawar in 1928. After twenty minutes or so of the technicalities of the sport, the lady's eyes began to glaze. He noticed and paused in concern. Had he, he wondered to himself, overdone it? After all the gel was probably too young to have been in India; perhaps he was boring her. He searched his mind for a subject that would engage her interest more closely; something she would know about.

'D'you go grouse shooting at all?' he asked.

The remainder of the evening dragged grimly on and when Johnnie eventually staggered to bed, Jose followed him, beckoning Gay out into the hall. 'Get that fucking woman out of my house by nine tomorrow morning,' she hissed.

After a cursory breakfast, during which his sole companion at the table wore her fur coat tightly around her as if to ward off a chill, Gay offered to drive her home – having first taken the sensible precaution of seeking Magsie's permission. He was keen that no marital misunderstanding born out of close proximity to a half-naked lady should distract him from the main business of the day. His behaviour would be exemplary. In the car though – despite his resolution – he couldn't help noticing how good her legs were; he wavered, looked again and was lost. As he slowed down, looking for a secluded spot, an army lorry overtook them, full of soldiers who – never slow to appreciate a good thing when they saw one – crowded to the tailboard of their truck, their gestures unmistakably lewd and to the point: 'We know what you're doing; we know what you're doing,' they chanted. Gay's nerve failed and he took her straight home.

It was perhaps just as well for on the racecourse that afternoon he needed all his strength to ride J'Arrive to victory in the three-mile handicap chase, a win that was confirmed only after the stewards had considered an objection from Jimmy Fitzgerald (the jockey of the second) for bumping and boring. The aggrieved owner of the beaten horse was so confident that the protest would be upheld that he wagered £500 on the outcome of the enquiry. In the jockeys' room they knew differently: 'You've no chance,' they advised Fitzgerald good humouredly. 'They'll never overturn Gay. No chance.' This good advice, born partly out of the fact that there was, in truth, little of a case to answer and partly from the professionals' perception of Gay as the golden boy who could do no wrong, was quickly relayed to the owner, who was able to lay off his bet by putting another £500 on J'Arrive at a generous evens.

Less than a week later Gay was back in the West Country (this time he decided to give the Bastards a miss and stay in a hotel) to ride at Devon and

Exeter. There he had two third places on his hurdlers, Handsome Prince and Pursebearer, and a win on the in-form J'Arrive who dutifully obliged in the Handicap Chase. This combination won again at Wincanton in September and a month later produced their fourth in a row in a two-horse chase at Cheltenham, once more on the firm going J'Arrive so relished. The little bay was then sent to Cecil Bonner to hunt with the Bicester and so qualify for hunter chases in February, a change of air he appreciated keenly, being – unlike so many racehorses – a brilliant hunter.

On 26 November at Kempton, Handsome Prince fell at the first in a two-mile hurdle and Gay, badly injuring a leg in a fall so spectacular that photographs of it appeared in newspapers published as far away as New Zealand and South Africa, missed a winning ride (taken by Alan Oughton) on the Kindersley-owned Steel Fortune. A trip to the Jockey's Garage was clearly indicated and Bill Tucker did his best – largely by prescribing pain-killers and extended rest – but even so the patient was out of the saddle for over three weeks. By his return in mid-December the going had softened considerably. The change clearly suited the stable, for Gallant Barney won a novice hurdle at Sandown and two days later Handsome Prince scooted home by two lengths at Windsor. By Christmas Day Gay had won six times, all on his own horses. The race for leading amateur was developing into a three-cornered contest which included his old friend Bob McCreery and the West Country rider, farmer and blacksmith Jim Renfree. The Renfree bid for the title was a proper old-fashioned family affair – Jim's father holding the licence and his sister Jenny doing the actual training while Jim himself (who hardly had time from his work to sit on a horse between races) did the steering and the shoeing.

On Boxing Day 1959 there were seven national hunt meetings in England. Gay and Don chose Wincanton, where the going was described as heavy, and entered four horses: Roberta and Gallant Barney in the seller and a 2½-mile handicap hurdle respectively; Steel Fortune in the Novice Chase and Donino's Serenade in the Handicap Chase. All were fancied and Gay had spent the previous day, not in the time-honoured fashion with turkey and plum pudding, but by giving the farm staff the day off, doing the milking and feeding the animals himself. It took his mind off the fact that he had to fast so seriously that eating anything, let alone a traditional Christmas dinner, was out of the question if he was even to approach the weight given to him in the handicaps.

At Luggala the spirit was notably different: the parties were in full swing and the house brimmed over with an ever-changing kaleidoscope of guests, including the American ambassador in Dublin. Patrick Cummins had organised a telephone line to Wincanton and was poised to bring Oonagh regular reports of her son's progress. At first he had little good news to convey. Roberta, whom the bookies had originally offered as favourite despite the fact that this was his first outing, faded in the race almost as fast as he had in the ring, finishing well down the field in a disappointing run as Oonagh and her guests sat down to a lunch of onion soup and turkey rissoles. By the time the beautifully browned main dish was being served, the butler had better tidings to pass on. As he proffered the rissoles to the notoriously fastidious ambassador, he leaned confidentially over to Oonagh.

'Mr Gay's turd,' he murmured quietly. But not quietly enough. The American paled as he paused, spoon in mid-air, before attempting hurriedly to return the offending article to the serving dish.

In fact Mr Gay was not third, or anything like it. Steel Fortune, never the most reliable of performers, had elected to run through the wings at the first fence. A little later Patrick corrected his mistake and apologised to Oonagh, the gleam in his eye suggesting that he was not entirely sincere. 'You know what it is, me lady; the telephone lines is terrible scratchy.'

From then on matters at Wincanton improved. Gallant Barney, despite carrying five pounds overweight, stayed on well to win his race by less than a length but at the very acceptable price of 5 to 1, and Donino's Serenade cantered home six lengths in front to be returned at evens favourite. Gay followed this double two days later with a win at Kempton on Speedwell – a three-year-old hurdler who also gave him his tenth success when, on 22 January, they won another seller at the same course, Speedwell being bought in agreeably cheaply on both occasions. This last, though, was the only win from seven rides in three successive days, following a week of cancellations because of snow. Things were no longer going to plan. There were also anxieties over Magsie's health as she approached the birth of Kim (in the event he was delivered safely) and about the fitness of some of the horses as Roberta and Brian Oge (a hope for the Cheltenham Gold Cup) broke down during races on the hard ground and had to be dispatched into the care of Frank Pullen at Fleet. Brian Oge had previously spent some time with Pullen, a vet who specialised in training unmanageable horses and in treating – often successfully – those suffering from apparently incurable leg trouble. In both fields he had gained a well-deserved reputation for restoring many to a full and reliable fitness. Despite the fact he had failed with both Brian Oge and indeed the ex-point-to-pointer Tartary, Pullen was to receive a further five from the Kindersley stable before the season was out – Gay's unquestioning faith in this Horse's Garage being equal to the unflinching loyalty he had shown to Bill Tucker over his own medical repairs.

With only one win in January and both Renfree and McCreery breathing down his neck, he looked forward to the return of the qualifiers, J'Arrive and Ice Pool, from Cecil Bonner to put him back on track. Meanwhile the reliable Speedwell delighted everyone by dead-heating with Wire Warrior (ridden by the promising professional Josh Gifford) in yet another seller; had Speedwell not hit the last hard he might well have been the sole winner. But it still counted – another to be added to the tally.

As March approached and with it the Cheltenham Festival, Gay and Don made plans to run Donino's Serenade in the Kim Muir and Cu Culahan (a novice who had performed promisingly under both Alan Oughton and his owner) in the National Hunt Chase, and they set about giving them an appropriate preparation. They appeared well set when Cu Culahan won at Newbury and Donino's Serenade took the Lord Stalbridge Memorial Gold Cup at Wincanton at a starting price of 6 to 1 – winning a great deal of money for the connexions – including Gay, who had staked his now habitual £300. Both, however, developed legs after these races and were consigned to Pullen for treatment. No Kindersley horse would run at the festival that year but hopes of at least taking part were immediately revived by an old training friend. The *Daily Mail* broke the news.

Trainer Fulke Walwyn has engaged Mr Gay Kindersley, the season's leading amateur, to ride Major J E M Bradish-Ellames' Grand National horse, Golden Drop, in the Kim Muir Memorial Challenge Cup at Cheltenham.

Golden Drop is one of the horses most in demand by Grand National backers and is currently on offer at 100–6. This decision could be lucky for Gay whose own horse, Donino's Serenade, misses the race. This enthusiastic rider has 13 wins on his own horses this season.

Sadly, enthusiasm was not enough. Golden Drop started a short-priced favourite and appeared to have every chance at the last, but he ran up the hill one-paced and was beaten a neck into fourth place by old ESB. He failed to make the National, not running again that year, and once more Gay's hopes of competing seriously for the greatest prize in steeplechasing were dashed.

There were other disappointments, too; and perhaps that felt most keenly at Priam Lodge was the poor form of the two-mile novice hurdler, the six-year-old O'Connell, who had cost very nearly as much as Gallant Barney but who in his six runs since mid-October had never finished better than fifth, often being tailed off. In training he performed well but in his races he constantly idled along, even after being given a reminder with the whip. Don Butchers, both as a jockey and a trainer, put the welfare of his horses above all else and was of the school that had little time for beating horses home – indeed many considered him to be over-protective of his charges, citing, for example, his fanatical distaste for the Grand National. He and Gay endlessly discussed the matter of O'Connell's apparent reluctance to give his all and Don decided that here an exception must be made. At the end of February at Windsor, Gay went out with orders to slap the horse hard every time he attempted to come off the bit. It worked; O'Connell, hard ridden to the post, came flying through the mud to beat horses who had regularly finished in front of him for the last five months. The price was 100 to 6 and the connexions left the course not only pleased but considerably richer. March produced four more winners: O'Connell (who had now got the message) at Wye and Plumpton, Handsome Prince by a short head and a long price at Hurst Park, and J'Arrive in the Past and Present at the Grand Military meeting at Sandown. Then came the Easter weekend in April which turned into something of a triumph after beginning badly when J'Arrive, taking one chance too many, crashed at Towcester on the Saturday. On Easter Monday, however, the team was at Huntingdon for that quaint little course's first meeting of the season and one that was not wildly popular with trainers because of the awkward siting of the fences. O'Connell and Handsome Prince both started as favourites in their races and duly obliged – Handsome Prince by only a neck. Gay then completed a treble for the only time in his career by taking the amateur hunter chase on Joint Account, owned by Mrs V Van den Bergh; it was one of the few outside rides he had taken all season and the only winner he had that year that was not his own. Five days later, at Stratford, he made his total twenty-two when J'Arrive cantered home by eight lengths.

By this time the few of his string which were still sound had become very jaded and clearly deserved a summer's rest. Desperate to increase his lead in the championship, he in fact ran J'Arrive and Handsome Prince once more each, but they were well past their best and Gay could do no more than watch helplessly as Bob McCreery – riding largely for other owners – crept closer. John Lawrence, in a *Daily Telegraph* article in early June devoted mainly to the equally exciting struggle for the professionals' title between Stan Mellor and Fred Winter (eventually won by Mellor by the closest possible margin), spared a few lines for his old friends and rivals:

Meanwhile in the amateur's table, a less publicised but no less hard-fought struggle is being waged between the two great friends, Gay Kindersley and Bob McCreery.

With 22 winners – all save one in his own colours – Mr Kindersley looked home and dry a month ago when Mr McCreery, who had already finished on top in two seasons, struck an irresistible patch of form, rode eight consecutive winners and is now only three behind.

That might seem to be an invincible lead to overcome but whereas Mr Kindersley has only one more ride – J'Arrive at Huntingdon – his rival has three at Fontwell today and another to finish up with at Uttoxeter tomorrow.

All four must win if Mr Kindersley is to be beaten and I know that Bob McCreery will not mind my saying that I sincerely hope they don't! No amateur ever put more energy and hard work into his riding than Gay Kindersley and to be robbed at the eleventh hour of this, his greatest ambition, would indeed be a cruel blow.

In the event the lead did prove to be invincible, McCreery finishing with twenty winners, followed by Jim Renfree on eighteen. Gay had ridden one hundred races, all but five on his own horses, winning twenty-two times and being placed in another fifteen. Of his wins, six had been on J'Arrive, four with O'Connell, three each on Handsome Prince and Speedwell, two each on Gallant Barney and Donino's Serenade, with Cu Culahan and Joint Account making up the balance. As an owner he had also won twenty-two times (Steel Fortune winning once under Alan Oughton). In terms of prize money (£5,050) he was a mere sixth in the list, the table being headed by Mrs Winifred Wallace who owned only one horse, Merryman II, which had won only one race – the £13,000 Grand National!

It was immensely gratifying to Gay that Don Butchers, too, had enjoyed his best season ever with thirty-two winners, bringing the yard over £8,000. Altogether it had been a fun and successful year which had thrilled not only Gay and his family but a huge number of friends, as well as the racing public who had cheered him on as they had once acclaimed Mildmay. The single-minded concentration on the championship, the worry over Magsie's pregnancy – and its happy outcome – had combined for a time at least to take his mind off the philandering that had become a way of life. The Kindersleys appeared to be on the crest of a wave as they prepared to enjoy the summer.

CHAPTER SIX

Nerve Endings

June 1950 saw Gay and Magsie once again happily immersed in village activities. They organised a donkey race-day in aid of local charities on the recreation ground of nearby Capel, dragooning their better-known friends and neighbours into acting as useful crowd pullers as well as lending a more practical hand. Lord Boothby – boomingly jovial – was the official starter; Derek Hart, the television reporter (who had taken a shine to Magsie), made a splendidly magisterial judge and a galaxy of owners and trainers – including Philip Kindersley, Freddie Laker (pre-Laker Airways) and Ryan Price – acted as stewards. Jockeys supported the event generously and the event rated almost as many column inches in the social and sporting pages as had the Epsom Derby the week before. The *Daily Express* reported that after the races 115 people stayed on to supper at Hullers.

Keeping himself busy during the summer months was seldom a problem for Gay. Soon after staying with Oonagh in the South of France he was back on the racecourse, riding a winner in an amateurs' flat race at Salisbury. Marlborough, in *The Daily Telegraph*, noted the event:

Just returned from a well-earned holiday in France, Mr Gay Kindersley, the leading National Hunt amateur, rode a flawless race to win the Carnarvon Cup on Kabale.

The same cannot be said for the rider of the unjustifiably short-priced favourite Sister Willow, who probably struck the front too soon and was a spent force when Kabale challenged in the final furlong. Fitness is a major factor in these summer amateur events and although Mr Kindersley's most recent practice was gained, I understand, on a mule in a Monte Carlo nightclub, I can testify to the strength of his finishing effort today.

This model of self-deprecation was written by John Lawrence, the beaten jockey of Sister Willow, whose fitness, if not exactly a by-word by more modern standards, was certainly superior to Gay's – particularly after the latter's three weeks' indulgence in the hands of his mother and Patrick Cummins. Amateur flat races were becoming popular with those who wanted to keep their race-riding skills polished during the non-jumping months and Gay enjoyed the different challenge they offered, despite their somewhat haphazard organisation. No official body existed at that time to look after purely amateur interests – a situation which he, Lawrence and Bob McCreery, among others, were to be instrumental in changing in due course.

Meanwhile there were visits to Luggala where Oonagh – escaping from France in her desperate attempts to distance herself from the presence and even the thought of Ferreras – continued to outdo herself and her socially competitive sisters in the scale and lavishness of her parties. After one notably hedonistic weekend, Sunday luncheon ended in something of a scramble as Gay, Magsie, his cousin Philippa (formidable and sober) and her husband Marco (companionable and drunk) found themselves running late for their flight to London. The arrival at the then tiny Dublin airport was noisily cheerful as a large group, including that great Irish party man 'Pleasure' Bent, piled in to see them off. The rumpus of their arrival was witnessed by the aircraft's captain as he walked through the public area on his way to start the engines. He paused. Gay, reversing unsteadily while organising the assembly into a choir, collided with him as Pleasure broke into a version of 'Paddy McGinty's Goat' probably not envisaged by the original composer. The pilot was unamused; he had recognised Gay from his frequent appearances in the gossip columns and had not been in the least impressed by the playboy image they portrayed. He attempted to make himself heard.

'Is your name Kindersley?'

Gay failed to respond.

His inquisitor's face darkened. 'You're not travelling on my flight,' he said. The words were soft but distinct.

Gay sobered up rapidly. 'But I'm booked. I have to get back to London. I've a race tomorrow.'

The pilot turned his back and Marco swayed forward, dishevelled but, as always, well meaning. He tapped a gold-braided shoulder. 'Now look here,' he began. 'I'm this young man's physician. He's perfectly sober. As a medical man I can vouch for him. He's quite all right.' He hiccuped gently.

The captain looked at him distastefully. 'He's not flying with me and that's an end of it.'

'But I'm a doctor.'

'I don't give a bugger if you're Catherine the Great. One more word out of you and you won't be coming either.'

'Shut up, Marco,' ordered Philippa as her husband opened his mouth. 'Shut up. You've got surgery in the morning.'

The pilot delivered his parting shot. 'I'm not having drunks on my plane. And that's it and all about it.'

Quivering with self-righteousness, he again turned away. Gay and Magsie slowly retrieved their luggage and prepared to return to Luggala. The party had gone suddenly flat but Marco, raging at the injustice of it all, directed a final salvo at the enemy.

'Imagine,' he shouted. 'Imagine. No drunks. On an Irish plane.' He shook his head disbelievingly.

At Priam Lodge preparations for the national hunt season were in full swing and the horse-power looked promising. To the remaining stars of the previous year – including J'Arrive, O'Connell and Gallant Barney – had been added some fresh blood, notably the Irish-bred Carrickbeg who had been bought among a £1,500 job lot of three and was still only 4 years old. Gay had won a bumper on him in Ireland the previous March and had already, even at this early stage, begun to nurse a keen anticipation – accepted with a resigned reluctance by Don Butchers – that here was a contender for a future Grand National. Carrickbeg – so dark brown as to be almost black but with a huge white blaze which should make him easy to pick out in even the biggest of fields – had his first outing over fences at Towcester in late October and was just beaten in a novice hurdle. But the feel was good; here was a youngster with genuine class.

The press and the racing public renewed their close interest as Gay began his battle to retain the leading amateur title, but the full glare of the spotlight had shifted temporarily to Don Butchers as he prepared the yard's star horse Saffron Tartan for the King George VI Chase at Kempton on Boxing Day. Owned by a partnership headed by Colonel Guy Westmacott and originally trained in Ireland by Vincent O'Brien, Saffron Tartan was a massive old-fashioned type with a rare speed for one so big, but he had a history of complicated physical problems which made him difficult to bring to peak performance. He had finished third in the 1960 Champion Hurdle and in this, his next season, his regular jockey was to be Fred Winter, perhaps the greatest-ever rider of close finishes: a master of the rare talent needed to persuade a tired horse to make a final desperate effort. In the King George, Saffron Tartan spared Winter the need to exercise his gift, winning with relative ease. It was now up to Butchers to bring the horse back to his best for the Cheltenham Gold Cup three months later. In this – the supreme test – Saffron Tartan was to be opposed by both Mandarin (who, until the advent of Arkle, was to win more prize money than any other steeplechaser in history) and the brilliantly brave but erratic Pas Seul. Saffron Tartan, now 10, only just stayed the Gold Cup distance, and on the great day Winter made the best possible use of his speed and outstanding jumping. Two fences out they were three lengths clear of Pas Seul but, going to the last, the jockey felt Saffron

Tartan's remaining strength draining away under him. Pas Seul was tiring too – the race had been run at breakneck speed – but he began to gain slowly and, it seemed to the spectators, inexorably up the long hill to the finish. Winter, driving as only Fred Winter could, picked up his exhausted partner and they held on to win by a length. This was Don Butchers's supreme training achievement and Gay, Magsie, and indeed the whole racing world, were thrilled for him. That year he was to finish third in the trainers' table.

Meanwhile in the amateur riders' ranks a new and apparently unstoppable threat to Gay retaining his title had developed in the shape of the young baronet Sir William Pigott-Brown. Curiously, his father John had been in the Western Desert with Philip Kindersley and the two men had talked together one evening while awaiting a German offensive. During the night, Pigott-Brown was killed by a shell and it was Philip who had undertaken the task of burying him.

William set about tackling the amateur championship with serious intent. Going to work for Frank Cundell who trained near Lambourn, he learned to race-ride to such good effect that Frank and his brother Ken (also a trainer) were able to recommend him confidently to a number of influential owners. In this way he amassed twenty-eight wins, only four of which were on his own two horses, comprehensively beating Gay (who had sixteen winners, all owner ridden) into second place. Having shown such early promise of becoming the most successful Corinthian since Mildmay, Pigott-Brown was to prove disappointing on account of his lack of staying power. Within a few short seasons he had gone – claimed, it was popularly supposed, by his other, less public, interests. He was not a universally liked figure: he once tricked Gay into consuming a large quantity of an hallucinating drug by concealing it in a dinner-party pudding – with unpleasant but happily relatively short-lived effects. This was widely seen as being beyond a joke by even the most liberated of spirits.

Being beaten so soundly by a beginner – even such a talented novice as Pigott-Brown – gave Gay food for thought. The more he dwelt on his recent riding performances, the more he suspected that his nerve might be failing. Such a realisation is the stuff of nightmares for anyone engaged in competitive equestrian activity. Loss of nerve can strike at almost any age or stage in a career. Always cautious to the point of pessimism, Don Butchers grimly agreed when Gay confided in him. He too had noticed that a spark was missing and, ever-mindful of his employer's well-being, was not disposed to disagree. Others had also noted the signs: more than one jockey had commented on how far back he was now leaning when approaching his fences, and even an elderly hunting lady who had watched him during one of her rare excursions to a racecourse asked him why he gave so much rein to the horse as he went over each jump. He himself was enjoying his races less and confided in a family friend (Kenneth Rose, the *Sunday Telegraph* columnist) after riding a double at Huntingdon at

Whitsun that he had felt frightened all the way round, whereas until recently the apprehension used to fade after the first fence. He was depressed at having to face this gloomy self-examination and felt that perhaps the time really had come to stop. But his courage, the streak of Irish obstinacy and the fact that he still desperately wanted a crack at the National led him to the delusion that his depression was more a reaction to a disappointing season than serious self-doubt. He employed again his ostrich-like talent for head burying, told Don not to give the matter another thought and set off with Magsie and the children to Ireland for the summer.

Among the guests at Luggala that year were the John Lawrences and Ann, wife of the 12th Marquess of Queensberry, who had been a contemporary of Gay at Eton. Luggala had always cast a romantic spell over the ever-vulnerable Gay and this time – despite the presence of his wife and the demanding distractions of his children – the beauty of the Wicklow Mountains and the peace of the tranquil waters of the sunlit lough combined to such devastating effect that he fell heavily in love with the slim, softly spoken, silken-haired marchioness. From that moment the holiday assumed a Wodehousian aspect as he mooned along the sandy shores wondering how he could engineer an opportunity to be alone with her. Never able to keep a secret and wishing to share what he imagined was his incredible good fortune, he confined in the Lawrences. John would frequently be asked to take Ann for a walk so that Gay could slip away, ostensibly alone, to an evening tryst without giving Magsie cause for suspicion. On one such mission, his rather reluctant accomplice was congratulating himself on successfully making the rendezvous on time when a black cloud of midges arrived simultaneously with his panting friend. Pausing only to light a cigarette as protection from the insects, the conspirator fled – reflecting that it would be hard to indulge in any serious naughtiness under such adverse conditions.

By the time the Kindersleys returned to England, Gay had become so besotted that he resolved to ask Magsie for a divorce. This was the first time that he had contemplated seriously such a far-reaching notion and it is doubtful whether he had thought the matter through, especially as to how such a course would affect his adoring children for whom he could do no wrong. When he confessed, Magsie was in turn hurt, shaken and angry. But having had an inkling in Ireland that something serious was in the wind, she was not entirely unprepared. As her husband stumbled through his confused recital, she became calmer, resolving to sit tight in the hope that the affair would run an eventually harmless course in the same way as its less intense predecessors. Gay, slightly surprised at this relative equanimity, went off to confront the Queensberrys. The marquess was even more placid than Magsie, appearing neither surprised nor in the least upset. After offering Gay a drink he wandered off to bed, leaving the errant couple to talk over their plans – a discussion which ended with them making love in front of the fire. On his return to Magsie, an attack of post-coital contrition led Gay to tell her – quite untruthfully – that he had ended the affair and this somehow moved him to take her in his arms in a demonstration of affection (not to mention lust), a testament to his virility if not his morality. Magsie, while doubting that this sudden show of tenderness was entirely genuine, welcomed his attentions as being anyway symptomatic of a change of heart. In a few weeks her patience was rewarded: the affair limped to a pallid conclusion and the Kindersleys resumed their now increasingly uneasy relationship together.

In addition to the tension resulting from Gay's erratic love life, further marital disharmony arose out of the Iveagh Trustees' decision that he should sell both Hullers and Priam Lodge and find a training establishment where the horse interests (running at a substantial loss) could be merged with a farming enterprise profitable enough to stem, if not reverse, the financial haemorrhages of the past few years. Gay – and Michael Bevan, the trustees' agent – had found what seemed to be the ideal establishment near the village of East Garston, some four miles from Lambourn. Gay had long wanted to live in the Lambourn valley, the centre of the national hunt racing world, and Parsonage Farm with its 1,100 acres lent itself to pleasantly imagined vistas of sweeping gallops, extensive schooling grounds and neatly fenced paddocks. There was even a pub close to the main gates – it was the perfect training environment.

The major problem was the house itself. Small, squat and red-brick, it adjoined a pair of ex-army Nissen huts which at one time housed German prisoners-of-war and were now homes to two families of farm workers. The huts would have displeased the least critical of eyes; to Magsie they presented an eye-sore which, together with the ugly little house, caused her to conclude that she could not contemplate living there; the very prospect brought about an uncharacteristic flash of mutiny.

By the time of the auction in September 1961, Gay had only partially convinced her that there would be money enough left over from the deal to allow some major alterations. She was by no means persuaded and spent the period of the sale sulkily tearing up her catalogue into small pieces and grinding them into the floor with her heel. After some tense and competitive bidding, Michael Bevan secured the property for £135,000 and the trustees congratulated themselves hugely on acquiring a bargain.

So pleased were they when they assembled to view the property for themselves that their chairman, who had been slightly uneasy over the rebellious expression which had hardly left Magsie's face during the visit, patted her on the shoulder and said: 'I know, Magsie, I know. And I absolutely agree. The house is a bit depressing but I tell you what; we're so pleased with the price and the fact that we'll be able to get rid of the other places, that you can have *carte blanche* with the house. *Carte blanche*, m'dear.'

Gay was appalled. 'Christ,' he thought, trying hard to look pleased for Magsie's sake. 'That's going a bit far. She'll turn the place into a bloody palace and I won't be able to afford to run it. God knows how many staff it'll need when she's finished.' Seriously alarmed, he looked at the complacent trustees. Why were they sounding so bloody generous? Another thought struck him. He cheered up. 'Perhaps I'm worth more than they're letting on.'

On this unfounded note of optimism he forgot his worries and threw himself wholeheartedly into helping Magsie spend a fortune. Fashionable architects and landscape gardeners descended like starlings. The little red house was gutted. A modern kitchen rose from the debris; a gracious drawing-room was added and, alongside it, a dining-room with floor-to-ceiling french doors. A whole new wing provided enough bedrooms for the family and their guests with bathrooms to match. Palladian columns rose to frame the main door. Pink-shirted interior designers, lispingly persuasive, flitted from room to room draped in pleated curtains and the most elegant of soft furnishings. Magsie loved it. This was, after all, her first chance to make a home of her own, and she blossomed with a new confidence. Gay, now scarcely pausing to give a thought to the bills, entered into the spirit of the enterprise with a will. The Nissen huts were bull-dozed and the men and their families rehoused in neat cottages; a swimming pool was dug and a tennis court laid; the drive was realigned and bordered immaculately by an imported beech hedge. It was all headily exciting – and very, very expensive. The work was not hurried – the best materials were worth waiting for – and the operation took a year to complete. It was not until the following September that the move was finally made.

The early part of the 1961–62 season saw Gay plagued by a number of minor injuries. A clue to that most dramatically acquired can be found in a footnote to *Chaseform* under the results of the 4.15 race at Carlisle on 9 October. 'Hillside Fairy', it reads. 'Withdrawn; not under orders; bolted before start.'

Hillside Fairy was a 6-year-old mare, a novice hurdler bought by Gay to win a seller but already entered by her previous owner in the race at Carlisle. He flew up to take advantage of the ride; the mare, he was assured, was just the thing for an amateur. The veracity of that assertion quickly become questionable, for on the way to the start she took off unstoppably. There are few more truly terrifying experiences than being completely out of control on a horse travelling at over 30 miles an hour, especially when the animal is racing the wrong way round a narrow country racecourse with little room between hurdles (all sloped towards the runaway) and where there is also a distinct prospect of colliding with the fearsome reverse aspects of steeplechase fences.

It was not long before the hapless pair – now the interested focus of all field-glasses in the stands – ran out of options and Gay prepared to take on a hurdle at top speed and with no brakes. With his eyes tightly shut, he both felt and heard the crash as Hillside Fairy misjudged her take-off. As he tried to sit still, her head came up and hit him so hard in the mouth that his teeth were forced back into their gums. Blood began to seep between his lips as he set out on a second lap. There was no slackening of the mare's stamina or speed and Gay's shoulder muscles – pinned together as they were by artificial fibres – showed every sign of giving out well before he could reclaim even the minimum of control. As they approached the patiently waiting starter for the second time, Gay adopted desperate measures: with all the strength remaining to him he attempted to use the rails to reduce speed, much as a driver of a rudderless speedboat might seek to rub up against a bank or a quayside. Boats, however, have fenders and Gay's left leg was not an adequate substitute. Now thoroughly frightened, he tried to lift it out of harm's way and Hillside Fairy, feeling the shift in balance, took this opportunity to rid herself of her burden once and for all.

As her relieved rider picked himself up from the, luckily, soft ground, he was in time to see her embark on a third lap with undiminished enthusiasm. The starter coughed. 'I think we might withdraw your horse, Mr Kindersley,' he said.

Gay agreed and was taken off by a St John Ambulance attendant to find a doctor, but as it was the last race of an otherwise uneventful day, the latter had taken a chance and gone home. In an attempt to stop the bleeding, the first-aid man stuffed his patient's mouth full of cotton wool, unwittingly causing further damage which necessitated some expensive subsequent treatment in Harley Street as gangrene began to set in.

Don Butchers persevered with Hillside Fairy – from that day on she was always known in the yard as Downhill Mary – and she was placed a number of times before being sold on as a brood mare, producing several successful progeny for her new owner. The Carlisle doctor's future was not quite so happy. Philip, on hearing of the events and the scandalous lack of qualified medical cover, rang the senior steward of the National Hunt Committee demanding retribution. The doctor was allowed to retire quietly.

Gay's injuries were painful enough to keep him grounded for several weeks but in November he entered a new sphere in his racing life by being appointed a steward at Kempton Park. Off came the battered trilby, the brothel-creeper shoes and the Dave Dick jacket (a combination of mackintosh and sheepskin made popular by the eponymous jockey), to make way for a bowler hat, leather brogues and a brand-new covert coat. He looked the part, even if he was young enough to be the son (in some cases the grandson) of most of his fellow stewards. In the majority of cases, the stewards were drawn from those with a

ABOVE LEFT: *The Honourable AE Guinness's yacht* Fantôme *1931.*

ABOVE RIGHT: *Oonagh with HRH Prince George, Duke of Kent, at Great Tangley Manor, 1933.*

LEFT: *1934 picture by Dorothy Wilding. Gay in his frilly page-boy suit and Oonagh.*

RIGHT: *Philip and Valsie dining out in London, 1934.*

LEFT: *Second husband. Oonagh with Daddy Dom (Lord Oranmore and Browne).*

BELOW: *Castle MacGarrett, 1937.*

LEFT: *Gay on Brown Jack, Castle MacGarrett, 1937.*

ABOVE: *The magical Luggala in the Wicklow Mountains. Given to Oonagh by her father.*

RIGHT: *Shooting party at Ashford Castle 1937. The Honourable Ernest Guinness, Gay and Lord Dorchester.*

Kindersley Legal Battle Ends

GAY HANDED OVER TO GRANDPARENTS

The Star

LEFT: *Press cutting, January 1944. Gay has to go to Eton.*

ABOVE: *Tessa and Tara. Luggala, 1947.*

BELOW: *Gay's leaving photograph, Eton, July 1948.*

BELOW: *Happy and proud: Tessa, having come third in the cobs' race at the South Mayo point-to-point, 1947 when only 15. Soon after this she tragically died.*

ABOVE: *Gay's first proper race – a bumper at Mullingar, 1949. He came third on his own Balheary Boy.*

ABOVE RIGHT: *Second Lieutenant Gay Kindersley, 7th Queen's Own Hussars. National Service, 1949.*

RIGHT: *Gay and Philip posing before competing in the same race at the Old Surrey and Burstow point-to-point, 1951. Half-sister Nicky is half-hidden.*

ABOVE: *Gay's first ride under national hunt rules, at Lingfield in December 1951. L–R: Edgar Springate, Brian Marshall, Joe Mahon, Gay on 'Tight Knight', Fred Winter.*

RIGHT: *Calgary stampede, 1952. Gay on Coyote – 'on for 8 seconds and out for 4 hours!'*

LEFT: *Mid-Surrey Farmers Draghounds Hunt Ball, Plaw Hatch, December 1952. L–R: Richard Fisher, Dilly Radford, Gay, Val Fisher.*

LEFT: *Mid-Surrey Draghounds meet at Warlingford, January 1955. L–R Ian Patullo (Whip), Philip (Master), Gay (Whip).*

RIGHT: *The courtyard at Luggala, December 1955. What remained of the house after fire broke out the night that Gay eloped with Magsie. L–R: Mr Williams (gardener), firemen from Bray, Patrick Cummins (in cap).*

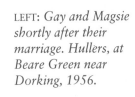

LEFT: *Gay and Magsie shortly after their marriage. Hullers, at Beare Green near Dorking, 1956.*

RIGHT: *Madrid, 1958. In the paddock for the running of Gama II. L–R: Tory Lawrence, Magsie, Bob McCreery, Gay, Ryan Price, Tom Masson (trainer of Gama II).*

BELOW: *Windsor, February 1959. Gay on Tartary at the last, winning from John Bosley on Middlegate* (centre) *and John Daniell on* College Master.

LEFT: *Cheltenham Festival meeting, March 1959; Kim Muir Handicap Chase. Gay jumping the last fence on Irish Coffee in front to win from Danny Moralee on ESB. Bill Tellwright jumping third.*

ABOVE: *Gay in action at Fontwell on Handsome Prince, November 1959. Finished second.*

BELOW: *Grand Military meeting, Sandown, March 1960. Gay on J'arrive (right) jumping the last to win from John Webber on Open Fire.*

LEFT: *Gay and Gallant Barney* (left) *take the last to win from Bill Rees on the Queen Mother's Silver Dome.*

BELOW: *Newbury, December 1961. Sir William Pigott-Brown on Blackheath* (leading) *falls, leaving Gay and O'Connell to go on to win from Tim Brookshaw* (right) *on Silver Reynard.*

RIGHT: *Michael Scudamore on Aristotle; Gay on floor.*

ABOVE: *Gay and Carrickbeg are led by Michael Scudamore over the last at Lingfield in December 1961, but then go on to win.*

ABOVE: *Heartbreak. Carrickbeg and John Lawrence are beaten by Ayala and Pat Buckley. Grand National, 1963.*

LEFT: *Summer 1964. The streetfighting major, alias Michael Webb, with the horse who took his name, Streetfighter, at Bill Payne's stables, Eastbury.*

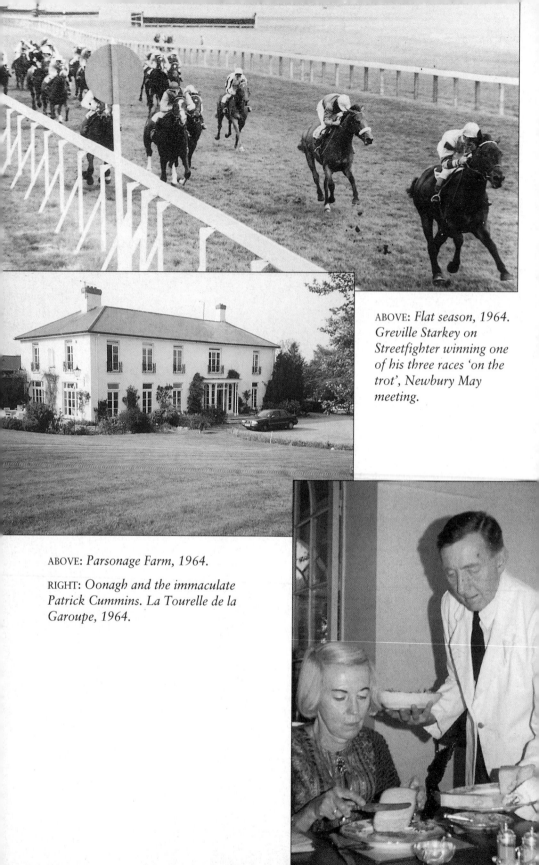

ABOVE: *Flat season, 1964. Greville Starkey on Streetfighter winning one of his three races 'on the trot', Newbury May meeting.*

ABOVE: *Parsonage Farm, 1964.*

RIGHT: *Oonagh and the immaculate Patrick Cummins. La Tourelle de la Garoupe, 1964.*

RIGHT: *La Tourelle from the air.*

ABOVE AND RIGHT: *Gay in his office at Parsonage and on his gallops with Joe Devaney.*

ABOVE: *Magsie at Epsom for the Moët & Chandon Silver Magnum, August 1964.*

TOP: *Gay greeting the Queen Mother at St James's Palace on the occasion of the Fegentri meeting, London, December 1972.*

ABOVE: *Sales in Ireland, 1975. Philippa and Gay.*

LEFT: *Second marriage, October 1976, Epsom Register Office. Gay and Philippa.*

ABOVE: *The wedding reception at the Punch Bowl, Oakwood Hill, October 1976. L–R: Jill Copestick, Marco Marshall (the best man), Oonagh, Oliver Reed, Gay.*

RIGHT: *Earthstopper (Des Paddock up) outside Parsonage, December 1985. L–R: The trainer, Philippa, Kim Allison, Joe Kavanagh, the head lad (in the cap).*

LEFT: *The Greatest Living Irishman! Terry Wogan at the Lambourn Valley Cricket Club Dinner at the Swan, Great Shefford, in 1986. He sings for his supper with Gay and John Fisher.*

ABOVE: *St James's Palace December 1991. Gay talks Fegentri business with the Princess Royal and Baron Henri de Montesquieu.*

RIGHT: *Gay in characteristic pose at his half-brother Christian Kindersley's wedding in Cape Town, March 1992.*

BELOW: *All six children in Scotland, August 1992. L–R: Oliver, Rory, Cathryn, Tania, Kim, Robin.*

background which had allowed them first-hand experience of some of the riding and behavioural problems peculiar to the racing fraternity. The same could not always be said for the stipendary stewards' secretaries or 'stipes', who were professional appointees whose duty it was to advise the stewards on disciplinary matters. With them young Mr Kindersley was often at loggerheads over such matters, for example, as when to exercise discretion in allowing the withdrawal of declared runners without penalty. He also sometimes found himself in sympathy with harassed trainers (often those with a war record) and senior jump jockeys with less-than-fond memories of their National Service days who were quick to take offence when barked at peremptorily by a stipe with an uncertain grasp of man management and a retired junior military rank. But his refreshing outlook, his natural good nature, a successful racing career and above all his classlessness and lack of side made him a popular, effective and respected member of the stewards' ranks. In a remarkably short time his performance was to come to the notice of the National Hunt Committee – the sport's ruling body and, at that time, the jumping equivalent of the Jockey Club.

On the racecourse itself he was not doing so well, suffering a further severe physical setback. Fit enough to return to the saddle and riding his own Eric's Star in a handicap chase at Hurst Park, he crashed spectacularly and, for the second time, broke his back. This time Bill Tucker and the consultants at Sister Agnes who were invited to gaze at this medical curiosity were adamant: no further racing that season and, possibly, not ever.

The other casualty of this accident was the owner of Blonde Warrior, a 10-year-old chaser entered for the Grand National. Gay had offered £5,000 for the animal but negotiations had to be first suspended and then broken off as the extent of his injuries became known. In the event, Blonde Warrior, still in his original ownership, finished a creditable twelfth in the race which was won by Kilmore; Gay dearly wished that he had been able to have the ride. The injury also kept him out of the Kim Muir, which Carrickbeg won in fine style under Giles Pitman before going on to the Whitbread Gold Cup in April and finishing second to Frenchman's Cove, this time partnered by Don Butchers's newest stable jockey, Peter Supple. For Gay, watching these events impotently on the side-lines, it was a case of mixed emotions – regret and disappointment however being easily dominant over pride of ownership. He gritted his teeth and, forswearing yet again the temptation to give up, promised himself that next year he would ride at Aintree, no matter what. The National was becoming an obsession.

In July his good start as a steward was rewarded when he was elected to the National Hunt Committee, an honour which met with the unanimous approval of the racing press and public alike as bringing to that body a much-needed injection of youth and current active involvement. The NHC, in common with the Jockey Club, had long been a cause of public wonderment in that it – a self-elected body of amateurs – should continue to be solely responsible for an increasingly professional business in which large sums of tax-free money were at stake. Nevertheless none of the critics had ever managed to come up with anything better and these two uniquely British institutions, served as they always had been by Messrs Weatherby, their secretaries, regulated the two strands of racing in Great Britain until their amalgamation in 1968. After that time they continued as simply the Jockey Club: still under fire, still amateur, still omnipotent. It was to be over twenty years before the club appointed its first professional chief executive.

Despite a popular perception that some sort of significant change had been effected by Gay's election, few of his qualifications (age excepted) set him apart from his colleagues on the committee; he was rich, he was aristocratic – in so far as the word had any remaining meaning – and he was firmly rooted in the establishment. Nevertheless he bought to the NHC a welcome wealth of hands-on experience and a close association with training which, while far from unique, meant that he was at least more in tune with current thinking and practice than were some of his more elderly fellow members. This, and the respect which his stewardship had brought, was to stand him in good stead during his first brush with the hierarchy.

His natural talent for self-effacement kept him relatively quiet during his first few meetings at the headquarters in Cavendish Square, but within eighteen months he had made a positive contribution as a voice for natural justice. In February 1964 a horse called Rosyth, trained by the sometimes unorthodox Ryan Price and ridden by Josh Gifford, won the Schweppes Gold Trophy (a handicap) at a starting price of 10 to 1. Somehow the word got round that Price had arranged for Rosyth to run well below form in his previous races in order to be awarded a low weight on the big day, thus creating the necessary conditions for the connexions to pull off a successful betting coup. The punters, whose favourite had gone down as Rosyth romped home by two lengths, were vocal in their disapproval and loudly – even threateningly – booed Gifford back to the winner's enclosure. The Newbury stewards, clearly influenced by this unusually public demonstration, referred the matter to Cavendish Square. The three stewards of the NHC – those responsible for maintaining the rules – considered the evidence available to them and exonerated Gifford. Price, however, was warned off indefinitely – a punishment so draconian as effectively to put an end to his career. The racing press, condemning the verdict as unduly savage, was quick to pillory the NHC and in no time the public changed its tune, now seeing Price as victim rather than villain. John Lawrence was particularly disapproving in his column in *The Daily Telegraph*, taking the line that, whatever the truth of the matter, an indefinite sentence with all the uncertainty that such an award implied was grossly unfair. There was, however, no official voice apparently willing to express that view until, under some pressure from his contemporaries outside the committee, Gay decided to speak.

At the March meeting he rose to his feet and suggested that the sentence imposed on Price should be reviewed by the stewards as a matter of urgency. Rarely had a disciplinary decision been questioned before and certainly not by so new and callow a member. There was an almost bewildered silence before the senior steward – the formidable Lord Cadogan – invoked a rule of procedure and closed the meeting peremptorily. Feeling friendless and not a little foolish, Gay was reassured when a number of members, including General Sir Richard McCreery (Bob's father) congratulated him and assured him of their support. After the meeting Cadogan – attempting to pass Gay's intervention off as a youthful indiscretion prompted by the press – succeeded only in being patronising. Gay did not respond in the way that was clearly expected; instead he gave the senior steward to understand that he had no intention of letting the matter drop. Six weeks later a discreet insertion in the *Racing Calendar* announced that Ryan Price would be allowed to apply for the return of his licence after one season. He did so, and it was returned. One up to the new boy.

The final summer at Beare Green was one of frantic activity – including a concluding meeting of the now famous Capel Charity Donkey Races in which Gay scaled new heights in persuading the theatrical profession to support the event, so attracting a larger-than-ever crowd. His induction into the entertainment world had been achieved through Magsie and her father, and he had immediately felt at home among those who enjoyed a similarly fast lifestyle often conducted, at least in part, in public via the gossip columns. He also nurtured show-business ambitions of his own, the first manifestations of which were an eagerness to perform 'Slattery's Mounted Fut' and other Irish folk songs with the minimum of invitation and the most fleeting of opportunity. He soon became a popular adornment to a variety of theatrical circles. His contacts were exemplified by the list of jockeys recruited for the 1962 Celebrity Donkey Oaks at Capel, which included Arnold Wesker, Tony Britton, José Ferrer and Michael Bentine as well as the ever-present Derek Hart and actor John Gregson.

Shortly before the move to Parsonage Farm his thirst for theatrical notoriety was unexpectedly assuaged by his father, who had been asked to make his drag-hounds available to help make the film *Tom Jones*, then being shot in Dorset. In fact two packs of hounds were to be involved: the Mid-Surrey were to supply the action and the smartly dressed ladies and gentlemen of the Cattistock Hunt were to provide the local colour. It was thought that drag hounds, trained as they were to follow an artificially produced lure, would – especially in summer – be more readily able to perform to order than the more specialist foxhounds. There were attendant disadvantages, however, and one which became particularly evident to all on the set was the 'drag' itself – an old wool stocking soaked regularly in a mixture of strong-smelling urine provided by the animals of London Zoo. But even this evil-smelling concoction was not certain to defeat the hot August days and Gay spent many frustrating hours trying to persuade the director that the cool of the early morning gave the best chance of providing a strong enough scent, which would be sure to lead to the fast-moving hunt required by the script. Nevertheless, he enjoyed himself mightily, galloping about at high speed, chasing his over-excited hounds – who were both stimulated and amazed by the novelty of being asked to perform among a welter of farm animals, including a herd of mildly surprised but co-operative Devon cattle, an alarmed flock of Portland sheep and hundreds of panic-stricken ducks and hens. He also found amiable and readily available drinking companions in the persons of the star, Albert Finney, and Welsh character actor Hugh Griffiths, who played the part of a drunken squire with exemplary realism. Kindersley the film star was having fun.

Gay's chasing about was not, of course, confined entirely to the pursuit of his hounds; the number of beautiful women who appeared to be both present and available almost overwhelmed him. He eventually settled for a particularly accommodating and inventive lady stage manager who took him on a picnic one evening to a well-known Dorset beauty spot, where he found himself drinking champagne while sitting on the tip of the most prominent anatomical feature of the Giant of Cerne Abbas. He had also (because he felt he ought) made a play for Susannah York and, indeed, became confident enough of ultimate success to take her out in London. Alas, on their return to her flat after a particularly encouraging dinner during which he ate and drank with lustful abandon, he was sick all over her new sofa.

Back in the real world Gay and Magsie – not without many tears of regret – said their goodbyes to Beare Green: the Donkey Races and the Cricket Club, the garage man, the publican and the farmers over whose land Gay had hunted with his father's drag over the last seven years. They also said farewell temporarily to Don Butchers, who was to remain at Priam Lodge for the time being as Gay embarked on the 1962–63 steeplechase season – which was, as it turned out, to be centred almost exclusively on Carrickbeg. Not fit enough to ride races before Christmas, Gay was aiming to do enough point-to-pointing in the New Year to enable him to do the horse justice in the Grand National. It was a modest enough plan but, in the event, even that proved to be over-optimistic.

Carrickbeg was still a six-year-old when, with Peter Supple on board, he opened his campaign in a handicap chase at Sandown in November. He was opposed by the even younger Mill House, to whom he was giving nearly half a stone. Ridden by Willie Robinson (later to become the great horse's regular partner in his heroic battles with Arkle), Mill House won easily; but Carrickbeg in finishing second was by no means disgraced and a fortnight later he came fourth in a strong Hennessy Gold Cup behind Springbok, whom he had beaten the previous spring in the Whitbread. He had one more race before Christmas, in which he was again bested by Mill House but beat the winner of the 1964 National, Team Spirit. Preparations were going well – perhaps even exceeding expectations – when there occurred an irritating disruption in the shape of the most severe winter in living memory. Every race meeting (save one at Ayr) between Christmas and the first week in March was cancelled. Snow lay everywhere over ground frozen to concrete.

Training to a planned programme became a major problem and Carrickbeg was moved from Epsom to Parsonage Farm, where for a time it was just possible to gallop him carefully on snow up the valley. It became clear however that although the horse's fitness was being precariously maintained, the same could not be said for his owner; Gay's plans to ride him in any race, let alone the Grand National, were proving to be just wishful thinking. As the weather worsened and the Kim Muir (thought to be an essential ingredient in the horse's programme) came closer, John Lawrence offered to buy a half-share in the horse and suggested that he should have the ride. Gay, characteristically generous in both thought and deed, could not conceive a happier outcome to his agonising dilemma and agreed – but not without another sharp pang of regret that yet again he was to miss a crack at Aintree. Don and the joint owners now put their heads together and decided to move the horse to Ireland where he could more easily continue his preparation and, at the same time, be entered for the Leopardstown Chase as a necessary warm-up for Liverpool. His training for this was now in the hands of Eamon Delaney at his yard near the sea. Carrickbeg had travelled reasonably well and, although clearly needing the run, he finished third behind another National hope, Owen Sedge, owned by Gregory Peck.

After the race, Gay and John decided to leave Carrickbeg in Ireland for nearly three weeks to work on the beaches before shipping him back for the Kim Muir, for which he started a short-priced but ultimately unsuccessful favourite, spreading a plate and unseating the unfortunate Lawrence. Putting aside this unexpected set-back, Don Butchers now got to work in earnest to produce the horse in peak condition for Liverpool. He was to carry 10 stone 3 pounds – a far cry from the 11 stone 12 pounds he had been allotted at Cheltenham and a weight which severely taxed his rider's powers of self-denial. Frugality was not, however, on the Kindersley agenda on the evening before the National as Gay and Magsie, helped by Gregory Peck and a dozen other highly charged owners and trainers, attempted to drink the Adelphi Hotel dry. By the time they assembled in the paddock with the connexions of forty-six other runners and had wished Lawrence all the luck in the world, the strain of the long build-up was beginning to tell.

Carrickbeg was in magnificent shape and Don, despite his distaste for the race, was confident – almost cheerful – as he and Magsie did their best to jolly along the now rather disconsolate Gay, who was suffering from a delayed dose of self-pity as he watched his horse going down to the start. The favourite was Springbok (Gerry Scott) with Kilmore (Fred Winter), little Team Spirit (Willie Robinson), Loving Record and Frenchman's Cove all fancied. Carrickbeg and Owen's Sedge both started at 20 to 1.

From the first fence Carrickbeg – the youngest horse in the race – jumped quite beautifully. In the stands, however, there was some gloom among the Kindersley party as the race commentator found it difficult to pick up the dark colours and Carrickbeg, despite the white blaze, failed to get a mention. Gay, glasses glued to his eyes, was able to reassure those around him as it became clear that Lawrence had the horse handy throughout the first circuit. He was going easily in twelfth place as they passed the stands. By the Canal Turn the second time he had moved smoothly up to fifth and his rider began to believe – with a sudden tingle up his spine – that they had a realistic chance of winning. Five fences out he had to check severely to avoid the fallen Out and About but soon made up the deficit and, two from home, he passed first Springbok and then the 19-year-old Pat Buckley on Ayala to take the lead. As Carrickbeg swept past, Buckley, exemplifying the spirit usually shown by jump jockeys, shouted, 'Go on then, John, you've won it.'

In the stands, the crowd also thought the race was over. The veteran trainer Fred Rimell leaned forward from his place behind the Kindersleys and said quietly, 'Well done, Gay, you've done it.' Gay, in a daze of delight, laced with just a little touch of regretful envy, watched as his horse drew away from Ayala on the long run-in past the famous Aintree elbow; he turned to push his way through the crowd to be first to lead the winner in. As he struggled in the crush, he slowly became aware that the cheering, which had been on a steadily rising note, was now changing to a hysterically excited pitch. He paused as he recognised the new sound as one that had become familiar to him in a number of close finishes, his mind registering a chilling foreboding as the implications became clear. He was all too right. For more than two-thirds of the pull up the testing Aintree finish, John Lawrence felt Carrickbeg still strong beneath him; the dream of a life-time was to be realised and in a fleeting moment of compassion he felt for his friend in the stands who had shared that wish with him for so many years. Then, unbelievably, only fifty yards short of the post, Carrickbeg came to the end of his brave young tether. He faltered and changed legs. Lawrence, in those final agonising seconds, could only watch as the equally gallant Ayala under the hard-working Buckley who – despite his generous exhortation – had never given up, struggled past in the last few strides to win by an official three-quarters of a length.

There were some who were quick to blame the amateur for weakening before his horse – twenty-five years later he was to encounter a late-night drunk in the Piccadilly Circus underground station who stopped and goggled at him. 'I know you,' he said, 'I know you, you're the booger that got knackered before his horse.' It might just be true that a Fred Winter (but probably only Fred Winter) could have picked Carrickbeg up for long enough to hold off the challenge, but that is to give less than due credit to the cruelly unfortunate pair – a young horse who had given not an ounce less than his all and a rider who had produced him at exactly the right time, having steered him superbly over thirty of the stiffest fences in the world. Numb as he was with disappointment, Gay – neither on that black afternoon nor at any time since, in public or in private – has never joined the detractors of Lawrence's performance. But he and his co-owner could have done without the final little twist that fate still held in store that day.

Ayala, who had broken a small bone in his foot and was never to win another race, was owned in partnership by his trainer Keith Piggott (himself a first-rate steeplechase jockey and father of Lester) and Mr 'Teasie Weasie' Raymond, whom John Lawrence, in a fit of perfectly understandable pique, later dismissed as a 'bloody barber'. The horse had run in Mr Raymond's colours (he being the principal partner) and it was at that time the tradition that the winning owner should give a party at the Adelphi, paid for by custom out of the prize money, which in 1963 amounted to a handsome £21,315, 7 shillings and 6 pence. Mr Raymond failed to turn up and the bill was handed to Messrs Kindersley and Lawrence who between them had won but £2,000. In drowning their sorrows they had a good deal of fun – but very little change.

Despite the shattering disappointment of Liverpool and acting against all the advice given to him by his wife, his trainer and his doctors that the chances of his being either killed or seriously disabled by another fall were now odds-on, Gay had started to point-to-point in March and by mid-April was reunited with his old friend O'Connell at Towcester. The racing press was quick to marvel at his courage, although many informed commentators strongly doubted his judgement. Few had access to Gay's own feelings and might have been none the wiser if they had. To keep going under the handicap of his physical disabilities could be considered brave. Set against his privately held belief that his nerve was failing, it was almost suicidal.

Leaving aside the thought processes of an amateur for the moment, it has always been difficult to explain with any pretence of logic the motivation of professional steeplechase jockeys: the risks are incomparably greater than those faced by their counterparts on the flat and the rewards are inversely meagre. The familiar answers – love of horses, fascination with speed, too big to ride on the flat, office life is boring – rehearsed a thousand times for curious journalists, each contribute a little to the truth but the sum total is unconvincing. The reality behind the apparent death-wish is more likely to be an ungovernable compulsion to confront danger head-on, and therein lies another more enduring peril. Once embarked on his hazardous career, the professional finds himself in a trap: his obsession is also his living; responsibilities multiply with age and money is needed to fulfil them; the imperative to go on increases at a time when the appetite begins to diminish. The mental price of physical courage is heavy indeed.

The amateur – and certainly Kindersley the Guinness heir – is largely spared this material concern. So how could it be that, throughout a summer spent haymaking and harvesting at home and riding the occasional flat race, he was really only passing the time while gearing himself up for another £300 handicap hurdle at Towcester during which he knew perfectly well he would be putting his severely damaged vertebrae (and probably his life) at risk? And even if he got away with it, all that he could look forward to with any certainty was another round of almost intolerable pain in his twisted shoulders, the mucking-out on frozen mornings, the riding-out in horizontal rain, the starving to the point of weakness and the paying of ever more demanding bills while waiting for another chance to fall.

In the heyday of the Corinthians it was not necessary to excuse or explain away a taste for danger. In a later, obsessively rational, security-conscious age where self-examination is almost obligatory, what was once accepted without question as wholly admirable is often called foolhardy; risks are to be avoided, not taken. Intellectual gymnastics hold little appeal for either professional or amateur steeplechase jockeys; in this they are at one because their motives are basically identical: if the amateur were broke he would try to become a professional and if the professional were rich he would be an amateur. In addition to the addiction to risk there is another bond – the horse, the instrument of that risk. Gay had both the obsessions in full measure. But in his case, the reluctance to give up was further hardened, not only by a perverse determination never to surrender to his fears, but also by his preoccupation with the Grand National. Nevertheless he occasionally articulated a certain resignation to his probable fate: 'It's not that I want to die or be dreadfully hurt but if it happens, I'm ready – and so is Magsie.'

And so to her eternal credit was Magsie; not exactly enjoying the tension in the stands as they lined up at the start on a freezing day at Plumpton, but drawing heartwarming strength from the other wives who, because their husbands had to do it, suffered the uncertainty and the agony even more acutely. Magsie never once, despite her constant apprehensions, made an issue out of her husband's obduracy. The fact that she was not alone in her terror was some small comfort but Gay's injuries had now – for the first time – made her fearful of the probable outcome.

Despite his refusal to give in, there were signs that Gay was beginning to hedge his bets by widening the scope of his racing-related activities. The previous summer, he and a number of other leading enthusiasts had founded the Amateur Riders' Association of Great Britain (ARA) with the primary aim of forming an official organisation which could co-ordinate races in this country for members of the Fegentri so that the British could play a full part in the international circuit, the benefits of which they had so long enjoyed.

The member nations of the Fegentri held a number of annual races (steeplechases, hurdle and flat) in their respective countries – the occasion in Madrid, for example – to which they invariably invited British riders; no reciprocal machinery existed and the leading amateurs felt that this was both stand-offish and unfair. There was resistance to change from some quarters of the racing establishment who believed that such a move would accentuate the differences between professional and amateur riders to the detriment of the former; there was already some feeling in the NHC that amateurs had too much influence and a disproportionate share of the spoils. There was also the practical difficulty that xenophobic British national hunt trainers were just not prepared to put up overseas jockeys of whom they knew little, assuming (not without some, but often overstated, justification) that both their race-riding skills and their experience left a great deal to be desired.

In the light of this at best luke-warm support, the newly formed association – appointing Gay as its first secretary – decided that Fegentri races in Great Britain should, anyway to begin with, be on the flat only. There was an urgent need to find appropriate sponsors and at this delicate operation Gay was a resounding success. He exercised his easy blend of enthusiasm and persuasive charm to such good effect that, within two years, backers from travel companies to whisky distillers had been found for four races. With one he struck gold – or to be more accurate, silver – when Moët & Chandon readily agreed to sponsor a race to be run annually over one-and-a-half miles at Epsom. The Moët & Chandon Silver Magnum, first run in 1963 and soon to become known as the Amateur Riders' Derby, has taken place without a break ever since. Together with the Richmond-Brissac Trophy at Goodwood in August, it remained in 1994 one of the two major Fegentri races held regularly in England. Abroad, in as many as seventeen countries from Sweden to the United States – with occasional participation from Australia and New Zealand – federation races are run over steeplechase courses (the Pardubice in the Czech Republic is one), hurdle tracks and flat racecourses with points being awarded for an amateur riders' championship. The close and happy alliance of this circuit with the great champagne house has been maintained over thirty years – in 1993 the Baron de Montesquieu of Moët & Chandon was the president of Fegentri whilst Gay Kindersley, one of the world's most assiduous purchasers of the product, became president of the ARA.

Carrickbeg's second campaign for the National began at Towcester in October. Ridden by John Lawrence in not much more than a pipe-opening exercise, he finished fourth and the joint owners, together with their wives, retired for dinner at a pub to plan the next moves. Morale was high and they were about to leave after a pleasingly euphoric evening when Don Butchers telephoned to say that the horse had heat in a leg. The trainer quickly added that in his opinion there was nothing to worry about, but a gloom descended on the little party as the first inkling of premonition stole over them.

It was January before Carrickbeg was judged to have recovered fully and at Sandown John Lawrence was again aboard. The rider's account in *The Daily Telegraph* the next day tells the story as it happened:

For the second time in ten months, for Carrickbeg and those whose hopes rest on his back, a dream became a nightmare here today. Giving nearly a stone all round, Gay Kindersley's wonderful horse ran away with the Stanley Handicap Chase – but broke down in the process and will not race again for at least a year.

It happened, I think, between the last two fences when, after just about as fine a display of jumping as has ever been seen at Sandown, Carrickbeg was clear with the race at his mercy. Suddenly he faltered – there was no doubt about it – and the sensation is one you do not easily forget. Nor shall I forget the leap he made – on three legs – at the last fence. Halfway up the hill with every stride more painful than the one before, he lost his action altogether – but this time at least there was no Ayala behind us.

What might have been means nothing in racing but for what it is worth in my opinion, Carrickbeg had shown himself a far better horse than ever before this afternoon. He has always been a superb jumper but the effortless speed with which today he left them floundering round the final bend was something new.

From start to finish he had made the fences look and feel about six inches high and, however harshly the Aintree handicapper may have treated him, no other jockey than his could have more confidence on March 21. But now that is all over and one can only hope that time, care and rest may bring another chance.

John Lawrence's painfully honest account would, in even sadder circumstances, have made a fitting obituary for a magnificently courageous and still young horse but happily – although Carrickbeg never raced again – he went eventually to the Mid-Surrey Drag, where he performed superbly for the whipper-in during a long and contented life.

Gay, again bitterly disappointed, briefly considered buying in a National entry but his still uncertain fitness persuaded him against such a move – he had, perhaps for the first time in his life, temporarily lost heart. Instead he decided to concentrate his immediate attention on an acquisition he had made at the Goffs September Sales in Ireland. The horse, a yearling named Streetfighter (as much after his antecedants as after Gay's old friend) was intended for bumpers and had been bought for him by Bill Payne who trained at Eastbury. But it became evident that the colt was something special and he was sent a mile down the road to Payne's yard to be prepared for the flat. Gay's high opinion was confirmed when, early in the New Year on the gallops, he made some particularly decent horses from neighbouring yards look very ordinary indeed.

Gay, Bill and Don Butchers, who had rejoined the Kindersleys, now hatched a plan aimed principally at bringing off a betting coup of impressive proportions. The horse with Greville Starkey on board was entered in a five-furlong sprint for two-year-olds at the first flat meeting of the year at Newbury in April. It was a wet spring and the ground was bottomless, suiting Streetfighter – who had feet that his blacksmith swore were every bit as big as those of the gigantic Mill House. The omens were good; Gay struck a bet of £300 to win £10,000 and the other connexions quietly laid their own bets on the course as the runners went down to the start. At that point luck deserted them; there were no stalls then and as the tapes went up a horse whipped round, colliding with the bewildered Streetfighter and turning him through 90 degrees.

In a field of 25 and in a race run over only 1,100 yards, it is asking a lot of even a wonder horse to make up the distance lost by being inadvertently facing the wrong way when he should be jumping off. Streetfighter and a furious Starkey did their best, finishing eighth as they flew past the post. The bookies failed to draw the right conclusions and barely a week later at Sandown Park (and before the bookmaker's account arrived) they ran him again on similar ground. This time there was no mistake and Streetfighter, huge feet making light of the conditions, shot home by five lengths at 8 to 1. His owner had increased his wager but could not be present to witness the triumph, being laid up with a particularly virulent strain of mumps which was not only causing him severe physical pain but considerable mental anguish every time he recalled his doctor's warning that the illness might well impair his ability to indulge as enthusiastically or as often as before, in his second favourite sport. Streetfighter, who – it was eventually established – could really only act in the mud, won a few more races before becoming a successful sire, first in Australia and then back in England.

Gay's betting rarely had as rewarding an outcome as that at Sandown but he was an inveterate and optimistic organiser of a possible 'touch'. One such occasion brought about a final break in his dealings with his credit bookmaker – much to the subsequent financial disadvantage of an otherwise shrewd company.

The Irish trainer Paddy Sleator had acquired a horse called Wisdom which he was certain would bolt up in a bumper at the Limerick Junction course (now called Tipperary). Gay was to ride him and organise the laying of the bets in a way which would not disturb the market unduly before the off. He went to his bookmaker friends and asked them to arrange for £3,000 to be placed on Wisdom in small lots around the country so as not to ruin the starting price (at which the wagers would be settled). He was assured that his wishes would be carried out and flew to Dublin, aiming to arrive at the course as late as possible to avoid having to answer potentially embarrassing questions.

As he entered the jockeys' room it become obvious that something or someone had leaked. 'You're on to a good thing in the last then, Gay?' they suggested. He demurred but was not believed; winks were exchanged, elbows nudged. On his way to the paddock it was no different; strangers and acquaintances alike came up for reassurance that Wisdom was the hot thing of the day. Gay mumbled something unconvincing about not knowing anything about the horse and wanting to get away on holiday immediately after the race; he was only there to do Paddy a favour. He even had a very public large brandy in the bar to show the world he wasn't taking things seriously. All to no avail; Wisdom started at only 11 to 8, and although he won easily there were no fortunes to be made. Gay's London friends had hardly been discreet; they had contacted a notorious ring of Irish gamblers known mainly for their interest in dog tracks (and therefore not so familiar on the racecourse) to do the business. The boys had arrived at Limerick Junction in three cars from Dublin, waited until a few minutes before the off and then moved in, rubbing out the prices on the bookies' boards faster than they could be replaced, laying a total of nearly £7,000 at odds ranging from 5 to 1 down the to starting price. Gay had won something substantially less than the £12,000 or £15,000 he could reasonably have expected.

In November 1964 he finally made up his mind that he would retire from riding over fences at the end of that season and made his decision public. Magsie and Don Butchers were overwhelmingly relieved but the trainer's satisfaction lasted only until a chestnut gelding called Some Slipper arrived unannounced in the yard. Gay, slightly embarrassed, explained that this was to be his mount for the next Grand National. Don sighed at the *fait accompli* and resignedly set about preparing the horse. Some Slipper was not an easy animal to train and Gay felt uneasy on him despite the warm words of Josh Gifford, who had ridden him into third place in the Great Sefton Chase at Liverpool in October. At least he had proved that he could negotiate the Aintree fences.

Some Slipper's final outing before the National was at Kempton a fortnight before the big race. Things went well and, for the first time, Gay believed that he had at last got through to the horse – they had felt almost like a team. His worries faded away; he could now hardly wait for Liverpool as he excitedly explained the importance of the big race to the children while having supper with them that evening.

The elation was not to last; even before they had finished eating Don came to see him, saying, 'Some Slipper's just got back. He's dead lame; I think he's split his cannon bone.'

Gay's first thought was for the horse and he went out to comfort him, moved to tears as he fondled the stricken animal. Tears, he recollected at last, as he pulled himself together, were going to get him nowhere if he was to take his last chance at the National. Would he be able to afford to buy a credible entry at what would certainly be an inflated price so close to the race? Would he be able even to find one? He spent the next week constantly on the telephone and there were several false leads before he finally got through to Arthur Stephenson in County Durham.

'Pity you didn't ring yesterday, Gay,' said the trainer who had supplied him with several horses of varying quality in the past – including J'Arrive at one end of the scale and the unforgettable Downhill Mary at the other. 'I've got just the thing; he's called Mr Jones. Trouble is someone called Chris Collins has been in touch and I've given him first refusal. He's only seen the horse once and isn't sure but he's coming back in the morning to make his mind up. If he doesn't want him, he's yours. I've got another; quite small but a good jumper. You'd better come straight up and try them.'

With only six days to go, Gay, Magsie and the vet, Frank Mahon, travelled to Darlington on the night sleeper. When they arrived at Stephenson's yard it was sheeting with rain and Collins had already left for his ride on Mr Jones. Gay got up on the small horse, Ronald's Boy, and his heart sank; there was nothing of the animal, nothing to give a man with only shreds of a once-iron nerve any confidence. Attempting to comfort himself, he tried to remember Ronald's Boy's form as recited by Stephenson (he had won a handicap at Wolverhampton in February and run reasonably decently since), gulped and went out to the schooling fences. In a downpour so heavy that it was difficult to judge distance, Ronald's Boy ran out through the wings at the first and eventually had to be violently encouraged before condescending to jump either of the two obstacles he was put at. It was not a good start, and when at breakfast afterwards Chris Collins announced his intention of buying Mr Jones, Gay was faced with an unpalatable decision. But if he was not to surrender this final attempt at the National he had no alternative and – capitulation not being in his nature – he sat down to write a cheque for £6,000.

With so little time left, Ronald's Boy stayed with Stephenson. Pre-race nerves began to affect Gay in a way they had rarely done previously; at the Adelphi the evening before the race his voice began to disappear and the next morning he could only manage a barely comprehensible squeak when being interviewed after early exercise. Back at the hotel he swallowed a couple of glasses of Buck's Fizz thoughtfully provided by Fulke Walwyn and felt marginally restored. His rocky confidence lasted only until his arrival at the course; from the jockeys' room he went to the loo three times in half an hour – finding himself always standing next to Michael Scudamore. The immensely experienced jockey explained kindly – and no doubt erroneously – that this was normal procedure before the National.

Having changed and weighed out, the forty-nine riders exchanged over-loud jocularities as they chaffed each other before settling down uneasily for the pre-race briefing. Lord Sefton boomed his way through the usual platitudes and, although the room was respectfully silent, not a man took in a single word. In indian file and with a noticeable absence of smiles as private hopes and fears fought their way through numbed minds, they trooped out to the paddock. Arthur Stephenson, standing alone, appeared to be strangely preoccupied and Gay, after a quick look round, understood why. 'Where's Ronald's Boy?' he asked.

'Just what I was wondering,' replied the trainer. 'I can't understand it. I saw he was all right with the girl – she's always been totally reliable – then I went to look at my other two runners. I don't understand it; I'll have to go and look.' After a hurried word with Chris Collins and a glance at Mr Jones, he sprinted off to the saddling boxes. Forty-eight jockeys mounted; the forty-ninth remained on his feet as the paddock emptied.

It emerged that the girl had fainted while tacking the horse up – no doubt overcome by concern for her charge and his chances of surviving the immediate future. Stephenson completed the saddling and led out Ronald's Boy, who appeared unworried to the point of indifference. Having been united with his increasingly agitated owner, he waited patiently as Gay was helped aboard in a flurry of girth tightening and leather shortening. They found their place in the parade. As they circled before the start Gay looked apprehensively down at his horse's ears; there seemed to be very little neck between them and his hands. He lengthened his leathers a notch; he couldn't afford to ride too short. Enviously he glanced across at Collins and the solid Mr Jones, a picture of a pair at ease with the world. He sighed and tried hard to remember that this was where he had wanted to be for most of his life. Two or three jockeys wished him luck and, as he looked up into the packed stands, the fear left him and he began to revel at last in the special comradeship of the biggest occasion in racing.

'Come on, jockeys, line up.' The starter mounted his rostrum as the field fiddled and jostled into some semblance of order. Gay nudged Ronald's Boy to a place close to the inside. Horses turned and skittered in their anxiety to be away.

Shouts of 'Wait, sir; wait, sir. Please' came from riders suddenly squeezed out by their neighbours. Then a final 'Come on then,' from the starter; the tapes flew up and they were off on the cavalry charge towards the Melling Road and on to the first fence. Ronald's Boy met it spot on, making little of the obstacle and clearly enjoying himself. Ears pricked, he set sail for the second and, as Gay caught the mood, his own confidence soared to the skies. At the fence they flew again – the horse foot-perfect. Gay's heart sang. This was what it was all about!

The third was an open ditch, as tall – if not quite so formidable – as its cousin, the Chair. The little horse, surprised by the size, found it all too much and as he rose uncertainly it became obvious to those behind that his courage had deserted him. David Nicholson, on Vultrix, afterwards described to Gay how it had appeared to him: 'Your horse lost heart over the first part of the fence and you lost heart over the rest!' As they crashed, only inches clear of the inside rail, Gay's terror at the realisation that they were not going to make it turned to frustrated anger and he beat the ground with impotent fists. His race – his obsession – was over and although he was unhurt and a knowing first-aid man told him gleefully that Ayala had fallen at the first, it was hardly a consolation.

From the ambulance he had a splendid view of the rest of the race as Ronald's Boy, also unhurt, cantered happily away into the centre of the course. The winner was Jay Trump, trained by Fred Winter and ridden by the American amateur Tommy Smith. Mr Jones came third and it was this, above all, that caused the Kindersley party to wallow for an uncharacteristically long time in a bout of what-might-have-been as they recalled the frantic activity of the previous fortnight.

Good humour was soon restored as Gay entered wholeheartedly into the Adelphi celebrations. He seemed possessed of an almost demoniacal energy, dancing non-stop, frantically living every moment and unwilling to let the night end. At 4 in the morning only he, Tommy Smith and a lady whom he had lusted after since dinner were still on their feet urging on the band. Magsie had long since gone to bed and the lady's husband had retired to his room to have a night-cap with John Gregson. Smith eventually said his goodnights – surely the happiest man in England – and Gay put the seduction plan (carefully worked out earlier with his willing companion) into operation. They would go up in the lift to the fourth floor (where neither was actually staying), search out one of the majestically imposing Victorian black-and-gold marble bathrooms for which the Adelphi was famed, and indulge their passion on the soft fluffy bathrug. Clinging to each other with by now impatient desire and undressed almost to the point of indecency, they rose at an agonisingly stately pace, floor by slowly passing floor. But Gay had pressed the wrong button and they fell out of the lift into the arms of Gregson and an immediately revengeful husband, who had no difficulty in recognising the situation for exactly what it was. A fitting end to a less-than-perfect day.

CHAPTER SEVEN

Rollercoaster

Giving up race-riding over fences did not quite signal Gay's complete departure from the competitive saddle. Two strands remained: bumpers in Ireland and amateur flat races – the latter mainly because of his involvement with the Fegentri. He had, however, come to terms at last with the fact that his pursuit of the twin obsessions which had so far dominated his riding ambitions was at an end. On the one hand he had succeeded in winning the amateur rider's championship – and had done so in the best Corinthian tradition, almost entirely from his own resources – but his other dream, having been subjected to a run of bad luck stretching over ten years, had ingloriously ended at Aintree's third fence. The decision to quit, hard to take as it undoubtedly was, had become progressively easier to face as his physical hurts and mental self-torture over the question of his nerve intruded more and more into his enjoyment.

The new life – he promised himself – should, whatever the changes, be lived to the full. George Rogers in Ireland would buy him an annual crop of likely yearlings and these would eventually be trained, some by George himself but the bulk by Paddy Sleator, to run in bumpers and then be sold on. In England his permit would enable him to train his own steeplechasers and he would also keep a few for the flat with his friend and adviser Bill Payne. Then there was the farm which, with a bit of luck, would largely fund not only these enterprises but one or two other particular interests to which he wanted to devote some serious time, notably music and the making of a film. The fact that both these projects were connected with show-business is a measure of how strongly he was attracted to his widening circle of theatrical and musical friends.

In June 1964 Gay and the racing commentator and author Michael Seth-Smith conceived the notion that the centenary of the National Hunt Committee, two years hence, should be celebrated by the making of a film. It would take the form of a documentary, first illustrating the historical background of steeplechasing and then giving an account of the contemporary scene using the Grand National as a central theme. David Foden, a businessman who owned and rode jumpers, became interested and undertook the administration, while the fourth member of Tetrarch Productions (the company formed to steer the project) was David Cammell of Cammell Hudson Associates, a film production group with a successful track record in making documentaries for the cinema. The first task was to write a script and this Hugh Hudson, Cammell's partner, completed inside a year using the working title *The Road to Liverpool*. It was a fictional account of the ambition of two men – one English, the other American – to win the Grand National. In the dramatic climax the Englishman failed while the American took first place. Gay found the story-line irritatingly evocative!

At first things went well. The NHC gave the scheme its blessing, together with the necessary permission to film in jockeys' changing and weighing-rooms – places normally out of bounds to cameras and reporters. The imperious Mrs Mirabelle Topham (she invariably began her letters to Gay 'Dear Kindersley'), who owned and ran Aintree as a personal fiefdom, gave her gracious assent to the plan over tea and cucumber sandwiches at her London home. Others in various high places who had been asked to read *The Road to Liverpool* were content that not only did it depict steeplechasing in a positive light but, because of the sympathetic portrayal of the American character, it might well appeal to the supposedly lucrative transatlantic market.

John Huston had offered to do the narration, but when Gay sent him a copy of the script he was less than impressed. His knowledge of the movie industry and its parlous economic state (it was at that time engaged in a losing and costly battle with television) persuaded him that such a film would not readily be taken up by distributors. His suspicions turned out to be depressingly accurate: sources of investment proved to be frustratingly elusive. Tetrarch Productions had budgeted the cost of turning the Hudson script into a 35-minute documentary as £25,000; the directors had put up some £5,000 between them and had to set about making extensive efforts to interest others. Gay and Magsie flew to the United States on a fund-raising mission aimed at the moneyed hunting and racing set of the east coast. Gay's promise to himself that he would tackle this task soberly and with a single-minded devotion to duty got off to a bad start when they spent the first two nights of the trip with the Clancy Brothers folk-group in New York. By the time he reached Virginia, he needed pep pills to keep him awake; indeed so exhausted was he that a keenly sporting blue-rinsed matron was able to persuade him to hunt her horse over some seventy huge obstacles without him even suspecting that the beast was only 3 years old and a complete novice over fences. After being congratulated on his performance ('Gee, Gay, didn't the youngster do well, it being his first time out and all'), he was so unnerved by the appalling risk he had unwittingly taken that he swallowed another handful of pills. When the time came for business to be conducted – over a working lunch and after a trio of bracing Dry Martini cocktails – he, not altogether surprisingly, failed to make the razor-sharp impression he had planned. He was listened to politely but there was not a flicker of financial interest.

The other partners, although perhaps conducting their search for funds in more orthodox fashion, met with a similar lack of success. The project was in danger of going under when Seth-Smith suggested that a new format, aimed at television and written by a well-known name, might stand a better chance. So it was that Ivor Herbert, author and journalist on racing matters (as well as being so successful a trainer that he produced Linwell to win the Cheltenham Gold Cup in 1957), wrote *The Grand National Story* which, after giving a brief history of the event, depicted the preparation of three horses for the race, each from a background which contrasted sharply with the other two. Again Huston was to narrate. Hopes for this fresh approach were high, particularly as CBS became interested and asked for more details. Herbert, too, was optimistic that his extensive media contacts could be relied upon to bring gentle pressure to bear in decisive artistic and financial quarters. It was all to no avail; no backers were unearthed; no television company was prepared to buy the idea; and by April 1966 the directors of Tetrarch had become tired of pouring money down what appeared to be a bottomless and unrewarding drain. The project was dropped.

Gay's other attempt to break into show-business was more successful – and certainly a great deal less expensive. It also gave him and a series of delighted audiences many years of (almost) innocent fun. Towards the end of 1964 he and Magsie had gone with a party to the Cheveley Country Club which, until somebody burned it down, stood near Newbury and had become popular with the Lambourn crowd. There they had been enthralled by a cabaret provided by two singers, one also playing a guitar, the other tapping a pair of bongos. This basic combination at a time when the musical scene was dominated by the complicated rhythms of the Beatles and the Rolling Stones had a refreshing appeal. Gay was particularly impressed with the pair's repertoire which, apart from the occasional standard folk song, was entirely comprised of politically incorrect (not to say outrageous and bawdily explicit) numbers of uncertain but probably barrack-room origin. Jimmy Smart and Percy Duncan were army sergeant parachute instructors at a nearby RAF station (they left the service soon after this meeting) who supplemented their income by playing one-night gigs at local clubs. Gay was captivated. Soon he had asked them to Parsonage Farm to listen to his Clancy and Dubliner records and, as a bonus, treated them to his own singular version of 'Slattery's Mounted Fut'. He asked them to play at the Mid-Surrey Farmers' Dinner where they were an uproarious success and they, in turn, insisted that he should join in one or two of their numbers. Later, after Gay had persuaded them to add some Irish classics to their act, they suggested that he should perform with them as regularly as his various commitments permitted. But, they said, before that could happen he must get himself an instrument; he looked awkwardly out of place, stuck up in front with nothing to do with his hands. As he couldn't play a guitar, why not build himself a one-stringed bass?

Gay, with some technical assistance from Don Butchers, assembled tea-chest, broom handle, length of nylon curtain cord and a rubber dog-bone (the key to a really successful bass!) and soon the three of them, with Gay as often as not in the role of lead vocalist, were performing at a variety of social events including a deb ball. So successful was their cabaret spot at this jewel of the London season that the dance-floor emptied as guests drifted out on to the lawn where the group had set up their pitch under a tree. The young audience wouldn't let them go and eventually an outraged band-leader, who clearly felt that his professional pride and reputation were at stake, came stalking out of the ballroom in search of the competition. He threatened to report them to the Musicians' Union. Gay claimed (inaccurately) that he and his friends were amateurs and as such did not need to be union members. Nevertheless the threat was serious as Jimmy and Perce were about to become dependent on their music for a living, and to avoid further friction they began to wind down their programme so that dancing could resume. Partly mollified but still muttering dark threats, the band-leader returned to his orchestra.

The London success led to a number of other paid engagements and the group also begun to play a significant role in the series of musical evenings that Gay had inaugurated at home. So popular were these events, not just with the Lambourn socialites but much wider afield, that the Clancy Brothers, the Dubliners and the New Seekers all came regularly to play and invitations were eagerly sought.

Although performing in public was now consuming much of Gay's time, the equine enterprises were far from neglected. In Ireland, where the volume of business was growing, George Rogers found that he was required to assign names to the Kindersley acquisitions that made no sense to him. Some, he mused to himself as he gazed gloomily over his paddock rails at the yearlings while trying to unravel the mysteries of a list he had received by that morning's post, involved words that he didn't even know existed: William Guppy, Dolge Orlick, Newman Noggs and Nicodemus Dumps would soon, it seemed, be joining Wackford Squeers and Betsy Cluppins. What could it all mean? George was not a literary man and neither, in truth, was his principal owner, but Gay had been much taken by a complete set of Dickens he'd come across and – his imagination fired – had spent hours thumbing through the volumes in search of the more exotically titled characters. Those who have been faced with inventing suitable (and acceptable) names for only two or three foals will recognise the neatness of his solution. Even when George was enlightened on the subject, it must be said that although at last he understood, he did not approve. For God's sake, how could a respectable horse be expected to perform when labouring under a handle like Arethusa Skimpole? So scandalised was he with this wanton cruelty to animals that when a particularly nice colt came his way and he had a mind to buy it for Gay, he declared that good as the horse was, he wouldn't get it if it was going to be saddled with one of those peculiar names. Gay promised that he would make an exception in this one instance. He kept his word; the newcomer was called Charles Dickens and became a successful steeplechaser, winning a number of races for his subsequent owner, Gay's old school-fellow and friend, Piers Bengough.

In England, Gay as secretary of the Amateur Riders' Association was working away with some success to increase the number of races open to his members. There was more than a little opposition from the professional jockeys, who considered that such a proliferation was prejudicial to their earning power, and also from a few racing journalists who were (with some justification) inclined to be sniffy about the fitness of some of the amateurs and their consequent inability to get the best out of their horses. Gay's credibility suffered a set-back in the shape of unwelcome publicity after the running of the Carnarvon Cup at Salisbury in July 1965, when he himself on Owen Davis was involved in a photo finish with his old adversary William Pigott-Brown riding Tropical Sky. Everyone on the racecourse believed that Gay had resisted a spirited challenge and held on to win by at least a neck, although there had been some question that Owen Davis may have illegally taken Tropical Sky's ground earlier in the run-in. The judge called for a photograph and, in the absence of an objection and to the amazement of the two riders and their trainers (Freddie Black and Frank Cundell), awarded the race to Tropical Sky. The crowd was not amused; their eyes had clearly told them that Owen Davis had won and many had not only backed the popular Kindersley but had then invested heavily on the outcome of the photograph.

The national racing correspondents were equally baffled and many took the opportunity afforded by the reporting of a fiasco to attack the very existence of amateur races. The *Financial Times*, in one of the more thoughtful pieces, recognised the shortcomings of amateurs but suggested nevertheless that such races had a place and advised punters who were in doubt to back the jockey rather than the horse, citing John Lawrence and Bob McCreery as the two to follow. *The Sporting Life*, however, seizing a heaven-sent opportunity to mount once again a familiar hobby-horse, was uncompromising in its condemnation. 'Racing,' it thundered, 'is now a business and best left to professionals. If amateurs wish to display their talents there are almost unlimited opportunities for them to do so during the point-to-point season.' It is as well that such bigotry did not prevail, although it made Gay's search for meetings willing to hold amateur races – and for adequate sponsorship to support them – all the more difficult.

The curious sequel to the finish at Salisbury was that when the racecourse staff removed the camera at the end of that flat season, the clerk of the course was horrified to discover that it had been aligned wrongly. Had it been properly placed, the race would, at least in the first instance, have been awarded to Owen Davis and there would have been little attendant publicity. The final words on the episode were spoken by Owen Davis's trainer Freddie Black, who was never one to duck an issue. 'With professionals up,' he pronounced, 'Tropical Sky would have won by eight lengths.' So perhaps justice was done after all – or could Black have been hoping that the handicapper was listening?

Magsie had a different problem on her mind. Far more worrying than the failure of the film venture or her husband's fight to put the ARA and the Fegentri on a sound footing was Gay's continued infidelity. Now, for the first time, she was facing a threat that completely overshadowed the hurt and irritation she had become used to living with as she struggled to come to terms with his brief affairs and one-night stands. She began to fear deeply for her marriage.

Ironically, the danger emanated from the very show-business circles into which she had first drawn her husband. John Irwin, a film and television producer and his actress wife Gwyneth Tighe (who later married Prince Yuri Galitzine and understandably amended her name to Princess Elizabeth) had asked the Kindersleys to a party one cold December evening at their house overlooking the Thames at Chiswick. Gay was particularly pleased to be going because he knew that among the guests would be Eammon Andrews, whose sympathies he hoped to enlist in promoting Jimmy and Perce. As usual, an ocean of champagne was consumed and, as the party gazed out of the brilliantly lit windows across a darkly glittering Thames, Irwin issued a challenge. 'A hundred pounds,' he announced. 'A hundred pounds to the man who gets to the other side first.'

A number of the men started to strip and others, less enthusiastic – or perhaps merely more sober – peered into the night to see if someone had left a boat about. Gay was out of his clothes in a flash (he had, of course, had more practice than most) and began to wade, clad only in his jockey shorts. The tide was out and the actual expanse of water in the river was relatively narrow. Sometimes swimming but more often wading chest deep through the clinging, freezing mud, he clambered out on to the far bank. 'I'm here,' he shouted. 'That's a hundred quid you owe me, John. Can someone please come and get me; it's bloody cold.' His teeth chattered uncontrollably and he began to regret his impetuosity. He was even more dismayed when Irwin shifted the goal-posts.

'No chance,' the producer yelled. 'The bet was there and back.'

Cursing horribly, Gay began the return trip and found, when he reached mid-stream, that the tide had begun to run strongly. The now much broader stretch of river was rising fast and the current gripped him. He struck out hard as he battled to make headway. He made little progress; slowly but inexorably he found himself being carried off. Weakening and very cold, he called again and again for help; for the first time in his life he felt sure that he was going to die. After a frantic search on the bank, a boat was found, someone dived in and between them the rescuers hauled him back to the shore and into the care of the by now distraught Magsie. Wrapped in a blanket, he swallowed a brace of large brandies and was laid out on a sofa to recover. He closed his eyes, dozed a little in ecstatic relief at his deliverance and then, relaxed and drowsy, it began to dawn on him that he must have died after all for now, surely, he was arriving in paradise. Intruding on his half-consciousness was the most entrancing voice he had ever heard and, unbelievably, it was singing his favourite folk songs. Slowly realising that he was neither dreaming nor deceased, he looked across the room and there, performing it seemed just for him, was a vision of blonde loveliness, playing a musical stringed instrument of a type he had never seen before but was the perfect complement for the heavenly voice. It was the Australian zither player Shirley Abicair, and Gay felt himself drifting helplessly into love.

Within days he had arranged a New Year's Eve dinner party at the Hyde Park Hotel and, through Grania Andrews, had engineered that Shirley should be there. His feelings were clearly and genuinely reciprocated, and while dancing they made a plan to meet at her flat in London four days later, when Gay would be on his way home having ridden in a bumper in Ireland. He had never, he persuaded himself (immediately forgetting all past declarations of undying passion), felt like this before. The intervening days, as well as the race itself, were passed in a fever of impatience until eventually he arrived at Dublin airport for the flight to Heathrow. Overflowing with the mixture of tingling excitement and hollow tummy which always so deliciously preceded his clandestine affairs, he checked in – to be told that there was fog in London and the flight was postponed indefinitely. Grinding his teeth with anger and frustration, he bullied the harassed staff into finding him a seat on a flight to Manchester, but by the time the plane arrived in England it was nearly midnight and the fog had spread from London up through the Midlands to the north. The airline was busy trying to organise its disgruntled passengers on to trains and coaches but Gay could wait no longer and ran to a taxi rank. Of the first three drivers he approached, one thought he was a madman and the others, sure that they were being accosted by a drunk, asked him less than politely to leave their cabs. The fourth gloomily agreed to take him to London ('You'll 'ave to direct me. Never been there before') at a price which made the air fare appear a bargain. They arrived at dawn but Shirley, who had waited up more than half the night and now had an early recording engagement, was in no mood to entertain her prospective lover in the way they had both longingly anticipated. Alone with his anti-climax in the early morning gloom, he was enveloped in a blanket of disappointment.

Despite this inauspicious start, the relationship soon gathered both pace and intensity as they met increasingly often – usually in Shirley's flat but occasionally in hotels – and Gay concocted wilder and wilder excuses for being away from Parsonage. As her husband grew more distant and preoccupied, Magsie came to realise that this time she had a real fight on her hands. There was a danger too that the affair would become public as gossip columnists began to drop hints. Gay was not being as discreet as usual, going so far, for example, as to pick his mistress up after her evening theatre engagements. Magsie asked him to put a stop to it; he refused. In desperation she said she would divorce him; he ignored her threats. He declared – and he may even have meant it – that he had no intention of ever allowing his marriage to break up. But neither, of course, was he prepared to be faithful.

They thus arrived at a mutually unsatisfactory impasse which soon infected the by this time impatient Abicair. She had begun to realise that the relationship was stuck in a groove that she could no longer accept. She confessed her frustrations to some friends, who took it upon themselves to speed up Gay's decision-making processes. He had a nasty surprise when, bouncing into her flat one afternoon, he found himself faced by a ring of uncompromising men who invited him politely to sit down and have a little talk. One moved menacingly to shut the door; Gay detected a certain tension in the air and concluded that he would do well to acquiesce with whatever the large gentlemen had in mind with as good a grace as he could muster. They carefully spelled out their views in tones that, Gay nervously recollected, were not dissimilar to those he had heard in films about the Mafia. The words themselves also rang a sinister bell.

'Shirley,' they said by way of summing-up, 'is too good to be merely your mistress. Either you divorce your wife and marry her or you stop seeing her. If you wish to remain in good health, you have no other choice.' Melodramatic, no doubt, but Gay found the threat alarmingly to the point. He decided, regretfully, to bail out of the affair.

Returning to Magsie and shedding the usual tears as he made his apologies and protestations, he failed to notice an increased grimness about his wife; to him the marriage seemed set to resume the uneven tenor of its ways. But, this time, there was to be a significant change in the relationship that was never to be reversed.

Magsie's habitual method of relieving her feelings during Gay's infidelities had been to embark on a gambling binge on London's roulette tables during which she would invariably lose spectacularly immodest amounts of her husband's money, taking grim satisfaction in the revenge thus exacted. The Abicair episode, however, had caused her so much distress that she felt herself close to a breakdown. She consulted her doctor. His unequivocal advice, while not perhaps entirely measuring up to the highest standards of medical ethics, was at least refreshingly direct.

'Go to London,' he said, 'and have an affair of your own. It'll do you the world of good.'

It is, of course, a wonder that Magsie had not had lovers before. Indeed a number of her friends – and even some of Gay's closest family – supposed that she had and linked her name with, among others, John Gregson, Derek Hart and the cricketer Colin Ingleby-Mackenzie. There is little evidence to support such conjectures but, as a classical beauty who was well known to be sadly neglected by her husband, she attracted a steady stream of offers and it is hardly surprising that rumours circulated. Whatever the past, this time there was no holding back and she embarked on a three-year romance which she was clever and discreet enough to hide almost entirely from the world at large and certainly from her sexually complacent husband.

Gay, completely unaware that his wife was paying him back in kind – had he even suspected he would have been genuinely astounded and not a little hurt – had put his own extra-marital curriculum on an almost institutional footing by renting a flat near Harley Street in which to indulge more comfortably in regular post-luncheon dalliances. Although this was a convenient arrangement and lasted for nearly ten years, it was to finish in tears. Towards the end of his tenure he allowed an occasional mistress, who had fallen on hard times after the death of her actor husband, to live in it rent free with her small daughter. When he was forced to ask her to leave so that he could return it with the desired vacant possession, the lady refused. The law was invoked, and the case wound its tortuous way into court as the owner sued. Gay was called as a witness by both the plaintiff and the defendant (in itself a legal curiosity), and in his anxiety to please his friend the landlord and his mistress he found himself in a dreadful muddle. The exasperated judge told him that he was the worst witness that he, the judge, had ever listened to in over forty years at law. After an ill-tempered contest during which Gay attracted wrath on every side, an eviction order was granted. It was years before either party spoke to him again.

With the Abicair romance behind them and an urgent need to relax their nerve-wracked bodies in benevolent sunshine, Gay, Magsie and the children spent part of the summer at Antibes. As they began to wind gratefully down, the holiday was interrupted by Oonagh, who telephoned from Ireland to ask Gay to fly to Luggala for a few days to help her run a charity picnic she was planning to give in support of a curious collection of French aristocrats who travelled

Western Europe persuading altruistic socialites to give subscription parties for their favourite causes.

The evening before the Luggala contribution to this extravaganza Gay was asked to escort a partnerless lady to a dance – another in the series of fund-raising events. Thus it was that Esme O'Flaherty came into his life, together with her glossy auburn hair, bewitching hazel eyes and seductively soft Irish voice. Divorced and thirtyish, she was not easy to resist; and Gay, true to form, succumbed instantly. He took her home that night and as he drove over the Wicklow hills back to a Luggala bathed in magical moonlight his heart sang, banishing finally any residual regret for the passing of Shirley Abicair. The next day the sun shone with the intense brilliance peculiar to Ireland as Patrick Cummins and the staff busied themselves unhurriedly in the marquee, polishing glasses and carefully unfolding the sparkling damask tablecloths. As the champagne cooled and the lobsters glistened pinkly on their silver dishes, the cars rolled down the long winding drive to the deep green valley enfolding the dark waters of the lough and the sugar-white house below. Gay was in a tremor of expectation as he waited for Esme to arrive – being only ever-so-slightly distracted by the sidelong glances he noticed being aimed at him by a sexily elfin French girl who was orchestrating the public relations of the visitors. Sighing, he made a mental note to remember to see what she might be doing after everyone else had gone home and with another glass or two of champagne he resumed his vigil. Soon Esme arrived, matching in every respect the voluptuous image he already carried of her and for him the day really began. The picnic itself fully lived up to the highest of Oonagh's standards and Gay, who had been made to perform extracts from his musical repertoire by his mother, decided that Jimmy and Perce should be sent for to add the final touch. He telephoned, giving instructions that they should catch the next plane to Dublin, and as the evening slipped seamlessly into velvety night, they arrived and began to sing. His cup was full.

Back at Antibes (he had been away for barely seventy-two hours, during which he had added two more irresistibly willing notches to his tally, the little French pixie having been conveniently on hand when Esme had to leave just before dawn), Magsie unpacked his suitcase and saw the lipstick on his white dinner-jacket. Rounding on him, she prepared for battle; he mumbled that he'd been forced to take a girl called Esme O'Flaherty to a dance. Open-mouthed she stopped in mid-reproach, dissolving into helpless laughter. 'You don't mean to tell me that you actually took someone called Esme O'Flaherty to one of the smartest dances in Ireland? Oh Gay, really. Esme! And O'Flaherty! What a hoot!' Still giggling, she went off to share the joke with the rest of the holiday party. Her own affair had already begun to have the beneficial effects that her doctor had foretold – she was calmer and more self-confident. Even so, she would have been horrified to know that Esme was to remain on Gay's agenda for many years. Gay himself was simply puzzled that he had been let off so lightly.

During January 1966 he was back in Ireland so that he, Jimmy and Perce – now known collectively as the Valley Minstrels – could appear on television. *The Late Late Show*, hosted by Gay Byrne, was RTE's prime-time flagship and Byrne – the only other Gay that Kindersley had ever met – wanted to do a piece on amateur riders who raced in Ireland. His researchers had turned to George Rogers for advice and he had recommended Gay. Byrne was enthusiastic; Gay, with his Guinness connexions, his playboy image and his impeccable racing pedigree, should attract a large audience; and when the presenter was told that there was also a folk group, he was sold. Both Gay and the Minstrels were booked.

On the day itself, they arrived at the studios in Dublin at around mid-afternoon and went into immediate rehearsal. After some three hours the song 'I Know Where I'm Going' was chosen for the evening show and soon, in the presence of a studio audience which included Magsie, Oonagh and Garech, the two Gays came face to face. The interview was a minor disaster. Byrne had done little homework and the questions he asked about race-riding were at best ill-informed and often banal. Gay, who was never able to include public speaking among his accomplishments (even when adequately prepared), was thrown by the absurdity of the topics and responded not patiently, as the situation demanded, but with competing idiocy. The audience became confused and it was a great relief to all when Byrne drew proceedings to a close and introduced the Valley Minstrels. In contrast to what had gone before, the musical finish was a great success. The song had some appealing harmonies and the three did themselves enough justice to be contacted by an agent who offered to fix them up with an almost immediate four-day tour. They agreed eagerly and Tommy Clancy (never one to miss an opportunity for unlimited free booze in some of Ireland's better watering holes) offered to act as their manager.

The engagements on the first three days went gratifyingly well, particularly at the South County Hotel outside Dublin where the evening rated a piece in the *Irish Times*:

Gay Kindersley and the Valley Minstrels (vocal trio with tea-chest bass and guitar) had good balance and the quiet 'I Know Where I'm Going' was their most pleasing number. It was set off, however, by generous helpings of comic relief, the number in which the leader strips to the waist being a riot of fun for young and old. Announcements of numbers are perhaps better left unembroidered unless the remarks have some point other than mere length …

Gay's unbounded (but largely unjustified) confidence in his ability to win an audience over by the charm of his oratory was tested again at the Clontarf Castle Hotel on the last night when, having consumed a number of jars in excess of those required to put a musician in good voice, Jimmy lost his plectrum and he and Perce, on hands and knees, were forced to scrabble about in the semi-darkness in search of this essential piece of the guitarist's equipment. They fell off the stage several times and, despite the advice of the *Irish Times* correspondent, Gay embarked on a rambling introduction to try to cover the gap. The audience grew restive. Tommy Clancy came in from the bar to witness the debacle. 'For God's sake, Gay,' he hissed, 'stop mimsing will ye. Tell them a story.'

Gay desperately searched his mind for something that would placate the now noisily discontented crowd. In a fever of indecision he alighted on a joke called 'Rotten for Daphne', told to him many years before by John Lawrence. While undoubtedly uproarious when related to a collection of well-lubricated Old Etonians (it concerns the travels of a retired Indian Army colonel and needs, for maximum effect, to be told in an exaggerated upper-class accent), it was never designed to raise a laugh out of a roomful of impatient Irish provincials who had paid good money to hear some of their favourite music and whose expectations were being comprehensively denied. The story died a predictable death, only Tommy Clancy – who had heard it a dozen times before – appreciating the punch-line with a cackle of glee. Gay, gazing at his feet in embarrassment and wondering how to deal with the increasing volume of cat-calls, suddenly saw the plectrum. It was quickly retrieved and, as they launched into 'Mountain Dew', general good humour was restored. At the end of the night the agent – a Yorkshirewoman imbued with a spirit of eternal optimism – thought that matters had gone really rather well and asked the hotel manager whether she should rebook the Valley Minstrels for him at some future occasion. 'Never,' he said, knowing from bitter experience how close he had been to footing yet another expensive damage repair bill. 'Absolutely never!'

When reports of Gay's professional musical activities across the Irish Sea percolated through the English establishment, a number of well-bred eyebrows rose. Even some trainers and professional jockeys – schooled in the well-defined social structure of the racing world where everyone knows their place – sniffed a little. Gay, after some consideration, saw that his role as a member of the NHC and well-respected pillar of the stewards' room was probably at odds with that of a whiskey-swigging folk singer strumming a broom handle in an Irish pub and vowed that in future he would play only charity events and hunt balls. This decision allowed Jimmy and Perce a freer rein for their own lives and a little later they won a heat of Hughie Green's *Opportunity Knocks*, which gave them a brief professional career while still allowing ample time for them to come to

Parsonage for musical evenings and to join Gay in a number of charitable engagements.

Life at East Garston did not suit Don Butchers. Having given up his own training licence shortly after leaving Epsom, he was now little more than head lad to the few horses Gay had in the Parsonage yard. He was also depressed by the strained atmosphere between Gay and Magsie and had (possibly wrongly) formed the impression that Magsie resented his undoubted influence over her husband. Much as he loved the Kindersleys, he felt that he needed a complete break from both them and horses. Despite Gay's pleadings that he should stay, he had made up his mind to leave the valley. When Matt and Mary Feakes, with whom he lodged in Lambourn, gave up training and moved to Kent, he went to live with them and took a job filling sausage skins for a local butcher. For a proud and private man who for many years had been respected and admired by some of the greatest in the land, this rather menial row was hard to hoe. In October 1967, within a year of his departure, he had a heart attack and died. As guide, mentor, friend and – at his best – one of the leading trainers of the day and one with a deep love for his horses, he had occupied a unique place in Gay's life and heart. There could never have been a more loyal companion and Gay missed him dreadfully.

By the summer of 1966 Magsie was again pregnant and at the end of the following January Tania was born. The general happiness at the birth was, however, considerably muted by the death of Tara in a motor accident barely a month earlier. Tara, only 21, was the younger son of Oonagh and Dom and was already married with two children. Indulged by his mother and supported by his Guinness inheritance, he had led a life notable for its recklessness on the one hand but also for the love and affection he inspired in others. Conventional he was not: he experimented widely with drugs and drew his friends from the pop music scene – the Rolling Stones had been at his twenty-first birthday party at Luggala earlier that year and the Beatles were to compose the song 'A Day in the Life' as a tribute after his death. In the absence of his widow Nicky, from whom Tara had been separated, Gay was required to identify the battered body and then to fly to Ireland to help his desolate mother organise the funeral. A monument similar to Tessa's was eventually erected at Luggala.

Oonagh's love of children and the fierce possessiveness she felt for members of her family led her to seek custody of Tara's children, Dorian and Julian, aged 3 and 2. She was only partially successful, and then only after a debilitating court case during which the judge granted her 'care and control'. In effect this meant that the children lived with Oonagh (where they joined the adopted Mexicans, Desmond and Manuela) but that Nicky was able to see them every two months if she so chose. That right of access, when it was invoked, was exercised mainly at Parsonage, to which the children had to be brought from Ireland or France. It was neither a tidy nor a happy arrangement.

By the time of Tania's christening in May, Gay had embroiled himself in two organisations, one of which at least was to make a significant demand on his time. Bill Tucker, still presiding over his Jockeys' Garage, was heavily involved with the British Institute of Sports Medicine and persuaded Gay to join it along with one or two more of his star patients. In a very short time Gay found himself head of the appeal committee which, during the next few years, was to raise over £150,000 to provide a central research unit for the post-graduate instruction of doctors in sport-related medicine. As a fund-raiser he was the ideal choice – gregarious, well connected, universally liked and, above all, a living example of the efficacy of treatment by a specialist. He was also able to exercise a hitherto unsuspected talent for persuading people to part with substantial sums of money to finance pet schemes of his own, providing, for example, portable X-ray units for racecourses as an immediate aid to diagnosis. Sadly this particular innovation, in the relatively early days of the appropriate technology, never really caught on, the results being adjudged by the medical experts as too unreliable to be used as a basis for possible life and death decisions.

If Gay found raising funds for charitable causes dear to his heart, both rewarding and relatively easy, the members of the Institute seemed to experience remarkable difficulty in reaching agreement on how exactly the money should be spent. This the appeals chairman found immensely frustrating and he resolved to take them to task over their lack of decisiveness, choosing as his forum a working dinner of the management committee to be held at the Reform Club.

The day started well as Gay fulfilled a luncheon engagement with a lady with whom he was in the habit of spending a few agreeable hours during the occasional afternoon in London. Today, though, because of a trustees' meeting, there would regretfully be no time for an extended tryst. Nevertheless he lunched well, if not very wisely, and arrived for the meeting exuding goodwill and brandy fumes. After the family business was concluded he and Garech (they had not seen each other for some time) embarked on a brotherly pub crawl. Then it was on to the Turf Club to change for dinner and be refreshed further by a couple of sharpeners with a racing crony. By the time he arrived at the Reform, he felt that he could take on not only the committee of the British Institute for Sports Medicine but the whole medical establishment, should it choose to bandy words with him.

The distinguished gathering, led by Lord Luke, the chairman, were imprudently warm in their welcome, furnishing Gay with several Dry Martini cocktails before sitting down to decide finally how the funds raised by their guest could be put to best use. Dinner was excellent; the smoked salmon and the most tender of tournedos were accompanied by the prize possessions of the Reform's cellar. Gay's confidence grew as he mentally, but by now rather hazily, rehearsed the broadside he was planning to deliver. After dispatching an admirable savoury, he lit a cigar and took a deep draught of the beakerful of brandy with which he had been thoughtfully provided by an attentive steward. The moment had arrived.

'I know,' he said, leaning expansively back in his chair, 'I know that you are all illustrious men, pre-eminent in your various fields. In your professional lives you are used to making important decisions. Some of you have in your hands the gift of life or, um, death.' Pausing, he made an unsuccessful effort to bring into focus the face of a particularly famous orthopaedic surgeon sitting across the table. He returned to his theme.

'So, what I cannot understand, gentlemen, is why, why when you have the relatively simple task of deciding how this money is to be used – money I have to remind you that I and my friends have spent months if not years in raising – your performance is absolutely pathetic? Pathetic; quite unacceptable.' He hiccuped loudly.

The committee looked at him in amazement. Gay leaned forward and swallowed another mouthful of brandy; he took a deep and satisfying pull on his Havana and prepared to expel a long stream of fragrant smoke into the room. All this was too much for his badly punished tummy, which seized that moment to rebel at the ill-treatment it had suffered during a long and self-indulgent day. It exacted a telling revenge over not only Gay but half the perfectly polished table and both his immediate neighbours.

There was a deep silence as Dr John Hunt, who had escaped almost unscathed, led him away to be cleaned up. Solicitously the president of the Royal College of General Practitioners sponged his unexpected patient down with the Reform's best linen towels and advised him with enviable composure that he would be unwise to catch his planned train to Newbury. He needed sleep; had he a club? If so he, John Hunt, would escort him there; it would, perhaps, be impolitic to trespass further on the Reform's hospitality. Gay was sick again during the cab journey to the Turf Club but eventually they staggered in through the doors in Carlton House Terrace. The head porter, the legendary Grace, took one look at the bedraggled figure clinging to its distinguished medical prop and took immediate charge. He picked up the telephone and dialled.

'Ah, Mrs Gay,' he said. 'Mr Gay will not be home this evening. We will look after him here and he shall catch a train in the morning. Goodnight, madam.' He summoned an underling. 'Edward, take Mr Gay up to Room 3. Goodnight, Mr Gay.' He turned his attention to the astonished physician. 'Dr Hunt, the Turf Club is obliged to you. Thank you very much indeed, sir.'

Gay spent several hours during the next (painful) morning composing and recomposing five sufficiently contrite letters of apology. He asked the porter to arrange their immediate dispatch, thanking him at the same time for having his suit cleaned and pressed. Grace had long been a loyal supporter of Kindersley the amateur rider, making a point of watching him ride on Easter Mondays over a number of years – as far as anyone could tell the only day in the year that the head porter was ever away from his duties. He died rich, amassing a tidy fortune from acting as a bookie's agent at his desk in the club (he took a commission on all losing bets) and from dealing as an unofficial foreign exchange bureau for members as they set off or returned from abroad. An archetypal London club servant, he found it difficult to come entirely to terms with 'progress' – a word he equated with diminishing standards. When he was instructed by the secretary to put up a notice informing members that ladies would now be permitted to use the bedrooms, he did so with great reluctance. An elderly cavalry brigadier paused to read it.

'Good Lord, Grace,' he joked, 'does that mean we can bring our floozies here, what?'

The porter looked at him with disfavour. 'Certainly, sir,' he said, 'providing, of course, that they are the wives of members.'

The Turf was one of many clubs that Philip Kindersley had decided his son should join when he was 21. Whites was another and Gay spent seventeen years on the waiting list. Philip loved this most aristocratic of institutions passionately and it was with the greatest of pleasure that one morning he was able to communicate some good news to his son. His letter, however, contained a word of warning, touching on an aspect of Gay's appearance which had been the cause of long-felt parental anguish.

Dearest Ghazi

You will be pleased to hear that news has just come through this morning from my good friend Dermot Chichester who is on the committee of Whites that you, at last after so many years, have been elected to the Club. I am so pleased.

I should point out one thing though. Several people at the National Hunt Committee have also noticed this. You do have those dreadful sideboards, generally known as buggers' grips; I really don't think that you can appear at Whites looking like that so for God's sake shave the bloody things off. Please come to luncheon there tomorrow.

Gay did his bit. He had his hair cut – short back and sides – and presented himself at the Whites bar, where he informed his delighted parent that as he was now a member lunch was on him. He bought their drinks and looked around.

An acquaintance, Bill Dugdale, hidden by *The Daily Telegraph* from Philip, was occupying an armchair and was sporting side-whiskers so flamboyant that they could have been modelled on those of Lord Cardigan at Balaclava; they made Gay's erstwhile efforts resemble the merest of bum fluff. As the Kindersleys passed Dugdale on the way to the dining-room, Gay drew his father's attention to the seated figure. 'I say, Dad, who's that chap there?'

Philip spluttered as he took in the excess of hair. 'What, where? No idea, some terrible fellow I expect. Must be a guest. Come along, we really must be going in.'

He knew Dugdale perfectly well!

At about the time that he joined the Institute for Sports Medicine, Gay also became a member of the Saints and Sinners Club, founded twenty years before by Percy Hoskins, a one-time crime reporter on the *Daily Express*. The club was a direct crib from that in New York bearing the same name and Hoskins – and the first chairman, the showman Jack Hylton – described it as 'an association of gentlemen connected with industry, literature, art, science, the theatre and the learned professions'. The really important qualification, however – first articulated by an early recruit, Lord Boothby – was that prospective members should be 'raffish'. This soon led to a virtual domination of the membership by the more colourful, and often patrician, elements of showbiz and sporting society leavened with a sprinkling of extrovert politicians and City entrepreneurs. If the Church of England could ever with any justification be described as the Tory Party at prayer, then the Saints and Sinners became the Tory Party at play. Although not primarily a charity, the club had by 1992 raised over £1 million for various causes, mainly through sponsored race meetings in the early days and subsequently by means of celebrity golf tournaments. Membership is limited to 100 and at the annual dinner self-professed Saints wear white carnations and Sinners red. Gay, who has never felt at ease in white, was recruited during his stewardship at Kempton Park – a venue for the charity race meetings – and at his first dinner, flanked by Arthur Askey and Bud Flanagan, he was much taken by the anarchy of the Crazy Gang members. Always the optimist, he entered eagerly into the club tradition of volunteering to open each function with a funny story. Gay's contributions – and some of those from more professional comedians – have not always received the applause he has felt they deserved. The reputation of which the Saints and Sinners is most proud is the quality of its guest speakers, who have included Princess Anne, Prince Charles, Ronald Reagan (generally acknowledged to have been the most successful performer of all) and a clutch of prime ministers including Margaret Thatcher.

Gay's fascination with the glitterati of the entertainment world was only in part sublimated by his membership of this organisation, but he was so popular that a steady stream of celebrities continued to beat a path to the doors of

Parsonage; invitations to the now well-established musical evenings and charity football and cricket matches were positively sought after; few cricket teams could boast of Peter Cook and Dudley Moore as an opening pair. Some of the stars were even interested in racing and one or two were keen enough to become owners.

In April 1966 Peter O'Toole had his first winner on the flat at a mixed (jumping and flat) meeting at Ascot. High on adrenalin and champagne, he roared his horse home with a stream of enthusiastic expletives not customarily heard in the then rather staid members' enclosure. He and Gay celebrated in earnest and immediately after the last race they went, at the actor's request, to see the weighing-room and the jockeys' changing areas. O'Toole was thrilled to meet Lester Piggott's valet and see the silks the great man had just worn still hanging on their peg. A few more celebratory sharpeners in the bar and then they weaved their way to the car park from where they were to drive (or be driven) home. As he got into his car, O'Toole produced a pair of racing boots from under his coat. 'Lester's,' he said triumphantly, throwing them at Gay. 'Couldn't resist 'em.' Laughing mightily, he drove off.

Gay was horrified; his mind reeled as he tried to take in the implications. Not only had he, a steward, broken the rules by taking a visitor into an inner sanctum, but the bloody man had robbed the greatest British jockey of an essential part of his kit. Lester, although doubtless owning several pairs of boots, was notorious for knowing exactly where they were and when. Further, he was definitely not renowned for a forgiving sense of humour. If the Jockey Club or the NHC got to hear about the incident, he would be for it. Sobering up rapidly, he grabbed the boots and ran back to the weighing-room. It was locked; everyone had gone.

Gay spent a sleepless night before searching the racing press the next day to see where Lester was riding. It appeared that he wasn't engaged but was down to perform at Folkestone the day after. Another anxious twenty-four hours were passed, during which Gay jumped nervously every time the telephone rang. The next day he wrapped the boots up in brown paper and set off for the south coast. He entered the Folkestone weighing-room and approached the valet. The man looked up and grinned. 'Hello, Mr Kindersley, thought we might see you. What's that you've got there then?' His smile broadened as he held up a pair of boots for Gay to see. 'These are Lester's. The ones you've got are an old pair we were going to throw away. Mr O'Toole's been having you on!'

The centenary year of the NHC, 1966, although not celebrated by the hoped-for film, did not pass entirely unnoticed. The *Sunday Telegraph* chose to mark the event with a full-page article on the youngest member and an exclusive interview was conducted by Neth (Kenneth) Rose – an old friend of both Oonagh and

Gay, soon to seal his connexion with the family by becoming Tania's godfather – who began by describing his subject as 'A man who has caught the public imagination with his courage and whose contribution to the prosperity of National Hunt racing is unrivalled'.

While it was accurate to suggest that Gay had become a popular folk-hero in racing when overcoming his appalling injuries to win the leading amateur title, it was perhaps going a little far to ascribe to him the role of supreme saviour. Lord Mildmay and Fred Winter, to name but two, would have superior claims to have been the greatest single contributor to the popularity and well-being of the sport. But there was yet another who was already indelibly identified in the public mind as national hunt racing's greatest-ever supporter, a woman who had helped substantially to carry the prestige of jumping to heights unthinkable before the Second World War; she was the guest of honour at the NHC's anniversary dinner: Her Majesty Queen Elizabeth, the Queen Mother.

Queen Elizabeth's close involvement was a legacy left to steeplechasing by Mildmay. While staying at Windsor Castle for Royal Ascot, he had talked so enthusiastically and eloquently about his first love that he had aroused the interest of the Queen (as she then was) and her daughter Princess Elizabeth. Mildmay and Peter Cazalet advised their new converts on the purchase of their first jointly owned steeplechaser, the successful Monaveen. When King George VI died the young Queen inherited the considerable royal flat-racing stable and chose to confine herself to that branch of the sport, leaving national hunt racing to her mother. Good as Monaveen undoubtedly was, it was the third horse bought by the Queen Mother which was to earn her world headlines and the sympathy and admiration of millions when Devon Loch, with the 1956 Grand National at his mercy, collapsed on the run up to the post at Aintree. No one can ever know the true reason behind this extraordinary failure. Was it, as the heartbroken rider Dick Francis believed, the tidal wave of sound that rolled from the stands to greet him as he carried the royal colours to apparently inevitable victory; was it a sudden and brief heart attack; was it an attempt to jump a phantom fence; was it a muscular spasm? All these possible explanations have their adherents; none quite fits all the facts. On the racecourse there was immediate and excited speculation, and it appeared that the only calm figure in the agitated crowd was Queen Elizabeth as she congratulated the winning owner of ESB and consoled her own stricken jockey. Despite the distressing end to her hopes for that afternoon, she betrayed no sign of her stunning disappointment; to the world she presented the same serene and smiling face – as old as the century – that thas won for her the admiration and the love of generations in every corner of the globe.

She had long been a friend of Philip Kindersley, her acquaintanceship stemming from the many times that she dined with the Cazalets at Fairlawne, where the Kindersleys were frequent guests. She had lunched, at Philip's invitation, with George Henderson and Company in the City and Gay had met her several times, noticing that she shared his taste for both Irish music and the occasional Dry Martini. In October 1968 Gay had put up £1,000 for the Sports Medicine Chase at Newbury – the whole meeting being devoted to the Institute's fund-raising effort – and it was natural that he, as a steward, should be expected to look after Her Majesty when she made it known that she would be present. More surprising (and very pleasing) was the fact that, through her private secretary, Sir Martin Gilliat, she had intimated that she would like to have tea – followed perhaps by a modicum of champagne – with Gay, Magsie and the children at Parsonage. She also made it clear that should the Kindersleys have a house party, she would prefer it if the guests would be good enough to make other arrangements for an hour or so – she wanted to be alone with her host and his immediate family. Gay and Magsie were thrilled; Parsonage was polished, the lawns trimmed and enquiries were made as to what sort of tea and brand of champagne would best please Her Majesty.

Conveniently, the Kindersleys had asked only two people to stay for that Newbury meeting: a divorced lady who was soon to marry an international figure with considerable racing interests, and her current lover with whom she was having a discreet final fling before her changed circumstances would make such an adventure impossible. When the royal command was issued, Gay briefed his guests carefully. After the races they were to go to the Walwyns for tea and drinks and were not to appear at Parsonage before dinner. The pair readily agreed; it was, after all, in everyone's interest that their presence should be kept as quiet as possible. All was arranged.

The day was a financial and social success. The Institute benefited to the tune of many thousands of pounds; Queen Elizabeth was in fine form and Gay was pleased, both with himself and with the general satisfaction that the afternoon had generated. After the last race he and Magsie left at speed so as to be at Parsonage when the royal party arrived. The children were lined up; Robin and Kim practised their nods assiduously, their chins practically touching their chests, and Catheryn bobbed up and down, perfecting her curtsey. Accompanied by Gilliat and a lady-in-waiting, the Queen Mother was precisely on time; the children behaved faultlessly; the sandwiches were just so and the tea much appreciated. Champagne was produced and after a glass or two Her Majesty asked whether she might see the stables. Half-expecting such a request, Gay had been prepared. He led her down to the yard where Len Adsett, the head lad, was waiting in his best suit. She asked a number of knowledgeable questions and satisfactory answers were at hand. The party returned to the drawing-room.

'And now,' said the Queen Mother, 'I wonder whether I might see the rest of this lovely house?'

Magsie and Gay, trying hard to remember whether all the beds were made, said 'Of course', and they all set off on the unscheduled tour.

'This is the dining-room; this the children's play-room.' They continued through the office and into the hall, where the royal visitor was interested to hear about the musical evenings and inspected the famous tea-chest standing in its corner. Then the party mounted the stairs and headed for the upper regions.

'These are the children's rooms and this is Nanny's.' They turned and processed in stately fashion towards the front of the house. 'This is our own bedroom and bathroom and this, Ma'am, is the biggest of the guest rooms.' Gay opened the door and Queen Elizabeth took a step forward and peered inside. She paused; the room was occupied, the bed a scene of furious activity. The house guests had come back prematurely and crept up the stairs while the royal party was at the stables. That their return had been prompted by an undeniable urgency was easily deduced; they were entirely naked and entwined; she was on her back, he was going for his life between her waving legs. The eyes of the wife-to-be widened as, over her lover's shoulder, she saw the unmistakable powder-blue clad figure framed in the doorway. She gasped. Taking this as a sign of appreciation, her partner redoubled his efforts. Gay and Magsie looked at each other helplessly and the lady-in-waiting's hand flew to her mouth as she stifled a shriek.

'How nice,' murmured the Queen Mother. 'But I think perhaps we should not go further.'

The best-loved figure in British racing was not easily fazed but she could, when the fancy took her, be disconcertingly unpredictable. At the Windsor course on an Arctic day in January 1969 when Gay had again been detailed to look after her, she watched her horse run and then decided that she would skip the next race and that she and Gay should move instead to the stewards' room for tea. As they made themselves comfortable she thanked him for sending her a gramophone record of 'Slattery's Mounted Fut'. 'Such a good tune,' she mused. 'Oh Gay, do sing it for me.'

Gay was startled; he put down his tea-cup. 'But I'm hardly prepared, Ma'am. I have no music; we need at least a guitar.'

She brushed him aside. 'Never mind all that, just sing it.'

Gay made one more effort. 'But Ma'am, could I not just say the words for you?'

The royal patience was exhausted; the smile took on a touch of steeliness. 'No, Gay,' she said. 'I want you to sing it. Now.'

Recognising none too soon that a directive was not a basis for discussion and that an appropriately enthusiastic response was quickly required, he launched into the familiar words.

> You've heard of Julius Caesar and of great Napoleon too,
> And how the Cork Militia beat the Turks at Waterloo ...

A stipendary steward, ensconced in his box next door, heard the unusual noise and came bristling in prepared to deliver a rocket to whoever was behaving in so unseemly a manner. Didn't they know, he muttered to himself, that Queen Elizabeth was likely to be having tea there shortly? He took two paces into the room before taking root in a state of suspended disbelief. Gay was on his feet, getting stuck into the histrionic heroics so essential to the rendering of his favourite epic. His audience of one was waving a sandwich in time to the words. Both were so absorbed that neither so much as looked up as the bewildered steward slowly withdrew, shaking his head. Another door opened and a waiter arrived with more tea. Gay paused; the Queen Mother did not.

'Go on, go on,' she exclaimed impatiently. 'He can't hear anyway; he's deaf.'

The royal sense of humour, never far from the surface, was often exercised on the racecourse. Gay, acting as senior steward at Kempton, once had occasion to fine Peter Cazalet £30 for withdrawing one of Her Majesty's horses without proper explanation. She was disappointed; it was her only entry that afternoon. Cazalet, something of a martinet and not to be trifled with by young stewards, was quietly fuming. Gay, seeing owner and trainer deep in conversation, prepared to take evasive action but Queen Elizabeth spotted him and beckoned.

'Ah, Gay,' she said, 'we were just working out how to find the money to pay your fine.'

Well as he got on with their mother, he found both the Queen and Princess Margaret difficult to talk to. Princess Margaret was patently bored by racing and when looking after her at Windsor Races (she had come one day with the Queen Mother), Gay found it hard to keep her attention engaged, let alone amuse her – although she did show a keen interest in the possible reasons for one of the runners having been named Sixty-Nine. When she appeared to be absorbed by the company of some friends, he dropped back, allowing her to be alone with them in the paddock. Side-tracked by the need to down a glass or two to restore his conversational courage, he failed to rejoin her party until she had arrived back at the royal box. She was cross. 'How dare you leave my side. You're supposed to be looking after me.'

Years later Tania Kindersley was introduced to Princess Margaret when on holiday in the West Indies. 'Ah, yes,' said the Princess. ' "Slattery's Mounted Fut". My mother still plays it non-stop. We have to march round the dining-room table.'

The Queen herself possesses a justifiably famous sense of impish humour but, unlike her mother's, it does not seem to have extended to appreciating Gay's company. He became painfully aware that he was not top of Her Majesty's pops when the Queen Mother arranged for Gay, Magsie and their three eldest children to join the Queen in the royal box at Ascot for a December jumping meeting. At luncheon, Gay and Catheryn were at the top table and from the beginning he found the going extremely heavy. Her Majesty seemed disinclined to discuss the day's card and different attempts made by him and some of the others to engage in small-talk were not encouraged. Gay was relieved when racing started and he was able to escape from the immediate royal presence. Summoned again for tea, he was slightly late and, to his discomfort, he found that the seating arrangements were unchanged and that the chair on the Queen's right was unoccupied. Mumbling his apologies, he slid into it and found that sustained conversation was once more difficult. Desperately he dredged his mind for some topic that might amuse. Should he try to tell a funny story? Was there one that would be remotely suitable for royal ears? Then he remembered a joke told to him by Jimmy Ellis, the actor who first made his name as the Irish PC Lynch of *Z Cars*.

'Are you familiar with the Belfast accent, Ma'am?' he asked.

The Queen looked at him quizzically. 'Oh yes,' she said. 'Of course. Why?'

'Well, Ma'am, I thought you might not have heard a rather jolly Irish story I was told the other day.'

His monarch evinced no obvious enthusiasm and Catheryn covered her eyes with her hands; she had heard it before. Her father, now committed, ploughed on.

'It seems, Ma'am, that there were two ducks flying over Northern Ireland and as luck would have it, they found themselves caught in cross-fire between the police and the IRA. Bullets everywhere. They were very frightened.

' "Quack, quack," says one duck to the other in terror.

' "God help us, I'm flying as quack as I can," says the other.'

There was a brief silence. Catheryn peeped through her fingers. The Queen sipped her tea.

'The old ones are the best ones, Mr Kindersley,' she said.

Despite the slightly tense atmosphere in the royal box, the children had a marvellous day at Ascot. For them it was commonplace to have fun with their parents; they had always experienced a happy childhood with all the apparent manifestations of a united and loving family. Gay and Magsie positively enjoyed doing things with them: ponies at home, fishing for Gay and Robin in Scotland; holidays in France and Luggala with the doting and indulgent Oonagh. They had little reason to know or even suspect that by their twelfth wedding anniversary their parents were in a virtual state of unarmed combat. Both had taken the greatest of pains to hide their difficulties from the children (and indeed from most of their friends) but they now lived in worlds apart, neither of them enjoying the things they once loved to do together. Gay, always preoccupied with planning his next extra-marital adventure, paid his wife scant attention. Magsie sulked when people came to stay and she no longer cared for the extended Sunday lunches and the riotous musical evenings which had been so much a part of their lives. Gay complained that she seemed to suspect him of having an affair with, or at least obviously fancying, all their female guests and accused her of making life uncomfortable for them. He added nothing to the plausibility of his pleas of innocence by allowing his wife to discover him in the play-room kissing the very attractive lead singer of the New Seekers.

The simple truth seems to be that after the Abicair affair Magsie never really felt safe again and retreated into a protective but insecure shell from which she wholly failed to emerge. From that time on, they had independently decided on a damage limitation exercise which neither found it possible to admit openly to the other. In public the proprieties of marriage were usually observed; in private the children, as children do, took the occasional row that spilled over in their presence in their stride, feeling secure in the love that Gay and Magsie so obviously felt for them. They continued to be responsible parents and Gay took his duties so seriously that he allowed himself to be elected to the board of governors of Cheam School at which, in 1968, both Robin and Kim were pupils. Almost immediately he was embroiled in controversy as the other parents brought pressure on him to lead a campaign to sack the headmaster, who had acquired a reputation for caning his charges unnecessarily. He found this an unsavoury episode – not made easier by his weakness for being oversympathetic to each of two warring parties – and the ensuing rows and the subsequent politicking over the headmaster's successor cured him from ever again accepting nomination as a governor. For Robin and Kim, however, their father's high profile at school added a new dimension to him and their lives.

Fegentri activities in England had, like Cheam, being going through a difficult period. In 1967 Moët & Chandon had been unhappy with the paucity of runners in the Silver Magnum. They understandably demanded an improvement, and it seemed to Gay that the next year would be make or break. To boost numbers he entered four of his own horses, three to be ridden by overseas amateurs. He himself would partner Phoebus II – a genuine flat horse – whilst Newman Noggs, Flying Barnie and General Kit, all jumpers, would be provided for guests, the last named going to the hospitable Spaniard, the Duque de Albuquerque. All carried the Kindersley colours and between them made up 25 per cent of the field for a race so valuable (over £1,500 to the winner) that it clearly deserved wider support from reluctant British owners and short-sighted trainers. In the event Phoebus II came third at a handsome 20 to 1 with the others well down the field. It was of some satisfaction to the altruistic owner (but little consolation to their Silver Magnum riders) that his horses so benefited from the run that they picked up two wins and a second over fences the following week.

Riding Phoebus II reminded Gay forcibly that his neck – a long-standing casualty of his jumping career – was giving him increasing trouble. Shortly after becoming a member of the Jockey Club when it absorbed the National Hunt Committee in 1969, he was made to face up to the fact that his race-riding days, even on the flat, must now be nearly over. The incident that acted as the final persuader happened at Folkestone where, almost at the last minute, he had been asked to ride a mare in a five-runner amateur flat race. Knowing that his shoulders and neck could no longer cope with a strong puller, he sought confirmation that his prospective mount did not take a hold. 'No, no,' he was assured. 'She's just the ride for an amateur. Make the running and you'll win. No problem.'

Thus promised, he set about losing seven pounds within twenty-four hours – never an easy task and all the more agonising as he approached 40. Feeling rather weak he clambered aboard in the paddock. Just before the lad freed the horse's head as he led it out on to the course, he looked up at Gay.

'Watch this one going down to the start,' he advised. 'She cocks her jaw and there isn't much steering.'

This was not at all what Gay wanted to hear. He took her down at a very gingerly controlled canter and at length they arrived in one piece. She was docile enough at the start and Gay began to feel that he had worried unnecessarily. Folkestone is a right-handed course and having taken the lead in front of the stands as instructed, he prepared to round the first bend. He gently steered her to the right; there was no response. He applied more pressure and might more profitably have been engaged in trying to turn a juggernaut; the horse continued in a determinedly straight line, carrying her rider towards the outside rail as the rest of the field slipped through on the inside. With both hands now tugging on the right rein, he hauled in as hard as his pain-racked body would allow. There was a sudden give as the bit came out the mare's mouth and he was hard put to retain his balance. He had no purchase as she careered on, completely out of control. With nothing to hang on to and his upper back giving him the feeling that it might at any moment disintegrate, he gripped grimly with his legs, both powerless and terrified, bouncing about like a badly filled sack of potatoes as his mount, entirely unaided, took her own line – managing, surprisingly, to finish third. As she pulled herself up, Gay rolled off and lay prone. Too exhausted to see the stewards who were calling an enquiry, he was attended by the course doctor. The stewards took a grave view and warned the trainer that the mare must never be entered for an amateur race again. Gay, although suffering no serious damage, went home that evening in an uncharacteristically thoughtful frame of mind.

The next week he was at Lingfield and met the gentle ex-professional jockey turned trainer, Brian Swift, whom he knew had also been at Folkestone. 'I didn't half feel a Charlie on that mare last week, Brian.'

Swift looked at him hard, put his arm round the shattered shoulders and smiled his kindly smile. 'You looked one, Gay,' he said quietly.

Gay rode only twice more: first on his own relatively sweet-tempered and certainly properly schooled Charley Winking in the Silver Magnum and, finally, on the same horse at Kempton in September. It was at Folkestone, though, that he realised he had crossed his own bridge too far.

Oonagh too had come to the end of an era. In 1970 the Guinness Trustees decided that her financial position, so seriously affected by the disastrous investment in Maison Ferreras, had now deteriorated to such an extent that it would be necessary for her to become a tax exile in France. Worse, she would have to give up Luggala. This was a dreadful blow to the family – even to Garech, whose home it now became. Gay found it particularly hard to bear; his mother and Luggala had been inseparable all his life and, since Dom's defection, the house had been the centre of her troubled world, a place where she could lose herself among artistic friends and keep at arm's length the harsher realities of her life. For Gay it had retained dream-like qualities which held him in their thrall – it was his own secret garden which never failed to work its magic. For both mother and son it guarded the dear memories of Tessa and now Tara too.

The trustees bought Oonagh La Tourelle de la Garoupe, a house by the sea on Cap d'Antibes. Patrick Cummins moved in and so did the ever-loyal Greta Fanning, whose job it was to look after the young children without whom Oonagh could hardly imagine life. A cook, chauffeur and gardener completed the permanent entourage and soon Patrick was urging his mistress to entertain 'in the ould ways'. Oonagh needed little prompting and La Tourelle quickly assumed much of the reputation for lavish parties that had once belonged to the lodge in the Wicklow Mountains. The Hustons, David Niven, Rex Harrison, Dirk Bogarde, Bryan Ferry, David Frost and even Lester Piggott joined those who now shifted the centre of their social gravity to the South of France. For the Kindersleys and their children it became the place of summer holidays on a grand scale.

Gay's fortieth birthday on 2 June 1970 prompted Magsie to pull out all the stops. In secret she planned a mammoth party; the guest list included practically everyone in racing and more than a light dusting of their friends from show-business. The Dubliners were invited and were pleased to announce that they would perform for as long as was necessary to give 'yer man' the time of his life. None of this was suspected by Gay as he was packed off to the Ascot Sales with Bill Payne. On his return that evening, proceedings were in full swing and the crack continued well into the following day. The Dubliners, true to their word, were unflagging but by lunchtime, ignoring the inviting green lawns and the sparkling blue pool of Parsonage, they were installed in the bar of the Queen's Arms from which to a man (and the odd girl-friend) they repelled all attempts at extrication. Their manager grew anxious; he had booked a very expensive recording studio in London for later that day and the touring programme did not allow them the luxury of an alternative date. He appealed to Gay. Len Adsett was summoned and the horse-box was filled with crates of Guinness and a case of whiskey. It was reversed up to the door of the pub; the ramps were lowered, the bottles broached and, as homing pigeons to a loft, on they trooped. But not quite all. One of the group was engaged in trying to telephone a girl at Galway University for reasons which remained both unexplained and unrequited. It became a lengthy process as the Newbury operator, scandalised at the language as the frustrated musician failed to make his connexion, pulled the plug at every repetition of the word 'fock'. Eventually the combination of GPO sensibilities and impenetrable university bureaucracy was given best and the remaining Dubliner climbed reluctantly aboard. The Queen's Arms had been drunk dry.

The next three years saw Gay consolidating his reputation as a successful permit holder, a reliable dealer in young horses in Ireland and England (where he leaned heavily on the advice of George Rogers and Bill Payne respectively) and, not least, as a prodigious punter. His winnings were impressive by any standards: £17,000 at Sandown when Sidney Carton beat the Queen Mother's horse after an agonising wait while the judge consulted a photograph; £8,000 as a result of a spectacular five-horse accumulator (all trained by Ken Oliver and ridden by Barry Brogan) at Wolverhampton and a £15,000 pay-out at the Cheltenham Festival in 1972. These well-remembered touches were, of course, more than balanced by the steady trickle of easily forgettable losses, notably one of £4,000 on his own Hit Parade and £2,000 on Nijinsky for the 1970 Prix de l'Arc de Triomphe – Nijinsky being the wonder horse with which Lester Piggott had already won the English and Irish Derbys, the 2,000 Guineas, the St Leger and the King George VI and Queen Elizabeth Stakes; but Lester chose this day to ride one of his very few ill-judged races. There were stable tragedies too: Wackford Squeers broke not one but both his forelegs at Folkestone and so affected was his owner by the loss that for over a year he could not bring himself to fill the horse's box at Parsonage. For Hit Parade there was a happier ending. He won a seller at Taunton and was bid for, surprisingly without prior consultation, by the father and son combination, David and Martin Pipe. Gay was incensed and pushed them up to a price he himself would certainly not have been prepared to pay. The last laugh though, was with the Pipes; three weeks later Hit Parade gave Martin his first winner under national hunt rules.

One of Gay's more successful equine investments at this time was Ventora, a little horse with an extraordinary metabolism. He had been bought very cheaply (and already named) by George Rogers and arrived with Gay when he was just 5, accompanied by a gloomy report from Rogers that he seemed to be impossible to train because of a feeding problem. His ribs stood out like a pair of combs and although he had once promised to be a good potential hurdler, he had lost so much condition that he could hardly canter. Gay soon saw that the problem appeared to be that Ventora's food ran straight through and came out the other end as an almost continuous stream of unpleasantly brown water. Various changes of diet in Ireland had proved ineffective but the Kindersley treatment (recommended by his vet Frank Mahon) was to feed him boiled barley – the traditional way to slow up a horse which was not required to show its best form in a race. Ventora, however, as if determined to repay the patience shown by his owner, thrived and began to put on weight. Starting to work in earnest, he was able to tolerate enough oats with his barley to keep him fit and build up his speed; he remained almost painfully thin but was getting stronger by the day. Soon he was winning selling hurdle races and because he looked so awful Gay seldom had to go beyond £800 to buy him in – a sum easily won back in bets at invariably generous odds. The hat-rack was turning into a nice little earner – until one day at Newton Abbot.

As usual Ventora had scooted home and his owner had done the now familiar arithmetic to ensure that his wager had brought him a sufficient return to cover expenses, including the expected buying-in price. This time, however, bidding was brisk – but not from anyone that Gay could recall ever having seen before. Loth to let Ventora go, he bid on but at £2,500 caved in, red-faced with rage. How could anyone spend that sort of money for such a skinny-looking creature? He followed the buyer as the man walked away, determined to gain some clue as to who he was, but was intercepted by the West Country trainer Billy Williams, whose face betrayed the fact that he had some important information to impart.

'I saw all that, Gay,' he said. 'Don't worry, you'll get your horse back. That chap was only let out of a loony-bin last week. He was at Taunton Hunter Sales yesterday, buying practically every animal in the place. He's pinched his wife's cheque book: they'll all bounce. The police are looking for him!'

Relieved as he was, Gay still had Ventora's diet to worry about; no doubt the tangle would take some time to sort out and meanwhile some trainer or racecourse lad would be stuffing oats and racehorse nuts into him. But within seventy-two hours the embarrassed Newton Abbot authorities telephoned to do a deal and the little horse was soon back at Parsonage happily wolfing his barley. The unfortunate lunatic apparently disappeared, the police having lost sight of him on the racecourse. A week later he was found up a tree in Hyde Park.

Gay's modest but solid successes as a permit holder, the relative prosperity of the farm at Parsonage and the sound reputation he had built as a trader in good steeplechasing prospects had combined to go some way into lulling him into a complacency with his lot. At the same time, having given up race-riding, he yearned for a more active and public role. Returning from a meeting at Wetherby with trainer David Gandolfo and jockey Bill Shoemark, Gay voiced his vague, unformed frustrations as they stopped for refreshments at a pub.

'Why don't you apply for a public trainer's licence?' they suggested.

He looked at them. Why not indeed?

CHAPTER EIGHT

Downhill to Divorce

In 1924 Lord Howard de Walden and Seaford contributed a notable piece of racing history when he became the first member of the Jockey Club to resign. He took this dramatic action – something of a *cause célèbre* at the time – because the club had elected to its membership Lord Dalmeny (later to become the 6th Earl of Rosebery), a man of whom de Walden strongly disapproved. He never made the reasons for his dislike clear – not even to his family – but they were alleged to be the aftermath of an incident which took place before the First World War. It is much to the earl's credit that many years later he successfully proposed the election of his adversary's son (the 9th baron), thereby illuminating the membership of the Jockey Club with a distinguished owner, breeder and three-times senior steward whose horses included the Derby winner Slip Anchor and the champion hurdler Lanzarote. It was to be forty-nine years before there was a second voluntary departure from Portman Square and this time it was Gay Kindersley.

In truth he had little choice. While it was apparently quite in order for him to be a member (and a steward at a number of racecourses) whilst training his own horses, doing so for other people provided grounds for disquiet – if not disqualification. When the club's senior steward, Sir Randle Feilden, asked him to consider resignation, Gay himself had no complaint, being persuaded that he could no longer run with the hare as well as hunt with the hounds. Others failed to see any justification for the pressure being applied. Jack Logan of *The Sporting Life* – always keen to take on the racing establishment – was particularly vehement, describing the virtual banning of professional trainers from membership as poppycock and regretting that Gay had not seen fit to make a stand. If he had, Logan reasoned, it might have led to a judgment in the High Court as important in its way as that which gave women the right to hold a trainer's licence.

It was not in the Kindersley nature to cause a commotion. Of far greater importance to Gay was the possibility that he might just be in line to follow Peter Cazalet as the Queen Mother's trainer. Cazalet had recently died and the popular newspapers were busy speculating (inaccurately) that Gay had been involved in 'top-level discussions' and had become favourite for the job ahead of a distinguished field among whom were Fulke Walwyn, Fred Winter, Stan Mellor and Cazalet's assistant, Richard Head. He was sufficient of a realist not to take the rumours too seriously and it came as no real surprise when he learned that a love of Irish music was not enough to swing the decision his way when compared with a long and successful training career. Walwyn got the job and the fifteen horses that went with it.

Gay's closest friends were not concerned so much with his resignation from the Jockey Club or failure to secure royal patronage as with his capacity for survival. They knew that financially he was up against it; Parsonage Farm was an expensive place to run and his unbusinesslike attempts to make his various enterprises pay had usually failed; the stable alone was losing £15,000 a year. His unstinting lifestyle was outrunning his inheritances, especially since his expectations had been considerably trimmed by Oonagh's disastrous investment in *haute couture*. He had expensive tastes in parties, women and holidays; his generosity to Magsie over such matters as her dress allowance was legendary and his betting accounts were sought after eagerly by every bookmaker in the land. Ends were far from being remotely acquainted, let alone meeting.

Gay too was worried, but his never-failing optimism prevented him from facing entirely up to reality. It is true that he had made sporadic efforts to cut down his expenditure by, for example, occasionally closing down his credit accounts and betting only in cash. Such bouts of uncharacteristically careful husbandry, however, did not last long. From time to time he partially confided his problems to Michael Allsopp and others in the City, but these conversations always fell short of asking for detailed financial advice – in any event, it is unlikely that he would have been capable of presenting a full enough picture for them to have been able to help in any serious way – but the process made him feel better and he would then go home and put theory into practice by virtuously giving up bacon for breakfast or cancelling the *Daily Mail*. Of one thing he was sure: professional training was what he wanted to do and, somehow, this new career – his first full-time employment – would turn his predicament around and balance the books.

The hard-headed racing fraternity thought otherwise. A favourite old shibboleth, always trotted out with more than a touch of *schadenfreude* in the pubs of the Lambourn valley when a trainer goes broke, was eagerly invoked as the pundits considered Gay's decision. 'The only way to make a small fortune in national hunt training,' it runs, 'is to begin with a large one.' Examples spanning the years are readily offered: famous names that to a greater or lesser extent fit the hypothesis. Others, whose profitable side-lines (or fairy godmothers) have stood between their training enterprises and similar insolvency, are held up as further evidence and the extraordinary success of Martin Pipe is dismissed as the exception that proves the rule. Hyperbole is rife but there is enough truth in the old adage for even judicious men to believe that screws have to be loose to the point of rattling before anyone could embark on the business of training jumpers with a view to actually making money. Job satisfaction – yes; respect – possibly, even with moderate results; fame – again possibly, and certainly if the yard has the good fortune to be responsible for an outstanding horse or two. But, in general, a most agreeable way to lose money is probably the most that anyone can hope for. Frank Mahon, a close friend for nearly thirty years until he died in 1993 and among the most respected of racing vets, feared the worst for the Parsonage plans. He was certain that Gay was temperamentally unsuited to the cut and thrust of a profession in which, for example, it might sometimes be necessary to enhance the chances of success by poaching owners from other trainers. He was not, it seemed to Mahon, ruthless enough. He was too trusting; just too damned nice. And, to make the venture even more problematical, there would be no Don Butchers to help and advise him.

Gay set with a will about his self-imposed task of proving everybody wrong. Naturally enough his methods involved the spending of a great deal of money – a fair proportion of it going into the provision of an all-weather training gallop with inadequate drainage which rendered it all but useless after rain. He then put in another which, in those early days of such technology, froze after only forty-eight hours of sub-zero temperatures. 'Good old Gay,' his critics said. 'He'll fall for anything.' But in gathering together his team he also displayed a surprisingly cut-throat streak by persuading Roy Pethwick to join him as head lad to replace Len Adsett, who had decided that the move up the training league was not for him. Pethwick had held this key position with Paul Cole in Lambourn and the move raised a number of eyebrows in the valley, seriously annoying Cole and making Gay – perhaps for the first time in his life – genuinely (but only briefly) unpopular with people other than disgruntled husbands.

Amongst the doubts and uncertainties, the occasional unpleasantness and the constantly gloomy advice of his friends, Magsie stood unwaveringly behind her man. Although suspecting that they were living beyond their means, she was not fully aware of the precariousness of Gay's situation. In all their rows (now increasingly bitter), he had never remonstrated with her over her extravagances and he had her full support as he set out to fill the twenty-five boxes in the Parsonage yard. Magsie saw her role as one of setting the stage on which Gay could best perform. She was a charming hostess who possessed a talent – often found in accomplished actresses – for instilling in people a desire to please, and she now planned to use that gift to seduce both current and potential owners into sending Gay more horses.

But even Magsie found it hard to make progress at a time when the national economy was in the doldrums and the racing industry – shedding disillusioned trainers like confetti – was far from buoyant. Inevitably Gay entered the lists owning or part-owning a high proportion of the fourteen horses he had acquired at the beginning of the season – well short of the number which, he calculated, would be necessary to ensure a decent return on his investment. Yet despite the difficulties there was a buzz of expectant bustle about the yard; the tack-room had the ordered appearance of an advertisement for a glossy kitchen and the boxes were airy and freshly painted; the horses looked well and the staff were smartly turned out as they eagerly set about their tasks. Ivor Herbert, in a lengthy article in the *Sunday Express*, was clearly impressed. 'I will be astonished,' he wrote, 'if Gay Kindersley does not make this a very good first season. He has got a real grip of the job.'

Gay had concentrated on securing horses who acted well on hard ground and which he hoped would give him the flying start he needed to establish a quick reputation. In the event they could hardly have done him better; for a glorious half-hour he even became the leading national hunt trainer when Ventora won the first race at the opening meeting of the year at Newton Abbot. By the end of September he had saddled nine winners from sixteen runners. By December, with the ground now going soft, he was second to Gordon Richards in the trainers' table, well ahead of established favourites such as Toby Balding, Fred Rimell and Frank Cundell, and with more than twice as many winners as Fulke Walwyn. Parsonage was on a roll.

The star of the string was Traumatic (owned by Gay in partnership with William Hill, the landlord of the Queen's Arms), a young hurdler who won seven times before Christmas, six of the victories being off the reel. But old favourites such as Ventora, Hit Parade and Sidney Carton all played their parts and the racing and social press were agog, devoting hundreds of column inches to this new twist in the Kindersley story, often stressing the unexpected nature of his apparent transition from playboy to hard-working man of the people. Not untypical was a piece in January by Monty Court, the racing editor of the aggressively egalitarian *Sunday Mirror*:

Any fool can be born rich. And many are. There are lots of men, women and dont knows [sic] in racing to prove the point. On the other hand there are people like Gay Kindersley, ever-smiling Guinness heir, former member of the Jockey Club and ex-amateur champion jockey.

In his time Gay was one of the most colourful of the upper-crust fun-makers – the kind who could yahoo-it-up all night and ride, red-eyed and hung-over the following day; the kind that would leap into a swimming pool in the middle of a party blowing a hunting horn and wearing a bowler hat; the kind who struck bets with such audacity that he had himself and the bookies either stiff with apprehension or giggling with relief.

There is no doubt that the ante-natal gods were in a generous mood when they were dishing out the rations to the embryo Kindersley. Among other things they gave him an extra portion of wit and guts ('one more fall will kill you,' said the doctors) that disproves the old theory that you have to be hungry to be a good fighter ... ...

And that is why he is making a remarkable success of it [training] in his first season – sixteen winners so far and more on the way. He is up there among the big boys ... Since his resignation from the Jockey Club, Gay is amazed at the changes in attitudes that have taken place in his relationships with people, even close friends. 'It's as though an invisible screen has been removed,' he says. 'People tell me things which they would never have dreamt of mentioning before.'

And he laughs at the change that has taken place in himself. 'I don't have to think it's time I had a haircut or about how I dress. If I want to go to Wincanton in cap and gumboots, I go in cap and gumboots ...' The over-crowded world of racing has been forced to make room for the ex-amateur who has become a totally dedicated pro.

Despite the public plaudits, owners were still hard to pin down, a notable exception being Tony Stratton Smith, a director of Charisma Records, who had made a number of enquiries in Lambourn in search of a suitable trainer and was eventually advised by Richard Pitman towards the end of 1973 to 'try Gay Kindersley; he never seems to stop training winners'. Bowled over by Magsie and the impressive results, Stratton Smith, an amusing, chain-smoking, vodka-guzzling bachelor, asked Gay to buy him two (later three) horses. The new partnership got off to a dream beginning when Fighting Chance – one of Arthur Stephenson's better offerings – won on his first outing at Doncaster in January. The six-year-old went on to take four races in all that season, including the Midlands Grand National at Uttoxeter, with Bill Shoemark in the saddle each time. The enthusiastic Stratton Smith, his huge bulk quivering with delight at every new success, became increasingly thrilled with his new venture. 'Better than having a record in the Top Twenty,' he declared.

With Magsie relatively happy in her portrayal of the ideal trainer's wife and Gay immersed in his demanding career there was a smoother domestic routine at Parsonage. Talk of separation and divorce faded as, for perhaps the first time in his adult life, Gay found that not only had he little time to devote to chasing other women but, surprisingly, the compulsive urge to commit adultery seemed to have subsided a little. But not to the point of disappearance. In January 1974, on Plumpton racecourse, he found Philippa Harper. Her unwitting impact on him was considerable.

The Parsonage team had not had a good afternoon. Drowning their sorrows, Gay and Magsie had met a steady stream of old friends and been introduced to Philippa and her mother, Peggy. He was immediately struck by the tall leggy blonde with a film star's figure and (following one of the basic rules of successful seduction) began to exercise his charm first on her mother. Several bottles of champagne later it had been decided that a small gang – including, naturally, Peggy and her daughter – should go out to dinner. Philippa, not having been consulted and having plans of her own, decided to be bolshie but was eventually persuaded to change her mind, though with a certain amount of bad grace which led her to isolate herself from the others during pre-dinner drinks in the restaurant by going to sit alone by the fire. Gay, becoming thoroughly overexcited every time he looked across, excused himself from the main party and joined her. She was unresponsive but Magsie, ever alert to potential threats, summoned her husband back to the bar and felt it necessary to do so again when she noticed that, once more, he had homed in on the blonde.

Before going in to eat, Magsie and Philippa found themselves together in the ladies' loo. Magsie asked how old she was and whether she was married. Philippa replied that she had not yet found anyone silly enough to take her on. Magsie paused as she finished applying a little more lipstick. She turned away from the mirror. 'No doubt,' she said, snapping her bag shut and heading for the door, 'one day you'll steal somebody's husband.' Philippa, mentally noting that the evening was turning out about as grim as she had expected, followed the older woman slowly into dinner. The next week she left England for a year in the United States.

The 1973–74 season, having promised so much, finished more modestly than had once seemed likely. The bare statistics showed that he had produced twenty-two wins from seven horses (mostly owned or part-owned by himself), gaining a respectable though hardly spectacular place in the trainers' table. Financially, though, matters had hardly improved and he was still losing money steadily.

The root of the problem was his continued inability to attract serious owners. The author Evelyn Anthony, of whom he had high hopes as a major patron, sent him just two horses (both so useless that they had to be replaced) and no other owner of any significance had appeared to join Stratton Smith. Even Magsie's charm had failed to make the break-through needed to overcome the twin disadvantages of his playboy image – now largely unjustified in that he was an undoubtedly conscientious and dedicated trainer, but which still clung to him like faded ivy – and his lack of a real equine star capable of making a show in, or better still winning, a major race. The inevitable result was an embarrassing number of animals with too few people to share the bills. Some of the horses had been left unexpectedly at Parsonage when prospective owners who had asked him to buy for them then withdrew from the deal ('My accountants tell me I mustn't go into racing after all').

Gay confessed to *The Sporting Life* in a painfully frank interview: 'It doesn't look too good when a trainer has so many horses running in his own name, does it? I'm losing more money now than when I was training under a permit.' Such a public articulation of his problems did little to alleviate them.

Despite the worries, he loved his work. Few relished the early mornings as he did; the riding-out, the crack with the lads, the juggling of entries, the afternoon's racing, the parties on the way home and the last walk round at night to check on the sleepy occupiers of the boxes in the quiet yard. Occasionally he had a slice of luck which added to the sum of his contentment, perhaps through an unexpected victory for an under-dog (of which he had more than a fair share) or by bringing off a well-planned betting coup. The brief career of Do So managed to combine both these ingredients.

Gay had gone to buy some hay from a neighbour who mentioned that he was trying to find a home – perhaps as a trainer's hack – for a broken-down, 10-year-old selling plater whose owner had bought him to run on hard ground but who had never won a race. Gay was led to a paddock where Do So grazed peacefully. He looked at the horse; the tendons were as bowed as bananas but there was something about him, his eyes bright and genuine as he ambled over to inspect the visitor. Gay parted with £400 and took him home to Parsonage where the lads gazed in disbelief as Do So clambered down the ramp of the lorry he had just shared with two hundred bales of hay. He soon became a favourite and throughout the summer the yard worked hard on him as Gay prayed for the rain that would make life a little easier for tired legs. It came and in the wettest August for years the horse was entered in a selling chase at Fontwell – as races go, about the bottom rung of the national hunt ladder. Do So was far from fast but he could jump and, unlike most in the field who had been readied for the fast ground usually encountered at that time of the year, he relished the bottomless going. Gay was hopeful to the tune of £100 at 8 to 1 and the horse, amply rewarding the faith shown in him, skidded home, paying for himself, the hay and a little more besides. At the subsequent auction no one wanted him and a few days later he won another seller, this time at Hereford. Again there was little interest although the auctioneer, perhaps sensing that the horse may not have been quite as bad as his previous form suggested, seemed curiously unwilling to allow him to be bought-in at all. Eventually Gay secured the deal and, still in

August and again in the soft, Do So obliged for a third time in an amateurs' chase at Fakenham. Thanks to the 'donkey' the season was off to a flying start.

The Kindersley hope for breaking into the big time in 1974–75 was the 8-year-old Black Tudor, a liver chestnut bought at Ascot Sales for around £7,000 which seemed to have practically unlimited potential over three miles and probably longer. The Grand National was to be the target but, as the long road of preparation began, the horse ran disappointingly. He was not alone: Sidney Carton, Thursday Christian (a novice chaser nursed back to health after a series of ruptured blood vessels) and Fighting Chance all performed below par, while Traumatic broke down, never to race again. Morale at Parsonage was low and, as is often the case, gloom gave rise to a brittle tension which permeated tempers to such an extent that during one of the constant bouts of bickering, one of the lads went for Roy Pethwick with a pitchfork. Happily he failed to cause serious injury, but worse was to come. Gay had taken Black Tudor out for a morning's roadwork and the horse, always full of himself, was spooked by a combination of a pair of ridden ponies and a passing car. The frightened animal tried to jump off the road and became caught up in barbed wire. The more he struggled, the more the wire cut into him, reducing his forelegs and chest to ribbons of dangling, bleeding flesh. Still he continued to fight and Gay jumped off, hoping then to be able to help untangle the coils. Nothing he was able to do had any calming effect; with the blood now pouring as if from a tap, Black Tudor thrashed about as Gay asked the driver of the car to go to the nearest telephone and call the vet. In time the horse recovered, though not to race again that season. There would be no National outing for the Parsonage team and rock-bottom morale now gave way almost to despair.

In early December the luck changed and the stable produced five winners within a week. This welcome upturn in fortune was followed by a remarkable win at Newbury after Christmas – an event not without drama and one which Gay was to look back on with decidedly mixed feelings. The horse concerned was British Smelter, a novice bought principally for Evelyn Anthony but in which a minority holding was owned by an oil executive who, it seemed to Gay, was interested not so much in the horse but in how much cash it could generate in the shortest possible time.

For his first run ever, British Smelter was entered in the Panama Cigar Hurdle and, because Bill Shoemark was otherwise engaged, he was to be ridden by a young Irish claiming rider who had been working for Gay since September. Nothing was expected of the horse – especially as he was up against a goodish field, including the Queen Mother's Sunyboy. The jockey's instructions were not to push the novice in any way which might result in his becoming sour; on the contrary, British Smelter was to be given every opportunity to enjoy the experience to the full.

Evelyn Anthony was very excited by the prospect of watching her new acquisition make his debut and was at the meeting with her husband, Michael Ward-Thomas. Ward-Thomas told Gay that the co-owner had telephoned from Paris to ask him to put £10 each-way on the horse if there was any chance of him coming close. Gay counselled so strongly against this complete waste of money that the bet was not placed. He had reckoned without the application of Sod's Law. British Smelter, leaving the remainder of the field for dead at the last bend, came roaring in five lengths clear.

The next morning the telephone rang in Gay's office. The oil man, still in his hotel in Paris, offered no congratulations, made no enquiries as to the well-being of the horse. 'Did you get my money on?' was his first and only question. Gay said no, explaining that there had been no reasonable chance of British Smelter being placed, let alone winning. Had there been, he himself would have been first to the bookmakers. The telephone exploded in a welter of expletives lasting a full five minutes and forcing Gay to hold the handset some distance from his ear. It was as well, he reflected when at last the line went dead, that the man had not known that although the official starting price was 33 to 1, the Tote, on which Ward-Thomas would have placed the bet, had paid a staggering 80 to 1; the winnings would have amounted to nearly £1,000!

Having to cope with the miserable owner was the lesser of the two matters on Gay's mind. The other he was anxious to deal with swiftly. He had been far from satisfied with his rider's account of how the race had been run and was still completely mystified. How could that green young horse have won so easily, particularly in the face of his pre-race instructions to the rider? He himself had been unable to pick out any incident which had yielded a clue and, as the mobile patrol camera had yet to come into general service, he would have to rely on eye-witnesses for an objective account. They were not slow to volunteer information; one jockey summed up the general view: 'As we went in to the last bend, he picked up his shillelagh and knocked shit out of your animal, Guv'nor.'

The racing correspondents, like the trainer, had not spotted the rider's actions and their columns were full of praise for his unexpected success. Gay, in possession of the facts, did not share their admiration; not only had his orders been ignored, there had clearly been at best a case of undue use of the whip. Called to account in a notably one-sided interview, the young man left his employer's office, ears ringing with a warning that should there be anything approaching a recurrence their association would be severed. A week later he was given a ride at Windsor by another trainer. Forming the erroneous impression that his mount was lazy, he beat it until it bled; the trainer was forced to call a vet and was almost incoherent as he rang Gay to complain. Gay was enraged to such a degree that he was barely able to restrain himself from physically assaulting the miscreant. Instead he managed to confine himself to assuring the man that his riding career was over. So indeed it proved.

By the end of 1974 the Kindersleys were forced to face up to the fact that, without an almost immediate narrowing of the gap between expenditure and income, the party was coming to an end. The trustees were unsympathetic, pointing out that while the children were well provided for (with funds outside the control of their parents), the same comfortable arrangement no longer applied to Gay and Magsie. While they would be unlikely to starve, horns would need to be drawn in almost to the point of disappearance. Gay, still certain that he could train successfully (had he not made an exceptional start?), cast desperately around for ideas. None was forthcoming but at this nadir of his hopes, fate took a hand in the unlikely shape of Alan Hopkins, a manufacturer of lavatory paper and a neighbour in the valley. Hopkins, unaware that he was about to set in train a chain of events with far-reaching consequences, leaned happily against the fireplace at Parsonage and expounded at length on the advantages of living and working in France. He gave it as his considered opinion that such a move would suit the Kindersleys well. Should they migrate across the Channel, they would benefit hugely – and not just Gay and Magsie, the children too. The tax laws could, he said, have been designed for a family in their circumstances and, of course, France was a lovely place to be. There must be something that Gay could do there. What about training? Not many jumpers perhaps but the competition would be less than hot. 'Think about it.' Hopkins levered himself upright, downed the remnants of his whiskey and went home.

Magsie's eyes had begun to gleam excitedly as she listened to this recital; now she sat still, trying hard to recall exactly what Hopkins had said. It had all sounded marvellous, especially the tax bit and the way the children would be helped. Gay, despite himself, was also impressed by the rosy financial picture that the man's words had conjured up. Parsonage could be sold – no doubt at a handsome profit; the overdrafts could be paid off and the trustees persuaded to roll the money over into a suitable establishment in France. A completely fresh start was surely within reach? He thought for a little longer, prompted by his already eager wife. The tax benefits would certainly attract the trustees – Oonagh had, after all, gone to La Tourelle partly at their behest. Perhaps they could be persuaded to provide a small base in England? The family would need one with the children still at school. And then the training; surely the French racing authorities would welcome him with open arms? He must sound out his friends in the Fegentri. There shouldn't be a problem.

In an astonishingly short space of time the scheme, conceived so casually – almost in passing – was gathering momentum. The trustees, as forecast, were supportive; property prices in France were very much lower than in England and

Parsonage, with its 1,300 acres, was a prime asset. Earmarked as the future Kindersley home in England was Mabberleys, a cottage with a small yard bought in the late 1960s by the trustees as a safeguard against encroachment and only a stone's throw from the Parsonage stables; the house had a tenant but the lease was short. Events moved so quickly that by April Magsie had been dispatched to France with Tania to establish the necessary residential qualification, making her home temporarily at La Tourelle. Gay remained in England to wind down the training operation and, at the same time, began to sound out the contacts who might be able to find him a suitable property across the Channel. It all seemed too easy; too good to be true. And, sure enough, it was.

The first tentative gropings towards a change of heart came as Gay achieved a greater number of winners than, at Christmas, had seemed possible – by the end of that second season he had twenty-four, a slight improvement on the year before. The press, which as yet had no inkling of his plans, continued to write up his chances of joining the cream of national hunt trainers in increasingly extravagant terms. His owners, notably Stratton Smith and Evelyn Anthony, were making buying noises – Miss Anthony had been so encouraged by her Silver Falcon's win at Worcester that she named a novel after him. Others seemed to be waiting in the wings. Never had his prospects seemed so buoyant. Gay began to believe that he could hardly fail.

Quite the opposite seemed to be the case as he examined more carefully the possibilities open to him in France. To a man, his racing friends there were pessimistic. To obtain a jumping licence, they informed him, was difficult enough for a Frenchman; for a foreigner – pouf. They shrugged their shoulders. Maybe, after a long wait and suitably correct impressions had been made on those in authority. But maybe not. Who knows?

This was far from the welcoming embrace he had naïvely supposed would await him. There was little point in his going if he couldn't train. Perhaps France was not such a panacea; there were after all many pleasing inducements to stay in England, particularly now that Magsie was safely ensconced with Oonagh – a situation that gave him an unusually wide-ranging pink ticket. Chief among his distractions as he struggled to make up his mind was Philippa Harper.

He had not forgotten her in the year that she had been in America. Shortly after his wife's departure he telephoned her home at Coldharbour to ask her to come to Plumpton Races. Philippa, who remembered vaguely that she had not been too impressed at their first meeting, said that she was sorry but she had to wait in all day for a vet who was coming to see one of her horses. Gay, too old and determined a campaigner to accept this excuse at face value, rang again a couple of hours later, hoping to get Peggy – who he had sensed would be an ally. He was lucky: 'Of course Philippa can come racing; the vet's here now. I'll tell her to meet you at the petrol station near the course.'

Her daughter was furious; not only did she not particularly want to go racing with an older man whose private life she hardly knew anything about (except that he was married to a rather fierce wife) but it was pouring with rain and Plumpton was not noted for the spaciousness of its covered accommodation. Short of being horribly ill-mannered, however, there appeared to be little alternative. She would be unable to contact him – he would have left Lambourn some time before. Crossly she climbed into her car and drove to the rendezvous. As she approached the garage she saw him, a forlorn figure standing in the teeming rain with a river of water running off his trilby hat and down his face; he was soaked. 'How pathetic,' she thought. 'The idiot.' Her heart gave a lurch. The anger evaporated and she fell immediately – and irretrievably – in love.

They had a funny, happy day and he asked her to have dinner with him. As Peggy had already arranged a supper party that evening, Philippa explained that she really couldn't let her mother down but, seeing his crestfallen expression, said that he could come too if he liked. After dinner, when the guests had left and Peggy had gone to bed, they sat alone at the drawing-room fire making tentative plans for another meeting, sleepily content in each other's company. This peaceful idyll was interrupted noisily as the door crashed open and, wearing only a bath-robe, in strode the bulky figure of actor Oliver Reed. He was not pleased with the scene that now presented itself.

For some time Reed, who lived in considerable style only a few hundred yards from the Harper cottage, had been conducting an affair with Philippa. Since her return to England she had found it difficult to define for herself a continuing role in his life in any way that gave her satisfaction. Accordingly she had decided to end the relationship. Reed, unwilling to let go, had watched the evening's party breaking up and, when he thought the coast was clear, had arrived with the intention of patching things up. Once introduced, the two men sat on either side of the room, mentally circling one another like cautious prize-fighters. Philippa sat between them, wondering how she could sensibly put an end to the evening as the stilted small-talk began to dry up. Her Alsatian puppy Athos, a present from Reed to celebrate his success in *The Three Musketeers* (he had taken Philippa to the première in Paris) lay snoring gently on the hearth. Abruptly the actor, tiring of impressing on the interloper that he had a prior claim to their hostess, rose, woke the dog and began to put him through a series of pointless obedience exercises. The puppy, still half-asleep, was unreceptive. Half-heartedly, and probably only for dramatic effect, Reed kicked it. Philippa, outraged, saw her chance. 'Out, you,' she ordered, propelling the protesting actor through the door. She turned to Gay. 'Stay if you want to, but I'm going to bed.'

Despite Reed's unsolicited but constant advice that Philippa was making a grave mistake and his plaintive cries that he couldn't understand what she saw in Kindersley, the affair rapidly accelerated. The lovers saw each other practically every day, taking turns to drive between Coldharbour and East Garston. For the sake of the children, they both felt that Philippa could not be seen to be staying at Parsonage (even then she once had to hide in a cupboard to avoid being seen by Catheryn) and so Gay borrowed a nearby cottage. As the relationship intensified, his already shaky resolve to sell and begin a new life in France dissolved. He came to realise as the weeks passed that he could not go back to living with Magsie. Circumstances had changed irrevocably; the grass, always apparently greener on the other side, had now not only been tasted but had made a considerable meal. He liked it; he liked it a lot.

The first problem to be faced – that of how he should break the news to his family – was taken out of his hands. In June he went to France to see Magsie, ostensibly to continue his search for a training establishment. He tried several times to embark on the discussion that, after over nineteen years of marriage, would end their life together but, somehow, the moment never seemed to present itself. The eagerness with which he had confessed his affairs with Ann Queensberry and Shirley Abicair (perhaps because he had always known that they were not as decisive as he had dramatised them to be at the time) had deserted him. The more he put it off, the more difficult it became to steel himself. In the event he was not to be put to the final test because Magsie, as she transferred the contents of his wallet to a new one she had bought for his birthday, found Philippa's name and telephone number. The name, at least, rang an ominous bell.

The row that followed was shrill in volume and tediously circular in form. Gay, confronted to begin with by evidence of what Magsie had taken for a casual affair, upped the ante and said it was more serious than she thought and that he wanted a divorce. Magsie pointed out that she was living in France not for her health but for the better future of the Kindersley family, especially the children. How could he think of throwing it all away? He must be mad. He said he knew all that but he just couldn't go on. Gradually the truth about Philippa emerged and the arguments went round and round until, at 3 in the morning, Magsie rang the number on the piece of paper she still clutched fiercely in her hand.

'This is the international operator. I have a person-to-person call for a Miss Philippa Harper from Mr Gay Kindersley. Is that Miss Harper?'

The actress in Magsie triumphed over her emotional turmoil, her voice rock-steady as she imitated the metallic tones. Philippa, struggling out of a deep sleep and not in any condition to be on her guard, reacted drowsily.

'Oh yes, thank you. Put him through. Hullo, darling, I miss you.'

There was a short silence and then Gay spoke: 'Philippa, that was Magsie. She wants to talk to you.'

This nasty little bombshell would have been difficult enough to cope with for someone in full possession of their faculties. In her sleepiness, Philippa thought at first that she was having a nightmare. The one-sided conversation that followed – from which she gathered that she was being summoned to Parsonage for some sort of conference – convinced her that the reality was likely to be worse. Long after the phone went down she lay awake, wondering apprehensively about the future.

Magsie had no doubts about her own course of action. From the moment she terminated the call and looked at the miserable Gay, she abandoned with only the slightest pang of regret all thoughts of the legal restrictions and monetary advantages that kept her abroad and, with them, the family's future in a tax haven. Instead she prepared to fight for her own and her children's way of life. The gloves, she mused grimly as she turned her back on the husband for whom she was going into battle, were off. She had won before; she would win again.

This time, however, Gay had made up his mind. Magsie, pleading for more time, extracted from the lovers a promise that they would not see each other for three months as she and Gay lived together again at Parsonage, hiding the true situation from the children as best they could. But the charade could not continue; the rows were constant and sometimes even violent. One night Magsie made her increasingly desperate husband go to bed in a spare room and then changed her mind, ordering him to come out and sleep with her. When he refused and locked his door, she tried to break it down with an oak chair. Gay had had enough. Knotting sheets together in the approved manner of an escaping prisoner, he left the house through a window and drove to Coldharbour.

The children were now told that their parents were to be divorced. Having been largely protected from marital strife by the commendable efforts not to quarrel openly, they found the situation hard to comprehend. Robin, 19, and Tania, still at day-school, appeared to their parents to take the news philosophically. In fact both were so shocked that they were hardly able to understand their feelings, still less give expression to them. Catheryn and Kim were more obviously distraught; both blamed their father entirely for breaking up what they had always serenely believed to be a happy and united family. Kim, in particular, could not begin to accept that Gay had behaved in any way honourably. A little later, at a most unfortunately conceived family lunch also attended by Philippa and Anthony Johnson (a Lambourn trainer who himself was in the middle of a divorce and on whose willing shoulders Magsie had taken to unburdening herself), it became obvious that Philippa, too, was being held by the children to blame.

Magsie, having lost the war – she would always believe that had she not gone to France she would have been able to save her marriage – now set out to limit the damage. She secured for herself a generous settlement (Gay was so keen to finalise affairs and get on with the rest of his life that he would have agreed to almost any demand), but her main concern was for the children. She and they – and especially the financially aware Catheryn – had realised that should Gay and Philippa have children of their own then the Guinness trusts set up for Robin, Catheryn, Kim and Tania would be diminished proportionately. She met Gay and tried in vain (her own recollection is that she actually succeeded) to extract a promise from him that he would have no more children. Whatever the true nature of that negotiation over lunch in the Savoy Hotel, she was not to have her way.

In the autumn of 1975 Gay and Philippa moved into a house in Aldbourne, a village between East Garston and Marlborough. He continued to train from the stables at Parsonage and planned to move into Mabberleys as soon as the sitting tenant could be persuaded to leave. Life was not easy; sympathy in the Lambourn valley lay almost entirely with Magsie. A popular view was voiced by the nudge-nudge, wink-wink brigade as they knowingly prophesied that Gay would soon return to the fold: 'He's only after her tits,' they declared. But there was a considerably more substantive opposition too; even the most loyal of his friends made it clear that they disapproved. Frank Mahon told Philippa that the best thing she could do was to 'put on your hat and coat and go back from where you came'. Mahon was certain that no one would ever forgive her for displacing Magsie and his words – easily construed as malice from a lesser man – were meant genuinely to suggest a way of putting an end to the general unhappiness. His advice was ignored and, in a surprisingly short period of time, Mahon – as he was the first to acknowledge – was to be proved comprehensively wrong.

Magsie, living alone in the home she had created at Parsonage, was seeing Gay on an almost daily basis, often giving him breakfast after he came back from supervising the first lot on the gallops. She was, however, now spending more and more time with Anthony Johnson and finally married him in June 1976. They stayed in Lambourn for four further years until Johnson finally gave up training and the couple moved to Barbados.

In September Gay and Philippa were able to take possession of Mabberleys. After a little dithering over dates, they decided to marry in October, gaining no more than the guarded acceptance of the children who, despite their mother's remarriage, still could not approve of another woman in her place. In contrast, Philip's letter to Gay after the divorce barely concealed his euphoria:

Dearest Ghazi

I gather that your divorce is through and you are preparing for another visit to the register office. The first thing to say is that I pray and hope that you will be happy – that is all that matters. No more 'emotional disturbances' as the Queen Mum says! I know you have had a very rough and unhappy time – alas I was sure it would be that way – but your Mum whipped you off to the register office because I was against it! However that is past history and it is no use crying over spilt milk. You have known Philippa for about two years and you must know your own mind by now!!

I have hardly met Philippa but everyone tells me she is very nice. You seem to get on well and at least you will have a happy time and peace of mind. Valsie and I wish you both every happiness and you know we would always love to see you both.

I feel you have been too generous to Magsie in view of her behaviour. She was always after the cash ... I would never interfere but in my opinion the ideal solution would be for the Trustees to sell Parsonage, stables, land and all, and buy another place further away. It must be awful, living in the same village ...

... Let me know when you are going to be married (last time only the *Evening Standard* told me!) and remember you have all our loving best wishes.

Love to you both,
Dad

It is sadly clear from this that, even after nearly twenty years, Philip had neither forgiven Oonagh for aiding and abetting Gay's first marriage nor lost his suspicion – first formed at that disastrous lunch party with the Wakefields at Hullers – that Magsie (and her family) had, all along, been in it solely for the money. Despite the perhaps overcharitable divorce settlement, this remains a simplistic distortion of the truth. Profligate as Magsie may have been, she was certainly no more so than her husband and – her love affair apart – she had steadfastly provided him with the unstinting support and loyalty he could not have survived without during either his racing career or his flamboyant and unconventional social life. Philip's verdict was a less-than-generous postscript to her contribution to the Kindersley family.

It was to take many years for the children to accept the new form their lives were having to take; indeed some may not have ever quite done so. There are letters, however, from Catheryn which indicate that at least she – at first the most emotionally disturbed by Gay's decision – might have come to forgive her father:

... I would like to make it up to Philippa out of the pressures of Berkshire. I now have a lovely feeling that everything will be alright; it is a cruel world but I know I can cope with it. I love you my darling Daddy so much ...

On 7 October 1976 Gay Kindersley and Philippa Harper were married at Epsom Register Office.

CHAPTER NINE

Parting with Parsonage

T he number of guests at the church blessing which followed the civil ceremony was hardly greater than the select few who had attended the muted celebrations at Caxton Hall twenty years before. Philip and Valsie were not able to come but this time they had at least been invited. Oonagh had arrived from La Tourelle and she and Peggy seemed equally content at the turn of events. In the church Marco Marshall, the best man, found himself reflecting on the number of times during the last two decades and more that he and his wife had provided spurious alibis as Gay pursued the Flying Fornicator and the many other passing fancies that had been his meat and drink. He wondered whether this new Mrs Kindersley would try to change her husband's compulsion for the chase and concluded that, even if she did, it was probably beyond the powers of any mortal being to put a stop to it. His reveries were brought abruptly to an end as Oliver Reed marched in, accompanied by a number of the minders and drinking companions he always described as his 'gardeners'. Reed, an often well-mannered man where women were concerned (he never swore in their presence), had found it difficult to come to terms with the notion that he had lost Philippa to a married, balding, older man with little – he thought – to commend him except perhaps a passably decent record as a jockey. The actor did his best to behave at the subsequent reception but inevitably the drink caused him to lose his always precarious self-control. As he prepared to leave, he leaned across the table, his head thrust between the bride and groom, his face contorted. 'I hope you both rot in hell,' he said.

From the time he had first met Gay, Reed's close but uneasy friendship with the Kindersleys was shot through with a strong undercurrent of conflict with the man he regarded as having stolen Philippa from him. Although he was to become a godfather to their younger son Oliver, the unaccustomed loss of a battle for a woman rankled obsessively. Years later, after becoming markedly overrefreshed at Newbury Races, he turned up naked outside Mabberleys on a cold November night. It was Philippa's birthday and he had experienced a little trouble finding the right house, startling a number of stable lads (male and female) in the neighbouring yard as he asked directions. When he finally found the right front door ('As it's your birthday, I've come in my birthday suit') the dramatic effect he desired was first deflated by young Rory Kindersley calling to his mother in a most matter-of-fact voice to say there was a funny man on the door-step without any clothes, and then by Philippa (not even bothering to investigate) responding from the kitchen, 'Oh, it must be you, Oliver. Aren't you cold? Why don't you put a coat on?' The point of the exercise was even further buried when Reed discovered that Gay was away and not able to take the hoped-for exception to his presence. At another time he picked a quarrel by accusing Gay of putting a hand up his girl-friend's skirt in the back of a car (this time he may well have been on firmer ground!) and made Philippa, who was driving, stop so that they could have a fight in the road. Both would-be pugilists were so drunk that they could hardly identify their targets, let alone land a blow, and the women were able to calm Reed down. *In vino*, the imagined *veritas* of the actor's humiliation at the hands of an older man always asserted itself.

For Gay, Mabberleys with its water-meadows and its sweeping views down the valley was the perfect home. The little flint-stone house had four bedrooms and no pretensions. There, his two new sons, Rory born in 1977 and Oliver in 1980, spent happy formative years in close proximity with their parents and with loyalties unmuddled by temporary attachments to transient nannies. There were occasional au pairs (off whom Gay found it relatively easy to keep his hands) but the intimate atmosphere – so different from the upstairs, downstairs routine fostered by Magsie at Parsonage – was something he came to cherish. This happy family scene was completed by Athos who, living up to the very highest standards of loyalty for which his breed is known, saved Rory's life when the 18-month-old child toddled off to see the ducks and fell into the stream which flowed through Mabberley's garden. Athos plunged after him, first nudging Rory to the bank and then keeping his head out of the water with his nose until Philippa arrived to complete the rescue.

As Philip had forecast, life was not entirely agreeable while living in the shadow of the Johnsons, particularly during the time that Magsie was still at Parsonage. But slowly, almost unconsciously, Gay's Lambourn friends lost their resentment of Philippa and the slate was wiped clean. When Magsie finally left, the trustees let Parsonage to a Canadian film magnate who stayed for five years, being replaced by a plastic surgeon. Both tenants and their wives enjoyed being surrounded by a working farm and loved being part of the atmosphere of the busy training yard down the hill; both were generous enough to allow the Kindersleys the use of the pool and the tennis court – a privilege that was keenly appreciated.

Life with Philippa could hardly have been a greater contrast to the state of intermittent and too often bitter conflict that had been the pattern during the last few years of marriage to Magsie. Philippa saw clearly that, as far as other women were concerned, Gay would remain incorrigibly footloose. She had convinced herself that the driving motivation during his affairs was the thrill of the chase, sexual gratification, if any, coming a distant second. As a result she was relaxed about his activities, satisfied in the knowledge that his love for her was in no measure diminished by them. As for his more endearing qualities, she not only loved her romantic, dashing husband but respected him for his kindness, his generosity and the determination he always showed in following a chosen path, however haphazard or tortuous the route. In his company she was content; apart from him she felt somehow incomplete. Her sympathetic understanding of Gay led to a marriage that some would come (inaccurately) to describe as 'open' but which, in fact, was based on a mutual regard and a remarkable trust – a trust that was to be put to some outlandishly severe tests. The trip to Thailand for example.

Accompanied by two men friends, Gay decided that he was off to explore Bangkok. It may be assumed that their itinerary was unlikely to be confined to Buddhist temples and Gay, whose fellow clients of the London salon known as the Wigmore Club had briefed him extensively, was looking forward to it with an anticipatory glee he found hard to conceal. Philippa, knowing what to expect, arranged for certain precautionary measures to be put into effect on his return. When she was invited suddenly by friends to spend some time on a boat in the Mediterranean, she telexed Gay to explain: 'Have booked you an appointment at the clinic in Swindon; suggest you keep it! Gone to France with Colin. See you a week on Friday.'

On his return from Thailand (which had lived up to, if not exceeded, his expectations) Gay dutifully clocked in at the doctor's and after forty-eight hours – the age of miracles being apparently not yet past – received a clean bill of health. A few days later he drove to Gatwick to meet Philippa and so pleased were they at their reunion that they made love in the car on the way home. This premature physical expression of a mutual need turned out to be a mistake. At the house there was a message asking Gay to contact the clinic urgently; there had, after all, been no divine intervention, just an administrative error. He had contracted non-specific urethritis; would he please come and collect a month's supply of tablets? He was the lucky one – the preventive course on which poor Philippa now had to embark lasted a full three months.

The joy and laughter which had come into his life and which gave rise to a well-founded optimism that the Kindersleys were set for a long and contented marriage was sadly not mirrored by events on the training scene. The 1975–76 season produced only eleven winners and, worse, Gay's most generous owner, the fun-loving Tony Stratton Smith, had deserted him at the time of his final rift from Magsie. This was not a coincidence – even Gay's most ardent supporters felt that he could hardly be giving his full attention to training whilst conducting a long-distance courtship on the one hand and a most acrimonious divorce on the other. He failed to attract any significant replacements, having no time himself to devote to recruiting and little cash with which to buy the horses which might have brought prospective benefactors flocking to his gates. Sidney Carton had broken down – soon to become the first horse to have a successful carbon implant operation on his legs – and the classy British Smelter was ruined when Gay succumbed to the clamourings of the mercenary part-owner and ran the horse for twelve months (in England and in Ireland) without a proper break.

Matters did not improve. The next three seasons produced only eighteen winners between them – nearly all from horses which Gay himself wholly owned or in which he had a substantial share. In early 1978 he engaged a public relations consultant to produce a brochure – *First in the Budget Stakes* – which was aimed at the corporate market, compellingly extolling the benefits of company and syndicate ownership and asking those who were interested to come to lunch at Mabberleys to discuss the matter further. Several hundred expensive booklets and a score of free lunches later, no new owners had been persuaded to invest, although Tony Stratton Smith made a welcome return to the fold – immediately striking up with Philippa the same easy friendship that he had enjoyed with Magsie. The marketing experiment was repeated two years later, this time with a greater emphasis on the *Team at Parsonage* (now led by a new head lad, Ian Cocks) but still directed principally at the corporate market. The invitations to lunch had been dropped but the photographs were glossy and the prose even more beguiling. The changes made no difference; there was no significant response.

The doldrums in the yard were punctuated by blasts of outright misfortune. Sidney Carton, having won a race on his new legs, broke down again, this time irretrievably. The promising Migrator, bought in Ireland, burst a blood vessel so severely that it was thought prudent to sell him on at a considerable loss to a West Country trainer for whom he subsequently never stopped winning. The Drunken Duck, a successful hunter chaser in the ownership of amateur rider Brod Munro Wilson, was first bought by Gay who then weakly capitulated to Wilson's promises that if he was allowed to buy it at the (very modest) price Gay paid for it, he, Wilson, would send Gay two horses to train. Only one was any good – Ramblix, who ran in the Norwegian Grand National – but he was not an amateur's ride and every time his owner was put up there was some sort of disaster, resulting eventually in a terminal row and the severing of the partnership.

Shortly after this unhappy sequence Gay made his first and only appearance at Portman Square in front of the disciplinary committee of the Jockey Club – although it was not unknown for him to be interviewed by local stewards over minor breaches of the rules. The Jockey Club on this occasion, however, wished to discuss a weightier matter, the subject being Ballynaclough, a calamity of a novice chaser that Gay had somehow been able to pass on into the ownership of a syndicate managed by four trustees. Having a lunchtime drink in the Queen's Arms, Gay was told that there was a rumour that Ballynaclough's senior owner had taken a fatal forward step while having an after-dinner pee on the edge of the cliff which formed the boundary of his garden. Gay was put in an immediate quandary. It was against the rules to run a horse owned in this way until legal steps had been taken to register a new trustee to replace the deceased – if in fact he had died. This procedure was likely to take a week or two and the horse was engaged to run at Nottingham within forty-eight hours. What was more, it was to be a two-horse race and the trainer of Ballynaclough's opponent had already telephoned to suggest that Gay should withdraw so that, with the minimum of effort, they could share the first-place prize money. Gay had refused; the other trainer obviously thought that his own horse would be beaten and Parsonage badly needed a winner. He decided to take a chance which, in complete accord with his current run of luck, did not pay off. Ballynaclough, although clear favourite, failed miserably and shortly afterwards Weatherbys caught up with the ownership irregularities; the trustee had indeed died. Gay, despite claiming not unreasonably that he could hardly be expected to act on a pub rumour, was fined £150 and warned as to his future conduct. In pleading his case, he had not advanced his cause by consistently forgetting the names of the members of the syndicate – including that of the deceased! He had always found it difficult to remember names, a Kindersley family failing which had manifested itself most startlingly in his paternal grandfather, who once forgot his own name when buying shirts in Jermyn Street, and being obliged to ask his chauffeur to remind him.

Oonagh, who by this time had reverted to calling herself Oonagh, Lady Oranmore and Browne, was – like her son – feeling the uncomfortable effects of depleted resources. Her own trustees had advised her that she could no longer afford to maintain La Tourelle and she had briefly flirted with a house in Switzerland before shipping her extensive household to Bermuda, a more advantageous tax haven than any to be found in Europe. She was never at ease on the island and when, after barely a year, she begun to suspect that Desmond (now aged 17) was falling into bad company, she moved again. Once more the furniture, the silver and the pictures were packed, this time for Guernsey and the beginning of a thirteen-year period of unhappy isolation during which she struggled to cope with the pressures of bringing up the four teenagers in her care. It particularly saddened her that she had now been largely deserted by the literary lions and show-business glitterati who had once been only too pleased to eat, drink and be entertained in the most sumptuous style at Luggala and Cap d'Antibes. She was sustained through these dark days by Greta Fanning, who faithfully remained to share the burden, but Patrick Cummins was now getting old and had plainly had his fill of foreign parts. He retired to his home in Mallow, occasionally visiting Guernsey and clucking sorrowfully over the gloomy dungeon of a house which Oonagh rarely left and from which she clearly longed to escape.

The fact that his training losses had placed Gay on a financial knife-edge was kept well hidden from the outside world and the full extent of his predicament was not fully appreciated, even by Philippa. He never discussed money – pushing the tedious implications to the back of his mind – but there were occasional incidents which brought the reality disagreeably to life. In 1980 in the Grosvenor House Hotel at a charity boxing evening in aid of a jockey paralysed by a fall, Gay so forgot himself in his enthusiasm to maximise the financial benefits for the stricken rider that he began to bid up a bronze statue being auctioned by the racing journalist Brough Scott. Predictably his critical judgement had been more than a little impaired by a cocktail or two, and he found that he had bought the piece for £1,500 – an amount he knew would be entirely beyond both the generosity and the inclination of his bank manager. As he collected the handsome statue from Scott ('Great man, Gay, well done') amidst approving applause, he sobered up enough to be able to ask the auctioneer in an undertone for the identity of the under-bidder. This was readily forthcoming and the next morning on the telephone he was able to unload his purchase for a net loss of only £300.

A much more pleasing aspect of that year was the marriage of Catheryn to Robert Millbourn, a businessman who mightily impressed his future father-in-law by telephoning from New York to ask formally for her hand. The wedding – and Catheryn's infectious joy – did much to restore his morale to the state of euphoric optimism which was its natural habitat and this was reinforced as he caught once more a whiff of the sweet smell of racing success when Boreen Daw (bought for Tony Stratton Smith) won a number of races over the next two years and went on to come second in the 1983 Arkle Chase at Cheltenham. In that season, Kindersley-trained horses won over £14,000, more than double the amount achieved in any of the previous eight years, and the credit lines to bookmakers were reopened with a vengeance. But in hard financial terms Boreen Daw and his stable companions provided only a relatively small alleviation of the deep-seated problem. What was needed was one truly class horse, one that could be turned into a household name. In August 1982 he came within a whisker of realising this, every small trainer's recurring dream.

At Saratoga, in the United States, he met an influential member of the

Maktoum family's entourage with whom he struck up an immediate rapport. The Arab said that he would like to get into national hunt racing and asked Gay to meet him at the Dublin Sales a little later in the year to choose one – perhaps even two – suitable horses. Gay took this commission extremely seriously, doing extensive research among his Irish contacts, and eventually found perhaps the most promising animal he had ever seen and certainly one that neither he nor his other owners would ordinarily be able to afford. At the sales they met as arranged and he was pointing out to his potential customer the advantages of buying this exciting prospect – explaining that the horse would cost around £50,000 and was likely to be worth every penny – when an English legal adviser to the Maktoums stepped in bossily and said: 'No, no. You can't ask him to pay that much; not for his first go at ownership. Why not start him off with a nice young horse at say a third of the price?' Gay was appalled, but the damage was done; the Arab took this unsought advice and the deal was off. In the event Lambourn trainer Nicky Henderson made the purchase; the horse was See You Then and he went on to win the Champion Hurdle three times in a row.

Gay found that, with one or two notable exceptions, dealing with his owners could be frustrating. Like most trainers in his position he was – to an extent that was sometimes barely tolerable – a slave to the most unreasonable of whims. The bigger (or richer) trainer is in the happy position of being able to tell difficult owners to take their horses elsewhere. Gay, not able to afford that freedom, was sometimes forced at an owner's behest to take decisions that did little to enhance his professional reputation – his treatment of British Smelter being an unfortunate case in point. Another concerned Orange Reef (son of Mill Reef), who Gay insisted would only act at his best on soft ground but was required for reasons of owner prestige to run on the firm at Cheltenham. There, not surprisingly, he failed to make an impression in the Triumph Hurdle and was entered again – so that the owners could enjoy another jolly day out – at Ascot on similar going, where he finally broke down.

Owners' idiosyncrasies did not always lead to such disastrous outcomes. Imperatives varied widely; the London Irish millionaire builder Pat Fahey, for example, was in the game to indulge more closely his passion for betting. He travelled to meetings in a gold-coloured Rolls-Royce and was incurably inclined to issue strict but often self-contradictory riding instructions to the jockey engaged to ride his sometimes indifferent animals. For failing to obey his orders to the letter he had taken against an excellent schooler of horses whom Gay employed for a while as a stable jockey, and insisted that his animal Pieroth should henceforth be ridden by Colin Brown – later to be the great Desert Orchid's first pilot and, after retirement from the saddle, the landlord of the Ibex Inn at Chaddleworth, home of the Lambourn Valley Monday Club. Unlike the unfortunate Orange Reef, Pieroth hated soft going but he had been entered for a race at Ludlow and the owner had reluctantly agreed to be present. The period of continuous rain which preceded the meeting resulted in as dark and muddy a day as Gay had ever experienced and seeing no realistic chance of a win in the conditions, he advised the owner not to have too outrageous a bet. Fahey was furious; in the first place he disliked being so far away from London, secondly the car had bogged down hopelessly in the car park and he had been obliged to walk a lot further than he would have chosen, turning his patent leather shoes into canoes of clay. Now this.

'If you think I've come all the way to this God-forsaken hole and not have a decent bet, Gay, you can think again. The bloody race is only worth 250 quid. It won't even pay the bloody petrol.'

He turned away crossly to find himself looking into the grinning face of Dodger McCartney, part-time manufacturer of Venetian blinds and full-time national hunt punter. Dodger had his own views on the probable winner but was quite prepared to help Fahey lose a packet if that was likely to make the day more fun. As the horses left the paddock (with Gay trying to make sure that Brown understood he was to ignore completely the instructions given to him by the owner), Fahey set off to find a public telephone down which, despite his trainer's advice, he intended to issue a significant directive to his bookmaker. Ludlow boasted only one working phone-box and there was a lengthy line of people waiting to use it.

McCartney acted decisively, sweeping the queue aside. 'Mr Fahey here has to make an emergency call,' he announced, handing the phone to the Irishman. Pausing only to hear £2,000 being placed on Pieroth, he rushed back to the ring, where he was delighted to see that the odds on his own fancy had eased a little. He placed his bets and hurried to the stand. This time he had comprehensively wasted his money; Pieroth, fighting gallantly through the mud, confounded both Dodger and the Parsonage pundits, winning by a neck and leaving the principals in this little episode to display widely differing emotions. Fahey went home grumbling that had Brown ridden to his instructions, the margin would have been wider; Gay sighed and wished fervently that he'd had a bet himself; while Dodger briefly contemplated suicide.

In May 1983 Gay set out once more on the road to the Grand National – the race that, despite the unhappy memories it held for him, continued to exercise an irresistible magnetism. At the Ascot Sales he bought Earthstopper, a 9-year-old chestnut gelding previously owned and ridden by the American amateur George Sloan. The horse – big, active and well bred – cost 22,000 guineas but had considerably more than mere promise to offer, having, for example, won the Mandarin Chase at Newbury in the previous season, beating a high-class field including Venture to Cognac. With no difficulty Gay found four owners keen to share this investment; half went to Chelle Wright, the

American wife of the English head of Chrysalis Records (record company bosses seemed attracted to Gay) and the remainder was split between three young businessmen.

Earthstopper summered well and Ivor Herbert, writing for the *Mail on Sunday*, persuaded the paper to allow him to report on the training of the horse right through to Aintree, giving his readers regular accounts of progress and, on their behalf, placing a £100 each-way bet – the proceeds to go to charities nominated by Gay. As winter approached and preparations began in earnest, every move was written up with sympathetic and knowledgeable interest. Earthstopper had particularly difficult feet and their treatment – as well as every other aspect of the care lavished on him – was followed closely by readers as all the connexions – including the new head lad Joe Kavanagh and Earthstopper's own lad, Des Paddock – were interviewed extensively. Details of the horse's daily routine were published, down even to the number of carrots he consumed at his evening feed. A fortnight before Liverpool Earthstopper cleared his last preliminary hurdle by running a creditable third to Special Cargo in a three-mile chase at Lingfield. He had now become something of a celebrity so that jockeys without a retainer for the National queued up to take the ride. It was eventually awarded to Richard Rowe.

On the great day Earthstopper was on top of his form; his coat gleamed and Des easily took the award for producing the best-turned-out horse. In the paddock, Rowe mounted and immediately felt comfortable. Earthstopper, on his toes, pranced out on to the course, but settled smoothly as they paraded in front of the stands before turning and cantering steadily down to the start. From the first fence horse and jockey gave each other a fantastic ride; they made steady progress until, three fences from home, it looked to those in the stands that they were bound to win. But suddenly and with no detectable warning, Earthstopper slowed perceptibly, before gradually – but with an effort that was evident even to the spectators – picking up gamely but running on to finish only fifth. The connexions were stunned. Gay, at a complete loss to explain the change of pace but suspecting a broken blood vessel, limped rapidly out on to the course (he had developed a troublesome hip) to question Richard Rowe. He was overtaken as Philippa and Des sprinted past. Before he was able to catch them, an Aintree official stopped him. 'Don't go any further, Gay,' the man said gently. 'I'm afraid your horse is dead.' At the autopsy it was established that Earthstopper had ruptured an artery; for the last few agonising furlongs he had struggled on as his lungs filled with blood. The owners, faces drawn with grief and disappointment, gathered in a tea-room. Gay tried to speak, to offer some words of sympathy, even of explanation; he could find nothing that was remotely adequate and instead burst into tears. It was to be his last attempt at the race which had brought him so much sadness.

Gay's battle to keep going at Parsonage and his regular and emotionally draining meetings with trustees and bank managers left him little time for the extra-mural activities that had been such important aspects of his life as a permit holder. He had resigned from the British Institute of Sports Medicine and handed over the secretaryship of the Amateur Riders' Association. His musical evenings, too, were largely things of the past – though he teamed up with John Fisher, a primary school headmaster he had met through Jimmy and Perce, to do the occasional cabaret. The diversions which afforded him the greatest pleasures now were his membership of the Monday Club – the weekly gathering of racing drinkers in the Desert Orchid bar of the Ibex – and his continued membership of the slightly more sophisticated Saints and Sinners. The lunches and dinners of the latter gave him some of his happiest moments as he revelled in the company of the talented and the famous and was pleased, even flattered, to find that they respected him and sought his friendship. It seldom occurred to Gay that he himself had much to offer – he put down his popularity merely to his gossip-column reputation and his Guinness connexions. He was wrong, of course; he had unaffected charm and an appealing lack of side, and it would have been difficult to find a more loyal friend. Some of the members became particularly close to him. Terry Wogan – famous for the easy manner and gentle wit exercised almost daily on radio and television to the delight of millions – took to him instantly. Wogan, a shy, well-mannered, almost painfully correct man, recognised Gay as at least a partially kindred spirit and, above all, someone he could respect – while always declining Gay's eager invitations to join him in a visit to the Wigmore Club. He and his wife Helen came to Mabberleys for family lunches and at first were surprised by the modest size of the house to the extent that Terry took to introducing him as 'my friend Gay Kindersley, the only poor Guinness!'

They got on so well that they took to sharing a table at the dinners organised periodically by the club at which it was possible to invite guests. Gay and Wogan would plan to ask three people each and swap names in advance. So correct in his behaviour and so unwilling to become involved in any public controversy was his friend that Gay found that he had to be surprisingly careful in his choice. He had met 'Bungalow' Bill Wiggins (so called because it was alleged that he had nothing upstairs) at the height of the latter's very public press notoriety in connexion with a well-endowed actress, and proposed to ask him to one such party. He telephoned Wogan to exchange lists.

'I'm having John Francome.'

'Ah, yes. He's a great man, Gay; a great man.'

'And John Oaksey.'

'Ah, good; great man, great man.'

'And Bungalow Bill Wiggins.'

There was a brief but heavy silence.

'Well now,' said Terry at last. 'He's a bit of a chancer, don't you think?'

This was a clear veto – based presumably on Wogan's careful unwillingness to be seen associating, even at a relatively private occasion, with the subject of prurient press interest. Gay capitulated and asked Marco Marshall instead.

As they became closer, Gay felt able to ask the Greatest Living Irishman to the annual Lambourn Cricket Club dinner held, as always, at the Swan at Great Shefford. It was the sort of event that Wogan would, under normal circumstances, have never considered attending and thus rather more than a bit of a coup. Tickets were quickly sold out and then resold at inflated prices. When trainer Paul Cole had to cancel at the last minute because of a summons from the Queen Mother (nothing less imperative would have deflected him), there was a rush to secure his seat. The race was won by Henry Ponsonby, a manager of racing syndicates and keen photographer. He asked Gay whether he might be allowed to take some shots during the dinner – something which the organising committee and the landlord of the Swan had decided against in deference to Wogan's wish to have no publicity. Gay gave guarded and heavily qualified permission that one photograph only could be taken and that only for eventual hanging on the pub wall.

On the night of the event it froze hard and the guest-of-honour arrived at Mabberleys in urgent need of external and internal warmth. Neither was readily forthcoming. Philippa was in hospital and Gay, having been racing all day, came home to find that he had run out of both logs and vodka. He was as embarrassed as Wogan was amused and they agreed to move quickly on to the Swan. The pub was packed – the diners having been joined in the bar by scores of drinkers anxious to see the man himself – and a hush descended of the variety normally reserved for the arrival of a member of the royal family, a notable manifestation of awe in such a hard-bitten and irreverent community. Gay's next concern was to make sure that Terry was not cornered by people who would insist on talking only about horses (not an easy task in the valley) or who, when over-refreshed (not so difficult), would be keen to score points by making worn-out jokes about Irish banks, in one of which Wogan had begun his working life. Frank Mahon came to the rescue and the evening went well, Wogan even taking a turn at the tea-chest bass during the Fisher–Kindersley cabaret.

Two days later in the *Racing Post* Gay was surprised to read an account of the dinner, complete with photographs. Ponsonby had taken the opportunity to make a clear profit on his ticket as well as scooping Steve Taylor of *The Sporting Life*, who had also been present but had respected the rules of the evening. Ponsonby, an otherwise affable man who shared Gay's taste for optimistic punting, was banned from the Swan for two years. He remained a racing and drinking friend and – perhaps in reparation – cut Gay in on an outrageous betting coup on a three-year-old called Alonzo running in a handicap at

Leicester; between them those in the know relieved the bookmakers of a total of £100,000.

In sharp contrast to the elegant dining arrangements of the Saints and Sinners, the staple diet of the members of the Monday Club was contained in either bottles or barrels. The club had been founded by a sporting local vicar, whose only weakness appeared to be a fondness for lunchtime boozing, and the crack was of a nature that would have appealed to the Wogan sense of humour – even if the language was sometimes a little colourful for Radio 2. It had always been a great place for a leg-pull – staffs of successive Tory prime ministers often being puzzled by irreverent motions passed by 'The Lambourn Branch of the Monday Club' – and it was not unknown for Gay, trusting as ever, to be the butt. It was the regulars who persuaded him, soon after he joined the local tennis club, that this innocent village institution was a hot-bed of wife-swapping. Gay, as anticipated, was entranced. This revelation opened up all manner of possibilities; he could hardly wait to be involved. Introduced at a local party to a man who was described to him as an enthusiastic tennis player, he was keen to display his inside information.

'Isn't it great?' he said. 'The tennis club being the centre of a wife-swapping ring. Are you a member?'

'Oh yes,' said the man. 'I'm the chairman. Tell me about it.'

Gay's naïvety made him an affectionately easy prey for the Ibex jokers. He was going through a period of addiction to Irish whiskey when someone asked him what he would like to drink. He turned to the dark-haired and disturbingly attractive barmaid. 'Have you got a Black Bush, Suzanne?' he asked. The Monday Club held its collective breath. Suzanne, unfazed, looked him straight in the eye. 'As a matter of fact, Mr Kindersley, I have,' she said.

The funny side of training was less easy to discern. By 1985 – after a season in which he managed only seven winners (worth about £7,000) – the writing on the wall was ominously clear for those who could bring themselves to read it. But even though he was increasingly in debt, Gay was still determined to believe that something – perhaps someone – would turn up. He began to lease out his horses, an arrangement whereby he retained ownership but the lessees paid the training bills; the prize money, if any, being shared. This compromise is widely regarded as at best a temporary plug in ownership gaps but in Gay's case there was no upturn in fortunes; indeed, the situation worsened in the following year, during which he managed only two winners.

In March 1986 a near-fatal accident to his wife relegated the constant battles with impatient bankers and anxious trustees to the back of his mind. Philippa had taken one of the horses to run in the Grand Military meeting at Sandown while Gay himself went with another to Chepstow. On the return journey she fell asleep on the M4 and the car left the road at speed. She was driving a small

Volkswagen Polo usually used by their au pair and because its seat-belts were filthy and Philippa was wearing a new silk shirt, she had – in an act of omission that was to save her life – not buckled the belt. As the car rolled down the bank, the door flew open and she fell out. Strapped in her seat she would undoubtedly have been killed; as it was she fractured her spine, split her liver and broke both legs, four ribs and her nose.

Gay, on his way back from Chepstow with Jack Denton (Peggy's husband) and a car-load of someone else's owners who were insisting that he should go dog-racing at Oxford, was unaware of the accident. Stopping at the Swan to unload Jack, he then went on to the greyhound track where Peggy eventually traced him. He was called to a phone via the public address system. Leaving his startled companions to their fun, he went by taxi to the hospital in Reading where Philippa lay in intensive care. Paul Cole was there with Peggy, and Gay, able to speak only briefly to his intermittently unconscious wife, stayed the night. It was days before she could be moved safely to the Nuffield Hospital in Oxford and weeks while a series of operations, performed by the surgeon Greg Houghton, slowly began to restore her. After three months she was allowed home, still in an enveloping plaster-cast, steel rods in her spine, metal pins holding her hips in place and a complicated arrangement involving a dog chain attached to the ceiling which enabled her to sit up in bed.

Gay was so pleased to see her back at Mabberleys and so keen to give her a fitting welcome that despite her armour he managed to make her pregnant. When Philippa later struggled along to see her gynaecologist with the help of a walking frame, the doctor was not so exercised by the need to terminate the birth – 'No problem,' he assured her – as by trying to work out how Gay could have done it. 'Ought to have been impossible,' he muttered.

Later that year Gay had his last notable racing success when Pactolus, owned by Jamaican businessman Robert de Lisser, won the Midlands Cesarewitch over two-and-a-quarter miles at Wolverhampton. Gay had bought the horse from trainer Guy Harwood who had thought Pactolus would not get the trip and had entered a runner of his own. Both the new owner and his trainer had made useful bets and optimism flooded through the team at Parsonage as hopes ran high for a repeat at the Newmarket Cesarewitch. De Lisser was a prodigious punter and it was only with difficulty that Gay dissuaded the Jamaican from backing Pactolus – who was moving up at least one step in class to take part in the Newmarket race – to the tune of £40,000. As Gay anticipated, with stiffer opposition and the ground against him Pactolus finished well down the field. De Lisser, despite being grateful to Gay for saving him a great deal of money, was finding it more and more difficult to place bets of his rare order of magnitude with British bookmakers; soon after the race he returned to the Caribbean.

In 1987 the trustees finally drew the bottom line. The training stables and the small stud run by Philippa were, between them, losing over £20,000 a year and it was time to assess how best the future could be provided for. There seemed at first to be no easy answer, but waiting in the wings, as if for his cue, there lurked a fairy godfather. On to the stage at precisely the right moment stepped the unlikely form of Bill Tulloch, a tough Scotsman who had made a fortune out of the fruit machines known as one-armed bandits. He owned racehorses (not trained by Gay) and had long coveted a land-holding in the Lambourn valley. In a complicated three-way transaction involving the trustees and Gay as an individual in his own right, in which a total of some £2 million changed hands, Tulloch became the owner of practically all the farmland and some of the cottages. Gay bought from the trustees – at a cost which reflected his privileged position as a long-term tenant – Parsonage farmhouse, the stables with their two cottages, the all-weather gallops, about a hundred acres and Mabberleys complete. It was a good deal.

Hindsight – or even a hard-headed foresight – should have dictated that this was the right moment to give up training altogether, but Gay, with all the stubbornness and the Jack Mytton-like wild optimism of which he was capable, determined to have one more go. Selling Mabberleys gave him the necessary cash and now that he and Philippa had moved into the relative grandeur of Parsonage, he hoped to be able to attract owners of greater substance. But his training record in those competitive times was not a persuasive recommendation and the stock-market crash of October 1987 – the effects of which were felt throughout the next year – did nothing to encourage people to invest in something as chancy as racing. By the end of the 1988–89 national hunt season he finally squared up to the facts. His last runner – Tommy's Dream in a seller at Huntingdon – was beaten by a neck into second place. It later went on to win a number of races for its new yard: the contemporary Kindersley luck in a nutshell.

As a trainer he had extensively failed to realise his hopes and in so doing had fulfilled to the letter the forecasts gloomily propounded by his friends some fifteen years earlier. Why had it all gone so disastrously wrong after what had seemed to be such a promising start?

Some of the factors have already been touched upon: for example, the failure to attract serious owners and therefore the cash, as well as the confidence, to buy really top-class horses. Instead he found himself with far too many owners of the 'Win or lose, we'll have some booze' variety: like fatally attracting like. There was a lack of steel too in his handling of people – too often and for too long he would retain staff, even jockeys, out of a misplaced loyalty when a more objective view would have led to his letting them go. Allied with this was a ready tendency to listen to whoever had given him the last piece of advice without necessarily examining its provenance. The desire to believe that all is for the best in the best of possible worlds was strongly pervasive. Finally, although there is little doubt that technically he was as good a trainer as anyone in the valley, the exercise of his judgement in the placing and running of his horses was often clouded by over-optimism and by the need to engineer – without of course breaking the rules – the right conditions for a successful bet on which, too often, survival depended. The sum total of these disadvantages – some circumstantial, others self-inflicted – was too much for him to overcome. In May the lads were given three months' notice and Gay began to look for a job.

He turned, not unnaturally, to the racing industry but soon discovered that retirement at 60 was the almost invariable rule. At only a little short of that, he could never be a serious contender for the sort of post for which he had imagined himself well suited. He and Philippa continued to run the stud for a while – he thought that operating even a small business would allow him to defray some of his running expenses – but it persistently refused even to come close to balancing the books and so it, too, was wound down. He now found himself living on little more than fresh air. Some of that air was, of course, securely enclosed within a cushion; the children, for example, had their own Guinness legacies which took care of the essentials of their lives, including education. Nevertheless, in order to maintain even a semblance of the lifestyle to which he and his family and friends had become accustomed, he needed a substantial income. Now that he owned Parsonage, the obvious answer was to sell it and look for something a little smaller, and he began to cast around for a buyer. Hardly had he decided to do so in the summer of 1990 than Bill Tulloch resurfaced, telling Gay that he now wanted to acquire Parsonage itself and all that still went with it. He mentioned a figure which took into substantial account an additional proposal that Gay should continue to live in the house for some years rent free. This condition did not appeal; Gay felt that he could not, with any peace of mind, stay on with a deadline hanging over him and, in any event, it would suit his circumstances better if the offer could be increased in terms of cash and he was to leave almost immediately. Tulloch quickly agreed and upped his bid to a figure which made Gay blink.

Philippa, however, was not altogether happy. Although she had no particular affinity with Parsonage – it was, after all, very much the house that Magsie created – she and, particularly, the children enjoyed what it had to offer. More importantly, she did not want to leave the valley where they had all made so many friends. She was not keen that Gay should come to any firm agreement with Tulloch until they had found a satisfactory home which fulfilled all their needs. Various options were considered. Philippa, liking the layout of Parsonage, was in favour of building a smaller model on some land barely a mile away from East Garston. Outline planning permission was obtained and architect's plans drawn up, but as the project advanced Gay became alarmed at the escalating costs and put an end to it. Philippa felt that if money was such a problem then perhaps Tulloch could be persuaded to increase his offer. Gay, who thought that the bid was already amazingly generous, was secretly worried that the delays they were imposing would cause Tulloch to change his mind – perhaps even compel him to withdraw altogether. He had somehow to reconcile these family differences, and to that end called in a company of independent assessors so that he would be on firmer ground if negotiations had to be reopened. Two young men arrived and tackled their assignment in a way that was gratifyingly thorough. They examined the house minutely and inspected even the roof of the stables; they looked at the damp-courses of the cottages and explored the gardens. Having dipped their fingers into the pool, they paced the tennis court. Self-importantly they took extensive notes and finally, sitting down with a family-sized Pimms each, they tapped gravely on their calculator keys. At last came their considered recommendation. It was unequivocal. If Tulloch, they said, had offered even a third less than he had in fact proposed, his offer should have been accepted without delay. As it was Gay, without even waiting for his lunch, should get into his car, drive to wherever Tulloch could be found and close the deal immediately. Almost before they had finished speaking, the relieved vendor had taken their advice and gone.

The search for a new home was not allowed to interfere with either Gay's philanderings or with the round of party giving at Parsonage. In the case of the former, matters did not always go according to plan. Gay had formed an attachment with a barmaid in a valley pub (not Suzanne!) which Philippa felt might be in danger of getting out of hand. She came to the conclusion that the best way of dealing with the problem – and at the same time preventing her husband from making too public a spectacle of himself – would be to include the object of his desire in a number of family activities. She was invited to a Sunday lunch party; they took her racing at Cheltenham; Philippa went out of her way to make her feel welcome. One day after a race meeting she came back to the house for supper, together with two trainers whose reputations with women almost rivalled Gay's. They were also considerably younger and more adept at pacing their alcoholic intake. The evening was a success from everyone's point of view – except that of the host. One of the trainers managed to get the girl into bed before reluctantly dragging himself home to his wife; the other spent the unexpired part of the night with her. In the morning Gay was silent as Philippa enthusiastically recounted the details of the bedroom farce which had escaped her sleeping husband.

Sadly he recounted the story to Steve Taylor as the journalist was driving him to a race meeting the next day. He became almost maudlin. Perhaps he was getting old? There was a time when those two young buggers would not have had a look in. As it was, they had got rather more than a look. What did Taylor think? Steve, feeling sorry for his rather demoralised friend, mentioned that he and a mate, Tom Butterfield – an Australian with no visible means of support but apparently unbounded hidden resources – were going to Tenerife for a week to stay in a borrowed flat. Designed for two, the accommodation was unlikely to be spacious but, if Gay would care to come, it might make it easier for him to forget this painful episode of unrequited love. Gay perked up; he liked Steve and Butters very much; this sounded fun.

Wearing a tropical linen suit, panama hat and Saints and Sinners tie, he eventually arrived on the island to join his rather more casually dressed friends. It was not long before Taylor and Butterfield began mildly to regret their invitation.

The trouble started in a German restaurant when Gay asked the waitress sitting on his knee how old she was. Hearing the answer and eliciting the fact that her family came from Hamburg, he became unshakeable in a belief that he must have known her mother during his National Service days. This suggestion did not endear itself to the management (in the person of the mother in question) and after an acrimonious exchange of views which had somehow widened to include Philip Kindersley's treatment as a prisoner-of-war in Brunswick, the friends were thrown out. Having made their way to a nightclub in search of a much-needed restorative, Gay headed for the dance-floor, where he unerringly homed in on two stupendously blonde and leggy Scandinavian girls. Effortlessly he detached them from their men, who became increasingly fretful at the hit that this crumbly but evidently persuasive Englishman was making with their companions. Taylor and Butterfield, recognising that they had only seconds to rescue Gay from physical assault, put an armlock on him and frog-marched him out, explaining that he was their redundant coal-miner father spending his severance pay and was quite unaccountable for his actions. The Swedes nodded sympathetically. They understood; the old were sometimes like that; OK, no problem. In the street Gay was peevish. He did not want to go to bed yet; he wanted to go back inside; he was doing all right; the girls liked him. Butters threw him into a cab and they all went home.

Having been seriously warned by Taylor and Butterfield that he was not to make a pass at the wife of the owner of their apartment, Gay became rapidly frustrated; he felt that he was not making the most of this extended pink ticket. After forty-eight hours his libido was at bursting point and he had begun asking whether Tenerife boasted establishments such as the Wigmore Club or, better still, a bar where a fellow might be able to have conversation with – and perhaps get to know a little better – a hostess or two. The assiduous Taylor, fearing for the virtue of the landlady and the consequent wrath of her husband, made enquiries and established that there was at least one such place. He and Butters would take Gay there.

The doorman welcomed them effusively. Gay beamed at him and went inside. He bought a round of drinks, looked up and saw that a girl had materialised at his side. Glossy long black hair, a red sheath dress split to the thigh and a look in her heavily mascaraed eyes for which the word 'smouldering' might have been invented were flaunted in his direction. She stroked his cheek; he bought her some champagne and they began to talk. Presently he joined Butterfield and Taylor.

'I think I'm in,' he announced, his eyes gleaming.

'Course you're in,' said Butters. 'It's a bloody knocking shop.'

Gay was unabashed. 'Yes, I know. It's going to cost me £70.'

His friends groaned and pointed out that he could probably buy most of the island for that. Gay looked thoughtful, had a drink and went back for further negotiations. At length he returned. He did not look happy.

'Everything all right?' This from a solicitous Butterfield.

'Well, not really; no.'

'Whaddye mean, not really?'

'She's a man.'

Steve Taylor was also involved in the elaborate intrigue devised by Philippa and the older children to give Gay a surprise sixtieth birthday party. They planned to ask around 150 people to Parsonage for lunch, while telling Gay that there was to be a small family gathering for which Oonagh would be flying in from Guernsey. In order to remove Gay from the house, Taylor was to collect him to go and play tennis on a friend's court. The game would be lengthy, there would be refreshment and Gay would be returned to Parsonage at around 2 o'clock, by which time all the guests would be assembled, having hidden their cars in the stable yard. By 10.15 on the appointed Sunday morning it had begun to rain and Taylor announced to his now rather reluctant partner as he picked him up a little late, that an indoor court had been booked in Swindon. After collecting the remainder of the quartet Taylor drove so slowly that Gay began to show signs of restlessness, complaining that unless they got a move on he would be late for his mother; he really must be home by about 1. At the tennis centre a convincing – but necessarily unrehearsed – row was staged in which the innocent staff were noisily berated for having no record of the booking and for negligently letting the court go to someone else. Leaving a bemused management searching their booking sheets for an explanation, the four meandered slowly back towards East Garston with Gay becoming ever more anxious at the lack of urgency. They pulled up at the Plough in Eastbury and dragged a protesting Gay inside ('Must have a sharpener, Maestro, before you see your mother; after all, it is your birthday'). The pub was full and Steve, looking round, realised that everyone there – literally everyone – was on the way to Parsonage. He made frantic keep-mum signals and, catching on, they all forebore to wish Gay a happy birthday. Slowly, without arousing suspicion, they trickled out but even so Gay was slightly surprised to see so many of his friends in an establishment they used only rarely. But more important matters were occupying his mind. He began again to look at his watch as he castigated his companions for drinking at about half their usual speed; would they please hurry? He was already getting on for an hour late for his mother. Philippa would have lunch organised; they must go.

Still in their tennis kit, they climbed back into Taylor's car. Because of the need to approach Parsonage from a direction different from that which would have been natural (to avoid a view of the stable yard now crammed with cars), they again embarked on a circuitous route. Gay was beside himself and his temper was further ruffled by the sight of a man disappearing through his front door as at last they arrived. 'Oh God, what the fucking hell is he doing here? This is meant to be just a family lunch. Another bloody hold-up.' They went in to the hall and there – led by Fulke Walwyn – the ranks of assembled well-wishers began to sing 'Happy Birthday'. Taylor and his partners in crime helped themselves to glasses of champagne, content with a job well done. Gay turned to them.

'Did you know anything about this?' he asked!

The happiness generated by such a splendid celebration – the party went on well into the following morning – was enhanced a few days later by his re-election to the Jockey Club. But there was sadness too as his father suffered a stroke so serious that it would be no longer possible for Valsie to look after him. She had to sell the house in Gloucestershire in which they had lived for most of Philip's retirement. He was moved into a nursing home in Aldbourne where Valsie, having rented a small house, was able to visit him every day and where his son, too, could keep a close watch on his health.

The search for a house for Gay and Philippa now started in earnest. Tulloch had formally completed the Parsonage deal in September and had generously given the Kindersleys until the following April to vacate. Gay for the first time for many years had immediate access to a great deal of ready cash and he found it difficult to resist the temptations that so unusual an opportunity presented. As the money, despite his best intentions, began to slip through his fingers, he realised that he must act quickly. His plan was to buy something only a little bigger than, say, Mabberleys – a place which would be easily manageable and with gardens and perhaps a paddock which could be run with the minimum of (preferably no) labour. The outlay which he had mentally set aside for this would leave him with enough capital to invest for an income sufficient to maintain a comfortable lifestyle for himself and the family.

The search did not prove easy and soon stretched into several tedious months of looking at a series of unsuitable properties laid before them by enthusiastic young estate agents. All had their disadvantages: some were too small, even for Gay's undemanding requirements; some too expensive and most – in common with many Lambourn valley houses past which strings of exercising horses parade every day – lacked even the most elementary privacy.

One morning when nothing remotely adequate seemed to be on the viewing books and they were wondering whether they might not cast their net a little wider, an excited agent rang to beg Gay to look at Laines, a house on the ridge between Aldbourne and Ogbourne St George. The recession-hit owner, it was explained, simply had to sell. The Kindersleys drove over with mixed feelings. On the one hand they had fond memories of Aldbourne; on the other the house was a little further away from their stamping ground than they would have wished.

Laines stood in nine acres, some three hundred yards from a quiet road. About two-thirds of the ground was given over to formal lawns divided by immaculate beech hedges and planted with a variety of trees fit to grace an arboretum. Beautifully tended beds promised a profusion of roses while a secluded kitchen garden boasted yards of raspberry canes. A swimming pool sparkled in the early spring sunshine and a heron flapped slowly off the water-garden which lay beyond the gravelled drive. Gay and Philippa were enchanted. Inevitably the price was higher than he had intended. Feverishly he did some calculations; he would need to put in a tennis court and perhaps a play-room for the boys – the garages could probably be converted – and he would have to build an office for himself and Evelyn Tabernacle, who had been his secretary for nearly thirty years and had no intention of leaving him just because he had given up training. Perhaps he could let the paddocks?

And so it was done. Economy was largely forgotten and, just as he had been carried away by Magsie at Parsonage, so he was here during the enthusiastic planning of the enhancements required to turn Laines into the perfect family home fit for the Kindersleys not only to live in, but to entertain in the unstinting style imbued in him by Oonagh at Luggala and La Tourelle. The long, slim house – one room wide from end to end – roofed with tiles in the style of Provence, was pleasingly refurnished; sweeping curtains elegantly framed the long graceful windows in perfect complement to the expensive carpets already in place. A hi-fidelity audio system devised by a master of his craft was installed to relay music to wherever it might be needed. The promised tennis court was laid; the office for Gay (and Mrs Tabernacle) and the games-room for Rory and Oliver materialised side by side overlooking the water-garden. With all – perhaps even despite – its gadgetry, its determined modernism and more than a touch of Southfork, Laines became a complete home for its new family, providing every conceivable comfort without straying too far into the realms of ostentation. It was a place too where a guest seeking brief relief from the overwhelmingly generous hospitality might find solitude in the deepest of armchairs or in walking the closely mowed lawns shaded by their carefully clipped hedges. Best of all perhaps – at any rate for the peace of mind of its owner – there were no stables, nowhere to be tempted to stray again into investing in the bottomless financial pits that are unsuccessful equine adventures.

Once the move had finally been completed in mid-1991, Gay again began to look for a job which would both interest him and provide a regular income. A South African acquaintance had conceived and designed a horse ambulance which, on racecourses and elsewhere, would do much to lessen the impact on the public of the sight of a badly injured animal. More importantly, it would allow a stricken (but still living) horse to be carried into the vehicle in relative comfort and with the minimum of pain – without, for example, having to be persuaded to struggle up a ramp. Such vehicles were naturally expensive to manufacture but a small company was set up in England to demonstrate, sell and lease the ambulances and Gay, having invested in the project, became a director with particular responsibilities for marketing. In the now familiar pattern of his business life, his timing was less than perfect. The recession was at its most far-reaching and racecourse authorities in the British Isles (and the rest of Europe) were feeling the effects. Worse, the Betting Levy Board had provided each track in England with a towed trailer to remove injured horses at no cost. Hard pressed clerks-of-courses and directors of racecourse companies, although impressed to the point of admitting that Gay's ambulances fully met both the practical and humane requirements in a way the lesser substitutes did not, were unwilling to find the money either for purchase or even for hiring by the day. Outside South Africa, the total sales in two years were three to Italy and one to Singapore.

On Saturday 28 August 1993 the president of the Amateur Riders' Association of Great Britain was at home awaiting the arrival of the first guests of the evening. That day the Richmond-Brissac Trophy Handicap for members of the Fegentri had been run at Goodwood and been won by young Luis Urbano from Spain on Her Majesty The Queen's Talent, trained by Lord Huntingdon. Gay was particularly pleased by the fact that he had publicly tipped the winner during an interview on the course's closed-circuit television. He had known Urbano's father (also called Luis), who had himself been a distinguished amateur and had made it round one circuit of the Grand National in Red Rum's second winning year. What he was not so happy about was the fact that the ARA had been unable to provide a ride for either the French or the American amateurs and, worse, there seemed no prospect of either of them being mounted for the Moët & Chandon Silver Magnum due to be run on the Monday over the Derby course at Epsom. This was particularly unfortunate since both races were sponsored by – and owed much to – the generosity of French companies. He sighed; there was nothing that he or the ARA secretary, Johnny Greenall, could do. Johnny had flown him down to Goodwood by helicopter in time for lunch with the Duke of Richmond and Gordon and they had each done some canvassing for late rides for the luckless pair but without success. Urbano, however, was to ride Bo Knows Best for trainer John Sutcliffe in the Silver Magnum and hoped to emulate his father, who had won the race twice in the 1970s. Gay didn't think Bo Knows Best was quite good enough, but he wished the young Spaniard luck. (In fact Urbano pulled off the remarkable double.) But now it was time to put his worries behind him; they were all back at Laines; it was party time.

The Barbecue Ball, which Gay was hosting, was designed to raise money to enable British amateurs to go abroad to compete in Fegentri races; around three hundred tickets had been sold and a handsome profit was assured. The party was to be held in a tent – although 'tent' was hardly the word to describe the red-and-white-striped structure that had gone up next to the tennis court, it had more the sprawling appearance of a Bedouin encampment. The bar was stocked, the disco almost ready and the food unloaded, soon to be cooked over the cut-down oil drums that served as charcoal burners.

At around 8 o'clock on this warm summer's evening, people began to arrive: trainers and their glamorous wives; journalists, breeders, punters; owners, jockeys and work riders; friends from London and parents of boys with whom Rory and Oliver were at school; young rockers and old swingers; the rich and the not-quite-so-rich. All were there not so much to contribute to the cause (some of the professionals positively disapproved of what the ARA stood for), but because the party was at the Kindersleys. Gay deserved support.

There were the small hiccups that invariably attend such gatherings; the food was slow and the queues – encouraged by the disc-jockey to form early – became a little restive. The same young man had forgotten the light that enabled him to see his record collection and one had to be hastily rigged up by an electrically minded guest. Some cars – their owners disregarding the harassed parking attendants – were blocking the drive. Philippa, in search of fresh air, saw a couple making energetic love on the tennis court bench. She smiled; they were clearly oblivious of the fact that it had been freshly painted only that afternoon. She wondered how they would explain the white streaks away when they returned to their table – and to the man's wife. None of this mattered; they were all there to enjoy themselves and, helped by a liberal consumption of remarkably cheap drink, enjoy themselves they did. The music was brash but seductively inviting – its insistent beat, reaching all corners of the tent, rendered conversation difficult but promoted intimacy as heads bent closer together to catch the words.

As night turned slowly into morning, Gay – after a seemly show of reluctance – was dragged on to the dance-floor. The music died away as people gathered expectantly, some sitting cross-legged on the ground, some standing, others clambering precariously on to tables and chairs to secure a better view. The disc-jockey handed him a microphone, pressed a button and, as the volume slowly increased, the lilting, martial strains that could only have come from Ireland began to fill the air.

Down from the mountain came the squadrons and platoons ...

It was the Queen Mother's favourite tune, and Lord Oaksey's choice for *Desert Island Discs*: 'Slattery's Mounted Fut'.

Those who by dint of long acquaintance were connoisseurs of the histrionic performance necessary to do full justice to this compelling piece of music swore that they had never seen better. Those who were witnessing for the first time the climactic tearing of the shirt (new Levi, specially chosen by young Rory for the occasion) as the singer sinks slowly to his knees cheered wildly, smug in the knowledge that, at last, they had been admitted to a charmed circle. The young, forgetting, in the glory of the moment, that they had been deprived for a time of their own urgent beat, led the frenzied demands for an encore. But the performer was too wily for that. What was it Tommy Clancy used to say? 'Always leave them wanting more, Gay boy.' He beamed with pleasure as he made his way back to his table, acknowledging the acclamation of the crowd. His crowd. The King was in his castle.

As Gay Kindersley shuffles into the autumn of his life, shoulders hunched, blue eyes twinkling behind the tortoise-shell spectacles, he remains the Peter Pan with whom age and maturity have tilted with no noticeable success. Doggedly optimistic that one day the authorities will see the light and equip themselves with his excellent ambulances, he is equally certain that the mother of all betting coups is just around the corner and, while he waits for that happy event, he goes on losing as cheerfully – and as regularly – as he always has done. But on the rare occasions when the winnings are substantial, he spends them immediately and generously on his family and friends – ever the bookmakers' dream and the trustees' nightmare.

Racing remains the dominant interest of his life. He is proud to be a member of the Jockey Club, while not necessarily agreeing with everything propounded in its name. He enjoys and feels privileged to be a local steward at modest Bath and within the grander settings at Newbury and Kempton. As president of the ARA and influential committee member of the Fegentri, he promotes the ethos (and the practicalities) of amateur flat racing as assiduously and as enthusiastically as ever. A regular attender at the Saints and Sinners table, he embodies the best that can be distilled from those uneasy but companionable bedfellows.

As Philippa so cleverly understood – almost from the day she fell in love with the bedraggled figure in the teeming rain at a Sussex petrol station – nothing can materially change the man. Willing as ever to accept a challenge and a drink with equal and cheerful facility; quite unable to resist a woman or a lark; totally trusting – not only of his friends but of the whole human race – he ploughs up and down the swimming pool every possible morning of his life, intent on maintaining for ever the self-discipline with which he has always restored his body after the excesses to which – just as regularly – he subjects it.

In *As You Like It*, Jaques neatly parcels the life of man into seven acts, from puking infant, through to second childishness to mere oblivion. By Shakespeare's reckoning Gay Kindersley, aged 63, had reached the penultimate of those pigeon-holes. But the bard would not have been at all pleased with this particular player. Far from progressing smoothly from one ordered stage to another, he has made little concession to his years, shedding few if any of the qualities, good or bad, that have characterised his own journey through life. When at last he plays the last scene of all – 'that ends this strange eventful history' – there is every reason to suppose that not only will it be 'sans teeth, sans eyes, sans taste' but also, as it has always been with him, sans enmity. Few men could ask for more. Fewer still will achieve it.

Index